eserving Polyphonies

NEW TRENDS IN TRANSLATION STUDIES

Volume 12

Series Editor:
Dr Jorge Díaz Cintas

Advisory Board:
Professor Susan Bassnett
Dr Lynne Bowker
Professor Frederic Chaume
Professor Aline Remael

PETER LANG

Oxford • Bern • Berlin • Bruxelles • Frankfurt am Main • New York • Wien

Preserving Polyphonies

Translating the Writings
of Claude Sarraute

Claire Ellender

PETER LANG

Oxford • Bern • Berlin • Bruxelles • Frankfurt am Main • New York • Wien

Bibliographic information published by Die Deutsche Nationalbibliothek.
Die Deutsche Nationalbibliothek lists this publication in the Deutsche National-
bibliografie; detailed bibliographic data is available on the Internet at
http://dnb.d-nb.de.

A catalogue record for this book is available from the British Library.

Library of Congress Control Number: 2013933467

ISSN 1664-249X
ISBN 978-3-0343-0940-0

© Peter Lang AG, International Academic Publishers, Bern 2013
Hochfeldstrasse 32, CH-3012 Bern, Switzerland
info@peterlang.com, www.peterlang.com, www.peterlang.net

This publication has been peer reviewed.

Printed in Germany

Contents

Tables

Acknowledgements

I am particularly grateful to the following people, without whom this book would not have been possible:

Dr Robert Crawshaw of Lancaster University, for his generous giving of time and academic guidance;

my Mum and Dad, for their immense emotional and financial support;

Claude Sarraute, for the enthusiasm with which she received my translations, and for granting me the English language rights to her works;

Vida, for her invaluable technical assistance;

other members of my family and my close friends, for their patience and encouragement.

Introduction

> Literature is one of the independent parts of the surrounding ideological reality, occupying a special place in it [...]. The literary structure, like every ideological structure, refracts the generating socioeconomic reality, and does so in its own way. But, at the same time, in its 'content', literature reflects and refracts the reflections and refractions of other ideological spheres (ethics, epistemology, political doctrines, religion, etc.). That is, in its 'content' literature reflects the whole of the ideological horizon of which it is itself a part.
>
> — MEDVEDEV 1928/1978: 16–17

Central to Pavel Medvedev's words, and the work from which they emanate, is the conviction that literary systems always occur within the ideological milieu of a given era.[1] Indeed, history offers ample evidence to confirm the axiom that literary texts are deeply imbued with the cultural values of the society in which they are produced. It was, for instance, no coincidence that works written in the fourteenth to sixteenth centuries were influenced by classical models, at a time when there was renewed interest in classical antiquity throughout Europe, nor that the literature of the Enlightenment emphasized reason and individualism rather than tradition, when these issues were dominating seventeenth- and eighteenth-century thought. It was not by chance that writers in the 1800s and 1900s were preoccupied with the notions of inspiration, subjectivity, and the primacy of the individual, nor that subsequent modernist writers favoured more experimental literary techniques. Works produced during the postmodern period are a further case in point. In his capacity as literary critic, Eagleton (1987, in

---

1   Medvedev belonged to the Bakhtin Circle whose work is discussed at length in Chapter 2.

Harvey 1989: 7–9) captures the essence of the notoriously complex post-modern 'artefact', which he sees as reflecting the nature of postmodern society at large:

> There is, perhaps, a degree of consensus that the typical post-modern artefact is playful, self-ironizing and even schizoid; and that it reacts to the austere autonomy of high modernism by impudently embracing the language of commerce and the commodity. Its stance towards cultural tradition is one of irreverent pastiche [...]. We are now in the process of waking from the nightmare of modernity, with its manipulative reason and fetish of the totality, into the laid-back pluralism of the post-modern, that heterogeneous range of life-styles and language games which has renounced the nostalgic urge to totalize and legitimate itself.

In short, the postmodern movement represents a departure from modernity and rejects homogeneity or unity. Rather, through literature, art, and other cultural media, it stresses the diverse and fragmented character of society. In its written form, the typical postmodern text is a thoroughly unstable entity which crosses generic boundaries and flouts discursive norms, calling into question the roles of the text's participants, hybridizing and satirizing societies and cultures, and playing with notions of time and space.

Similarly, the transfer of any text from one national language to another reflects the ethos of a given period (Gentzler 2001: 4). Pre-twentieth century theory centred on Bible translation and was dominated by the concepts of the divine word (St Jerome, fourth century; Luther, fourteenth century), and fidelity to the source text (ST) in the cause of classical education (Arnold, nineteenth century). For most of the twentieth century, the dominant interests in translation were largely rooted both in the German hermeneutic tradition (Benjamin 1923; Kelly 1979; Steiner 1975) and in structuralism (Jakobson 1959; Nida 1964; Vinay & Darbelnet 1958). Following the rise in functionalist and systemic approaches (Even-Zohar 1978; Reiss 1981; Vermeer 1989), a specific interest emerged in translation as a process of intercultural communication (Bassnett & Lefevere 1990; Snell-Hornby 1988). This could be seen as one effect of applying more radical, deconstructionist principles to the study of translation (Derrida 1985a; Lewis 1985). If translation has always been a challenging process, from the late twentieth century onwards it appears to have become particularly so.

Not only are translators now confronted with fragmented, decentred STs, they are also operating in a climate in which a plethora of conflicting approaches to translation coexist (Gentzler 2001; Munday 2001; Venuti 2000). Clearly, the existence of such exploded texts is not an entirely new phenomenon. Over the centuries, more radical writers have attempted to break with the literary traditions of their time (Cervantes; Rabelais) and translators have always rerendered these works in other languages. However, in the present era, this phenomenon is articulated more fully and coherently by critics, which clearly raises more specific questions for the analyst and the translator.

Against this background, the present work contends that translation theory currently offers no satisfactory response to the multidimensional challenge of rerendering postmodern texts. As the existence of linguistic and cultural plurality in these writings is now widely acknowledged, many theorists recognize the impossibility of achieving complete equivalence in translation. When rerendering the fragmented, decentred postmodern ST, a process of 'rewriting' is instead deemed more appropriate (Lefevere 1992b). Nevertheless, examination of a number of key concepts from some of the major phases of translation theory suggests that such an approach, if taken too far, may not always be the most suitable. This work seeks to determine effective means by which the translator can first read and analyse such unstable, fluctuating writings and subsequently preserve in the target language (TL) the intricacies of the postmodern ST. In order to provide a suitable and wide-ranging response to this challenge, it proceeds in a number of stages.

Chapter 1, 'Claude Sarraute and her Writings', concentrates on the life and work of the contemporary, postmodern French journalist and novelist, Claude Sarraute, and identifies certain major areas of interest which can assist in categorizing the peculiarities of her work, namely: 'The Text', 'The Participants', 'Social, Cultural, and Political Issues' and 'Time and Space'. Her writings are a *sui generis* amalgam of genres, linguistic varieties, voices, social and cultural references, and temporal and spatial settings.

Research confirms that Sarraute's work has, hitherto, been neither studied in depth nor translated into English.[2] There may be a number of reasons
for this. First, on a general level, it is widely acknowledged that demand for
translated foreign works is markedly lower in English-speaking countries
than elsewhere in the world. It is probable, then, that there has simply been
little or no call for English translations of Claude Sarraute. Second, more
specifically, Sarraute's works do not respect established literary norms, and
do not therefore class as conventional literature in the source language (SL)
culture. Due to their unconventional nature and the resulting lack of public-
ity which they have received outside France, it may be that Sarraute's works
have not been sufficiently well known to attract the attention of anglophone
translators. Alternatively, the unconventionality of her works may have
resulted in their being deemed less worthy of linguistic and cultural transfer than more traditional texts. Third, as this work demonstrates, Sarraute's
writings are particularly challenging to rerender in English. Over the years
they may therefore have appeared forbidding to those translators who did
happen to come into contact with them. Paradoxically, it is precisely for
this reason that the challenge of their translation deserves to be addressed.

In seeking a paradigm which can assist in theorizing Sarraute's writings, it is instructive to have recourse to the work of the Russian philosopher, Mikhail Bakhtin (1895–1975), and the Circle of thinkers to which he
belonged. Some of the tenets of this work constitute the principal focus
of Chapter 2, 'Dialogism and the Polyphonic Text'. The Bakhtin Circle's
diverse publications, which have seen a definitive resurgence in Europe over
the past thirty-five years following the opening up of the Soviet bloc,[3] are
unified by one key idea: that of 'dialogism'.[4] Originally, this concept was

---

2   All translations of Sarraute's spoken words and written texts contained in this book
     are my own. References without a name are all from Sarraute's works.
3   Since the 1980s, Bakhtin has become a prominent figure in the humanities. His phi-
     losophy has been, and continues to be, widely used by linguists, by those interested
     in the study of literature and narrative, and by social, cultural, and political theorists.
     See Vice (1997).
4   Pearce (1994) and Todorov (1939/1995) employ respectively the terms 'dialogic prin-
     ciple' and 'dialogical principle' to describe this idea. Todorov's work was, however,

founded on the belief that all language is intrinsically interactive in nature and reflective of the power-inscribed relationships which exist between its users. The Circle first identified the function of dialogue within language, at the level of the individual word. According to Voloshinov (1929/1973: 86), '*Word is a two-sided act* [...] a bridge thrown between myself and another'. Bakhtin (1929/1984: 6) himself proceeded to argue that dialogic relationships exist both between the many voices and consciousnesses of characters in novels, which he labelled 'polyphonic' and, in addition, at multiple levels of such texts. '*The polyphonic novel is dialogic through and through*' (ibid.: 40). Bakhtin (ibid.: 93) later established that these definitions are applicable not only to the novel, but also to other genres of writing. Subsequently, post-Bakhtinian theorists have identified dialogism to be at play within other areas of the Circle's work. Indeed, the notions of dialogue, interactivity and interrelatedness can be seen to reach yet further, that is, to the wider areas of subjectivity and identity, society and culture, time and space. These are all susceptible to, and determined by, mutual influences (Holquist 1990). Thus, as the Circle's work can help to account for many of the unstable and dynamic qualities of Sarraute's writings in the four areas previously identified in her work ('The Text', 'The Participants', 'Social, Cultural, and Political Issues' and 'Time and Space'), the present study is essentially Bakhtin-driven. The quadripartite approach to the classification of Sarraute's writings, which is a leitmotif throughout this book, is a product of the Bakhtin Circle's work and can later serve as a benchmark against which to assess the success of my translations of Sarraute.

In view of the above, Chapter 3, 'The Translator as Interlocutor: An Eclectic Approach to Reading and Translating Claude Sarraute', sets out to determine how one can read, and subsequently translate, Sarraute's polyphonic texts. Clearly, given their dynamic character and multiple layers of complexity, Sarraute's writings prove a challenging, and at times puzzling read for an SL audience. This chapter first reviews an eclectic range of theories of textual and stylistic analysis and reader-response criticism

---

originally written in French; 'dialogical principle' is Godzich's 1995 translation of the title of Todorov's work.

before proceeding to suggest which elements of these are more or less helpful in enabling each individual reader to arrive at a consistent and coherent understanding of Sarraute. As many of the theories considered only
partially assist this process, it is posited that, when considered together,
the different approaches to reading and stylistic analysis commended by
Mikhail Bakhtin and Jacques Derrida can offer a more fruitful framework
in which to examine texts as diverse and variegated in character as those
of Sarraute.

Bakhtin (1970–1/1986: 75) recognized the inherently 'responsive'
nature of the reading process: 'The work, like the rejoinder in dialogue
is oriented toward the response of the other (others), toward his active,
responsive understanding'. He therefore advocated dynamic approaches to
the study of literature (1941) and sociological analyses of style (1934–5). As
regards Derrida, application of his thought can both account for subjectivity in the reading of such writings, and assist identification of the peculiar
qualities of polyphonic texts themselves. In his coining of the neologism
différance, Derrida posits that the very nature of words makes any complete
representation of meaning in language impossible; consequently, all texts
lend themselves to infinite possible interpretations. The methodology of
deconstruction also derives from this principle. Derrida (1967a) argues
that, as all concepts in society are grounded in language, and as language is
inescapably unstable, all conceptual hierarchies in society can be destroyed,
or deconstructed. When applied to this study, the concept of *différance*
encourages the reader to form a communicative, interactive relationship
with Sarraute's writings, reading her texts subjectively, or openly, and supplementing them with new meaning. Moreover, adoption of Derrida's
approach enables close stylistic analysis of polyphonic texts. By breaking
down the text into its smallest components, deconstructing and interrogating it, the analyst can, it is argued, maximize their own understanding
of Sarraute and thus become a well-informed interlocutor of her writings.
Once this has been achieved, the reader/analyst will be in a position to
respond meaningfully to Sarraute's work.

The notion of dialogue, or interlocution, can be extended to the role
of the translator (Mounin 1963; Kelly 1979; Robinson 1991; Youzi 2006).
In order for the translator/interlocutor to rerender the various qualities of

the polyphonic ST convincingly in the TL, they will be required to employ particular instruments, and to possess certain insights, which can be supplied by translation theory. As previously discussed, it may first appear that, when faced with writings such as those of Sarraute, the translator would be best advised to employ a free and adaptive approach to rerendering these texts in the TL (Bassnett & Lefevere 1990; Lefevere 1992b). This was, moreover, the opinion which Sarraute (Interview with Claude Sarraute – ICS) herself expressed when I broached with her the subject of translating her work into English: 'You shouldn't translate it, you should rewrite it', she insisted. 'Personally, I don't see how it can be done. It should be completely transposed, you understand?'. However, through its examination of a number of concepts from some of the above-mentioned major phases of translation theory and its consideration of their greater or lesser applicability to Sarraute, this chapter investigates whether the translator/ interlocutor can be better equipped to approach such texts if they interact with, and apply, an eclectic blend of translation approaches.

In recent years, translation theorists and practitioners have also given increasing acknowledgement to the mutual benefits of their respective approaches (Chesterman & Wagner 2002). In this vein, Chapter 4, 'Polyphonies in Practice', complements the preceding theoretical investigation and considers the question of rerendering polyphonic texts from a practical perspective. It refers to an eclectic body of approximately thirty more or less well-known texts from the past, many of whose translations have attained the status of archetypes. Following the four categories of 'The Text', 'The Participants', 'Social, Cultural, and Political Issues' and 'Time and Space', the chapter illustrates how the particular qualities of these works, which are also features of Sarraute's writings and can be theorized by referring to the work of the Bakhtin Circle, have been rerendered variously in the TL. Chapter 4 concludes by proposing a balanced framework for the rerendering of Sarraute.

With these guidelines in place, Chapter 5, 'Rerendering Claude Sarraute', centres on a collection of ten extracts which have been selected from Sarraute's writings (Ellender 2006a: 308–67). It provides ten commentaries, one on each ST and my corresponding rerendering of it. In a Derridean sense, my ten commentaries therefore supplement my translations of Sarraute. The salient empirical findings made in the ten commentaries are synthesized in four tables which are intended to reinforce and enhance the discursive commentaries. Again, these tables reflect the four recurring categories which are used for analytical purposes throughout this work. The findings, which outline the nature of my translation choices, are ultimately expanded upon in this chapter. In its conclusion, *Preserving Polyphonies* returns to the essential problematic which it detailed at the outset: that of determining effective means by which the translator may read and analyse the complex, postmodern ST and subsequently preserve its intricacies in the TL. While recognizing the inevitable limitations of the present study, it draws on its findings in order to provide a wide-ranging response to this challenge which is grounded in both theoretical and practical evidence.

Claude Sarraute and her Writings

Claude Sarraute was born in Paris in 1927 to wealthy and successful parents. Her father was the owner of a legal firm and her mother, Nathalie Sarraute, the internationally acclaimed writer of experimental, psychological literature. Nathalie (née Tcherniak) was born in Ivanova, Russia, in 1900 and, as a young child, moved to France with her parents. The family was of Jewish descent and endeavoured to conceal this; in the intellectual and highly cultured circles in which the Tcherniaks moved, it was considered inappropriate to share such information. Claude herself did not learn of her Jewish heritage until she was eight years old. Anti-Semitism was prevalent in France at the time and the *extrême droite* was active and very vocal. In this climate, Claude found it particularly difficult to accept her Jewish identity. She captures her distress, albeit amusingly, in one of her earlier works:

> In a solemn mood, [my grandfather] told me: 'I'm Jewish, you're Jewish and Jesus Christ was Jewish'. I don't give a shit about Jesus Christ. Too bad for him. That's his problem. But me! What a disaster! I took half a century to get over it. (1987: 90)

Claude's family employed an English nanny to raise her and English became her first language. She pursued her interest in this at school and at university, studying law and English at the Sorbonne. Following her education she met and married an American, Stanley Kudrow, an editorial writer for *Time*, with whom she lived in New York and had two sons (Sarraute 2003: 99–100). This experience gave her increased exposure to English and allowed her interest in, and knowledge of, the United States to develop. Some years later, following the failure of her first marriage and her return to Paris, she married her second husband, Jean-François Revel,[1] a politician and writer, with whom she had a daughter and another son (Sarraute 2005: 95–6).

In 1949 Claude Sarraute embarked upon a career as a comedienne which was to be short lived. She once claimed: 'I was a better comedienne in real life than on the stage' (in Ruquier [n.d.], my translation). In the early 1950s she sought alternative employment with *Le Monde* and *The Sunday Express* in Paris. It is with a certain pride that she describes her involvement with, and various roles within *Le Monde*, which spanned a period of thirty-five years. In 1953 she began by working on theatre and cinema programmes. She then moved from untitled news to titled news and to the writing of previews, before working as a *critique de variétés* [critic of various cultural events]. Subsequently, after twelve years as a television critic, she became an editorial writer. For seven years, Sarraute suggested that she write a humorous column for the newspaper, but her idea was repeatedly rejected as the style of the proposed column was considered too forceful. When a new editor arrived at *Le Monde*, Sarraute was eventually invited to attempt the column. It was to become a huge success and she thrived on her work:

> You know, I'm not making it up, I made the newspaper sell. Every day, on the front page, you have the work of a humourist. You know, a cartoon. So, people used to look at the cartoon on the first page and then turn over the newspaper and read my column on the last page. That lasted several years. It made the newspaper sell. That had always been my dream. I love that job. It's wonderful. It's my passion. (ICS)

Given that Sarraute assumed many different roles as a writer, her style developed considerably over the years. In her position as *critique de variétés* for *Le Monde* she reviewed circus shows and musicals and her style was elaborate and literary: 'I had to convey the atmosphere, the smell of sweat and dung in the circuses, acrobats' performances, you see? It was very well written and the style was very pretty' (ICS). It was not until she became

---

1   Jean-François Revel (1924–2006) was a conservative French politician, journalist, author, prolific philosopher, and member of the Académie Française from 1998.

a television critic, reviewing documentaries and debates on social issues, and a columnist, that she deliberately altered her style:

> Before I changed my style, I used to say: 'He'll come back to you, don't worry'. [...] And after, instead of that, I said: 'He'll be back, don't stress'. So, it's more familiar. It's much more punchy, more powerful. My whole column was written in this style which was very spoken and very forceful. (ICS)

As Sarraute became well known and increasingly popular she was invited to participate in television and radio shows, notably the humorous radio programme, *Les Grosses têtes* [The Big Heads]. She amused and entertained the members of her audience, some of whom were not readers of *Le Monde* and therefore not familiar with her column. This prompted her to attempt to produce a novel, in order to make her work available to a wider public. She explains that: 'My books [...] are just an extension of my columns' (ICS). When preparing to write her column, she was sometimes short of ideas or pressed for time. She would then resort to a set formula and produce a piece entitled '*Allô c'est toi? C'est moi. Tu sais pas ce qui m'arrive avec Pierre-François?*' [Hello, is that you? It's me. You'll never guess what's happened with Pierre-François!]. This was written in a conversational style, contained gossip and was targeted at a female audience. '*Allô c'est toi? C'est moi*' was to become her 'trademark', and it was from this that her first novel *Allô Lolotte, c'est Coco* developed in 1987, when she was aged sixty. Since that time, Sarraute's writing of literature has continued to go from strength to strength. She has published eleven books: nine novels, a collection of her articles from *Le Monde*, and one social critique. All have sold well, a number have been best sellers and ten remain in publication today.

Sarraute's career with *Le Monde* ended in the mid-1990s. However, she continued her work as a writer of literature and, in addition to this, began to write a column in the monthly magazine, *Psychologies*. This column bears her distinctive style which originated in '*Allô c'est toi? C'est moi. Tu sais pas ce qui m'arrive avec Pierre-François*' and contains no explanatory foreword to her readers. They themselves must interpret the nature of the dialogue which takes place and the identity of the characters who participate in it. At all times, Sarraute uses these individuals in order to present a range of social issues and problems. Alongside her writing, Sarraute has participated in numerous television and radio shows and appeared regularly on the daily television programme, *On a tout essayé* [We've tried everything], on France 2, and radio programme, *On va se gêner* [We're not bothered], on Europe 1. These entertaining shows focused on current affairs and topical issues and were hosted by the popular presenter, Laurent Ruquier. During my discussion with Sarraute it emerged that she fully intends to remain involved in a broad range of professional activities.

It would be reasonable to assume that the many circles in which Sarraute has moved, and the different cultures with which she has come into contact throughout her childhood and her personal and professional life, have had a certain impact on her writings. Nevertheless, when I broached this subject with her she was extremely sceptical about any relationship between her life and work. She rejected the idea that she may have been affected by Jewish and English influences and insisted that her choice of style is conscious and deliberate, yet subordinate to the specific and intended meaning behind her writing:

> I'd worked all that out in my head. Style and form are of no interest to me. Form and style are there to bring out the content, to make it more obvious, more powerful. So, that's it. It was about finding a form which matched the content which I wanted to deal with. That's all.[2] (ICS)

Of all the potential influences on her writing, the one which Sarraute dismisses most forcefully is that of her mother. Despite describing Nathalie with affection and admiration (2003: 17–18), Claude insists that she was not at all inspired by her mother's work. On the contrary, she stresses their fundamental differences:

> Nathalie's works were very impenetrable, very very difficult. I only knew about them much much much... very late. I sort of did the opposite. Personally I've always, I'm like, I dunno, not even Walt Disney. It's like Donald Duck compared to Proust. (ICS)

2   Interestingly, this approach to style is closely in line with opinions which Sarraute expressed on the subject in June 1960. During an interview for *Le Monde* she stated that: 'Style [...] only serves to bring out of you what you want to show' (1960: 3).

At an early stage in her career, Sarraute's writing was heavily criticized in an article which appeared in the newspaper, *Libération*. She recalls that: 'They said that [...] when your mother was the queen of French literature, you could get away with writing like me!' (ICS). It is highly probable that such experiences, and the understandable tendency of critics to compare mother and daughter, have fed Claude's desire to distinguish herself from Nathalie Sarraute and have inspired the constantly reactive and subversive style of her writing. It is on this writing, and on the quick-witted, exuberant personality which she expresses through it, that Claude Sarraute has built her reputation in France over the past fifty years. She is now popular with people of all generations and from all walks of life.

An extensive but close reading of Sarraute's work reveals the four principal areas of interest mentioned before. When considered collectively, they form the cornerstone of her writings. Under the headings of 'The Text', 'The Participants', 'Social, Cultural, and Political Issues' and 'Time and Space', Sarraute's journalistic and literary writings will therefore be examined with a view to demonstrating the sense of continuity within, and the development of her work, and to establishing its reactive, iconoclastic nature. The term 'literary writings' will refer to all of Sarraute's published books which do not include her journalistic writing, that is, her nine novels and her work, *Des hommes en général et des femmes en particulier* (1996), an amusing study of the sexes.

The Text

A striking feature of all of Sarraute's work is its degree of self-consciousness. In her journalistic writing this is illustrated powerfully in an article for *Le Monde*, entitled '*Comment ça va?* [How's it going?]', in which she considers the challenges of the newspaper column, that is, the difficulty of finding inspiration to produce such writing and the means by which she searches for new ideas. She comments:

What kills me, is the people who say to me, like that, in passing: Hey, I thought of something for you, a subject for your column, wait a minute... What was it again? Oh, drat! I don't remember. I should have noted it down. Shame. It was funny though. It's unbelievable, they do it on purpose. Are they sadistic, or what? Because, well, ideas aren't easy. They don't jump out at you every morning when you get up. They are sniffed out, dug out, stolen, invented, noted down and stored up and they fall apart because topical issues quickly lose their relevance. I pinch ideas everywhere, all the time. (1985: 230)

This sense of self-awareness is further apparent in Sarraute's books, particularly her novels, in which it becomes a prominent and recurring feature. Sarraute is frequently required to define the generic identity of her works when communicating with her publisher ('Hey, darling, where are we? In the chapter of a novel or a newspaper article?' [1989: 21]), her characters ('By the way, is this a novel or a satirical tract?' [2003: 10]), and her readers ('Whereas here [...], it's a novel!' [1989: 117]). Equally self-reflexive is her writing process itself. When Sarraute's editor, Françoise Verny, appears as a character in the novel, editor and author discuss the novel's characters and plot. Verny advises Sarraute on such issues:

Listen, my little sweetheart, you know what you can do? You have a good think for another... Let's say... 98 pages. Or even, say, 114, let's be generous. Whatever you do, don't rush. No, it's true, it's a serious decision.. And if, then, you're still hesitating about going to the café with your two blokes, you come by and see me at Flammarion. (1987: 46–7)

Nevertheless, Sarraute does sometimes clarify that she alone is responsible for her writing and for the fate of her characters:

You can't imagine how bothered I am about this. How is Lolotte going to get back with JJ again? I just don't know. How can the deadlock in this situation be broken? Ask Verny? No way! After, people will say that she's the master of breathtaking suspense, not me. Hey, that's given me an idea! What if he, JJ, telephoned Lolotte? Yes, but what would he say to her? Well... Er... (1989: 131–2)

Collectively, the self-referential elements of Sarraute's writings have certain functions. They clarify the genre to which her work belongs and, in doing so, remind the reader that the text is a fictional one which revolves around invented characters, situations, and events. Sarraute's texts do not, however, merely focus on, nor refer to themselves. Each contains multiple intrageneric references. Her newspaper columns (1985) frequently cite not only other examples of the French press, but also a wealth of foreign sources including *The Herald Tribune*, *The Financial Times*, *Spiegel*, and *L'Espresso*. Similarly, her novels make explicit reference to other popular foreign literature, for instance the works of Barbara Cartland (1998: 213) and Helen Fielding's *Bridget Jones's Diary* (2003: 35–6). Sarraute's (1996) *Des hommes en général et des femmes en particulier*, an observant treatment of the sexes, mentions on a number of occasions John Gray's (1992) best seller, *Men are from Mars, Women are from Venus*, a book with which it shares many similarities.

Furthermore, Sarraute frequently draws on other genres, a technique which adds depth and texture to her writings. In her articles she makes direct references to, and uses quotations from, a wide range of sources. These include television programmes, reports and surveys containing statistics, and classical foreign literature such as that of Shakespeare (Sarraute 1985: 148). Such breadth of reference is equally apparent in her books. These mention songs, programmes, articles in the press, and an abundance of foreign literature, ranging from Danielle Steel, through Anthony Burgess and Aldous Huxley, to George Orwell. At times, Sarraute (1987: 64) provides her own assessment of these authors, demonstrating her erudition: 'I think just like Aldous Huxley. A genius. The genius. With a capital G. A neglected genius compared to George Orwell'.

In Sarraute's journalistic and literary texts, other intergeneric references occur in different, and sometimes less explicit, ways. In her articles, she reproduces a variety of styles, writing columns in the form of letters (1985: 203 & 234), and in her novels, she imitates the dramatic genre, presenting certain scenes as if they belonged to a play (1987: 152). In *Allô Lolotte, c'est Coco*, she recreates the child's adventure novel, in which the reader is free to follow the story as he pleases. She jests: 'If you find it funny, keep reading. If not, skip ahead and I'll see you on page 21 to have lunch with Lolotte and Ned, OK?' (ibid.: 14). In these novels, Sarraute is playful in her use of style, copying that of a telegram in order to reformulate ideas for her reader (1989: 33) and that of a text message, adding authenticity to the scenario which she describes (2003: 63). Often, her description and imitation of other styles and genres are also comical to the extent that she ridicules and appears to parody them. As will be seen in my discussion of Extract 8, Sarraute sometimes demonstrates an audacious and slightly vulgar sense of humour.

These many quotations, imitations and parodies, each of which is written in a distinct register, illustrate the extent of Sarraute's knowledge. However, the permanent self-consciousness, and intra- and intergenericity which she creates in her writing, and which result in a hybrid of contrasting genres, styles, and registers, suggest an alternative agenda. Not only does Sarraute's own contribution to popular literature help to valorize this genre, but her continual interweaving of distinct genres also appears to flout traditional written norms, both literary and non-literary. Therefore, she explodes the divide between traditional high and low literatures, rethinking and potentially suggesting some reorganization of traditional hierarchies.

If Sarraute's journalistic and literary texts contain many genres, styles, and registers of written language, they by no means focus uniquely on the written word; spoken language also features prominently throughout. First, both Sarraute and her characters display awareness of the ways in which their language is used. Sarraute adds footnotes to her novels, explaining the subtleties of pronoun use (1989: 148), and discusses the different tones with which one can speak when leaving a message on an answerphone (1987: 76–8). At times, the characters themselves reflect on and discuss the etymology of French expressions (1989: 149), the use of vulgar language (1995: 146), popular language, and *verlan*.[3]

This said, it is not so much contemplation of language as language in practice which infiltrates Sarraute's writing; transcribed oral conversations dominate both her journalistic and literary texts. Each of her novels, written between 1987 and 2005, teems with exchanges of colloquial language

---

3   In some bilingual dictionaries, *verlan* is approximately translated as '(back) slang'. A more precise definition of this particular use of language is: 'A slang procedure which consists in inverting phonetically the syllables of words' (Hachette: Le Dictionnaire du français. 1992: 1719, my translation).

and is an effortless pleasure to read. In an interview given to *Le Monde*, Sarraute (1960: 4) describes her technique of incorporating the spoken word into her writing:

> I put spoken language into writing. [...]. This transposition is hard to do, it's a lot of work. It doesn't look like it, but it's difficult. To make a novel like mine, you have to write 80,000 pages to get 800. When they're talking about me, people say: 'She has natural eloquence... she writes as she speaks... they are everyday words... we recognise them'. Only, there you are! It's 'transposed'!

Over forty years later Sarraute maintained this stance, explaining to me how she loves to create dialogues in her writing and stressing that: 'It's quite clever!' (ICS).

The oral French which features throughout Sarraute is not merely that spoken by natives. In her writing, Sarraute manipulates the speech of her foreign characters, as if transcribing phonetically their exotic use of French. West Indians speak (see Extract 1) as do certain Europeans (1989: 161). In order to further reinforce this impression of foreign presence, Sarraute blatantly juxtaposes national languages in her writings. The use of English occurs repeatedly in her articles and in her novels, and when a number of languages coexist and appear to clash, the result is a highly textured piece of writing which assumes a clearly multicultural dimension. This is exemplified when two female characters have difficulty communicating in an Italian restaurant. Not only does the woman speaking pidginize her mother tongue, so too does she attempt to make herself understood by using a combination of other European languages (see Extract 6).

In sum, in her journalistic and her later literary texts, Sarraute's use of genre and of the written and spoken word is both self-reflexive and extra-referential, that is, it refers to what is external to it, or to what is 'other'. This results in a true medley of genres, styles, languages, and voices; Sarraute's writings are cacophonous and have an inherently multidimensional and polyvalent character. Thus, through the production of such texts, Sarraute appears to transcend two important divides: that which traditionally exists between high and low literatures, and that which separates speech from writing. By constantly allowing the spoken word to be absorbed into her written texts, she blurs the conventional distinction between these two discourses.

The Participants

Given the prominence of the issues relating to genre and language in
Sarraute's writings, it is important to consider the participants in these
texts: Sarraute (the 'author'),[4] her characters and readers. Once again, it
will be seen that the nature and function of the individuals in Sarraute's
journalistic articles closely anticipate those of the participants in her later
literary works.

Throughout her writings, Sarraute herself is constantly present. As
these texts contain many personal and autobiographical references, the
reader gains a strong sense of the impact which Sarraute's reading, past
conversations, experiences, encounters, and friendships have had on her own
life (1985; 2003). Sarraute is not only subject to such influences before she
begins writing, but also appears to be affected by others during the writing
process. It is later witnessed that she continually relates to her characters
and readers, both through her linguistic interaction with them and on a
broader interpersonal level; she participates in a number of her texts alongside these figures. In her journalistic articles, Sarraute frequently appears
with other characters in her personal anecdotes and, in a number of her
novelistic writings, she herself is a character. She discusses her manuscript
with her editor (1989), signs her books which are for sale in the shop in
which her characters work (1991), and acts as the friend and confidante
of her characters (2003). Both prior to and during her writing, Sarraute
therefore emerges as an individual who is open, and receptive, to a number
of external influences.

As author, Sarraute also displays a high degree of self-consciousness.
It has previously been established that, as she writes, Sarraute is aware that
she is producing texts and that she acknowledges this explicitly. However,
her self-view and self-confidence are much more difficult to determine.
She frequently asserts her own opinions with clarity and force ('He's funny,

4   Sarraute's role as author (and narrator) fluctuates considerably in her writings. This
     issue is explored in greater depth in Chapter 5.

Chèvenement! I love him!' [1985: 46]); ('The Russians are really smutty. They've got dirty minds' [1985: 183]) and writes confidently of the success of her works ('I write novels. OK, they're little novels, but they sell rather well' [2003: 8]). Nevertheless, she does deride these works, joking that: 'Young secondary school pupils will have this masterpiece of French literature, this great classic, as part of their curriculum in 2999' (1987: 54), and makes playful, self-deprecating references to her own rhetorical function. One of her articles for *Le Monde* opens with such a reference: 'I'm there, very sensible, all alone in my corner, on the last page of the newspaper. I'm there telling you stories about dunces and dog muck' (1985: 74). At times, the characters in her novels also explicitly discuss and criticize Sarraute, her works, and her intervention in these, but do so with some affection:

> Oh yes, I see. A woman who's a bit bonkers, but rather nice. Except that she writes things, *Allô Coco, Allô Lolotte*, I can't remember. Big Maddo tried to read it. [...] You don't know who's talking. You can't understand anything. (1991: 187)

Thus, in her writing, Sarraute's confidence fluctuates considerably. Her position is consequently unstable and somewhat difficult to define. This is reinforced by the fact that she is a multivoiced personality. She provides orthodox narrative description, yet also allows her intrusive voice to dominate and her strong opinions to be heard, she directly transcribes some conversations, but indirectly reports others.

The characters in Sarraute's writings share similar characteristics with the author herself. They too are open to external influences, continually interacting with fellow characters, and are affected by the experiences which they have. Moreover, they display acute self-consciousness, acknowledging their existence within works but also debating whether they are real people or merely Sarraute's constructs. This renders their identity distinctly unstable:

Sarraute frequently enjoys a position of authority over her characters. Many of these individuals are stereotypical figures; emblems of diverse sectors of French society of whom she provides physical descriptions and biographical information. Sarraute (2000: 98–9) ridicules her characters' behaviour and is aware of her ability to determine their fate: 'At that point, I thought I should intervene. Not to make her feel better, not at all. On the contrary, it was to drive her further down, and to make her hit rock bottom. Otherwise, she wouldn't get through it'. Moreover, through free indirect speech, she uses these individuals as mouthpieces to express her own thoughts and opinions. Some characters, for instance, express their dislike and fear of hospitals (*Psychologies*, June 1999; 2000: 91), a theme which recurs in Sarraute's (1985: 25 & 253) earlier articles written for *Le Monde* in which her own opinions are clearly voiced.

In spite of her position of control, Sarraute often hints, somewhat contradictorily, that her characters are real people, independent of her creation. In both her journalistic and novelistic texts she incorporates explicit dialogue between herself and her characters, and this is developed considerably in her novels. She and her characters are frequently involved in a process of exchange and their positioning in relation to each other is open to constant renegotiation. Sarraute (2000: 86) sometimes befriends these people and appears protective towards them: 'Are you alright now? Have I made you feel a bit better, my little sweetheart?'. Occasionally she agrees with them but she prefers to give them advice. When they disagree with her, asserting themselves and their autonomy, she also chides them and enforces discipline. As will be seen in my discussion of Extract 4, Sarraute uses both her own voice and free indirect speech to recount an argument with one of her characters, Patrice. There is a subtle effect of irony, and it is suggested that a power struggle has taken place between herself and her character.

The third category of participant in Sarraute's texts is the reader. Traditionally independent of, and external to the texts which they read, these people, like the author and her characters, will have been influenced by that which they have read, conversations which they have had, and their past relationships and experiences. They will have been open to a variety of influences and come from a wide range of backgrounds, of which the author cannot be certain. Nevertheless, Sarraute does make assumptions about her readers' personal circumstances, presumes that they have certain knowledge and anticipates their responses to herself and to her writing. These may be interpreted as attempts to define and control her readership, which she views as both monolithic and varied and which is clearly plural and contradictory in nature.

This said, such control is frequently relinquished. A striking feature of all of Sarraute's writing is her tendency to address her readers directly, a device which she originally borrowed from Denis Diderot. Not only does she talk to and confide in her readers, she also advises them guides them through her works and encourages their active participation: 'Come on, don't tire yourself out. Or rather, do. Make an effort, try to guess. I'll give it to you in ten, a hundred... Come on, think!' (1989: 122). Moreover, she reproaches them for their inattention and sulks when she suspects that they may be disinterested.

There are, then, moments when Sarraute attempts to define and predict the behaviour of her readers, but many occasions on which she suggests that they are independent people who are at liberty to act and respond to her works as they please. Sarraute's position of authority is once again uncertain. She and the readers of her texts frequently compete for a position of control.

In a study of the participants in Sarraute's texts the question of gender is of particular importance. It closely affects both the relationships between, and the identities of, these individuals. Throughout her articles and books Sarraute situates herself in relation to people of the same and the opposite sex. Her behaviour towards each gender is distinctive, and it is clear that she has constructed her own gendered identity through such interaction. She refers to her friendships and conversations with female colleagues and explains how she used to appreciate male attention:

> When I say that I love being spoilt by men... I used to love it. I saw in it the most tangible, indisputable proof of passionate love. The price they were ready to put on having the privilege of being with me for a while. Yes, I know, that sounds very tarty. I was, I still am, an old tart. (2003: 40)

In her texts, Sarraute positions herself similarly in relation to her characters, befriending and gossiping with the females, but adopting a different stance toward the males. Gendered relationships between Sarraute's characters themselves are equally noteworthy. Identities are constructed between characters of the same gender – friends, work colleagues, and relatives – and within male-female relationships. Sarraute's characters are often gendered stereotypes and are spoofed. These humorous creations are built on her ironic observations of roles and behaviour in society at large:

It's crazy when you think about it, the responsibilities that we girls have. To think that men have the cheek to complain that they're weighed down by things: industry, defence, government, education, leadership of the EU and all that. I'd like to see them in our shoes. How we stand the strain, I don't know. Have a little flick through our magazines, you'll see, it's alarming. 'Your plant is bored, speak to it'. 'Become a sex bomb'. 'How to strengthen your relationship'. 'You are thirty-eight kilos too heavy. Lose the weight in four days'. [...] 'Find your G-spot'. 'Keep a check on the size of your thighs'. 'How to make your relationship work'. (1989: 180)

Therefore, in her journalistic and novelistic writings, Sarraute plays with and manipulates her portrayal of the sexes. She reverses roles, alternately sides with, or ridicules males and females, and defends the rights of each gender (1985: 135 & 222). Significantly, she devotes her *Des hommes en général et des femmes en particulier* (1996) to providing a detailed and amusing presentation of many aspects of gendered identities and relationships. Sarraute also presumes that her works are read by both men and women. Although many of her texts may be applicable to both male and female readers, she occasionally addresses a specifically male readership, or, alternatively, a uniquely female one. Through this varied treatment of the sexes and refusal to favour either, Sarraute contributes towards destroying any hierarchical positioning of the genders.

The participants in Claude Sarraute's texts permanently interact with one another and are constantly open to the influence of others. Although these tendencies can be witnessed in her journalistic writings for *Le Monde*, they are developed and much more apparent in her books and in her later articles for *Psychologies*. In these writings, the roles of the author, characters, and readers have an inherently unstable and fluctuating nature and all participants enjoy varying degrees of control. In Sarraute, traditional roles, according to which the author enjoys a permanent position of authority and characters and readers are subservient, are therefore disrupted, as is any male-female dichotomy in which the male enjoys a position of superiority over his female counterparts. By creating such fluctuating individuals, it seems that Sarraute attempts to alter established roles and disrupt existing power structures within society. In doing so, she deliberately destabilizes her own writings and, by extension, the notion of genre itself.

Social, Cultural, and Political Issues

In both Sarraute's journalistic and literary texts, social and cultural issues constitute the core of her subject matter. 'That's what interests me', she claims, 'relationships between people, society as it really is' (ICS). In this respect, her articles written for *Le Monde* and *Psychologies* once again act as forerunners of her later works. In her writings, Sarraute provides a highly observant portrayal of France. She covers a broad range of issues from banal routines and aspects of daily life through particular customs and cultural figures, to political rule. Interestingly, specific social issues are touched on in individual articles and are then revisited and greatly expanded upon in her books.[5] Articles on the following themes appear to directly anticipate her later works: male/female relationships, feminism, a variety of taboo issues including incontinence and sexual techniques, daily life, children, schooling, hospitals, illness, and old age. Frequently these are set within a social (class-related) framework or against a clearly political (and specifically governmental) backdrop. Through her detailed treatment of the behaviour, customs, attitudes, and concerns of the French, Sarraute demonstrates her intimate knowledge of the country in which she grew up and provides her readership with an insider's perspective on France.

Alongside this detailed consideration of French society and culture, frequent references to other peoples, and to their languages, cultures, and customs, are also made. If the range of nationalities which Sarraute discusses is impressive in its scope, her principal focus is nevertheless on the Jews, the English and, somewhat overwhelmingly, on the Americans. From cultural traditions to public figures, and from recently published newspaper articles and books to governmental politics, Sarraute displays her familiarity with other cultures and, through her incorporation of personal anecdotes,

---

5   Certain themes which Sarraute originally treated in her articles for *Le Monde* and
     which she deals with in her later books are also revisited in her articles for *Psychologies*.
     Sarraute writes on the cusp of these two genres and the close interrelationships
     between all of her texts can be observed.

suggests that her writings build directly on her own intercultural knowledge and experience. Furthermore, at various stages throughout her texts,
Sarraute considers the presence of other nationalities and cultures within
France and refers to herself as a foreign (Jewish) presence in the country.
Her presentation of France as a true linguistic, social, and cultural hybrid
is most striking in *C'est pas bientôt fini!* (1998), a novel in which pupils of
many ethnic backgrounds are gathered together in a *collège* in an underprivileged suburb of Paris. This work, of which an extract is later discussed
(Extract 7), encourages heightened awareness of the social and cultural
issues concerning, and problems faced by, these other peoples. Moreover,
by juxtaposing these nationalities, the work arguably fosters greater self-
awareness. In this novel the French self, so accurately captured by Sarraute,
can be perceived in relation to what it is not.

Sarraute's depiction of French and foreign societies and cultures is
not, however, without ambiguity. Through her adoption of anti-serious
and ironic tones, she derides many aspects of contemporary France; her
writings are distinctly subversive and reactive. First, she suggests that her
own behaviour and moral position may be dubious: 'Are you a liar? Really?
So am I. I lie through my teeth' (1985: 163), and she seemingly encourages
her readers to behave unethically: 'No personnel manager is going to ask
for a medical certificate if you're off work for less than forty-eight hours.
[...]' (1987: 20–1).

Second, she blatantly attacks the French class-system and mocks the
upper classes: 'Have you noticed, in France, the more you climb the social
ladder, the more barriers, checks and petty procedures are multiplied. When
you get to the top, nobody should be able to contact you. You should be
inaccessible' (1989: 95).[6] Third, Sarraute uses the writing process as a means
of expressing her negative views on a number of French institutions. In her
articles for *Le Monde*, she blatantly criticizes hospitals, education, transport,

6   It is interesting to note that Sarraute's choice of words in this extract from her novel,
     Maman Coq (1989), reproduces almost exactly the way in which one of her earlier
     newspaper articles on the same subject was phrased (1985: 226).

and the public services as a whole. On a purely political level, she voices her discontent and ridicules the government, individual political figures, their decisions and ideas.

Thus, through her attack on the class system, social institutions, and the government, Sarraute displays a distinctly reactionary approach and, in her iconoclastic writings, appears to challenge social and political hierarchies in France.

Sarraute's treatment of other nationalities has similar nuances. If her tendency to incorporate foreign peoples, languages, and cultures in her writings suggests her familiarity with these and her knowledge and acceptance of them, at times she nevertheless attacks these others, adopting a deliberately provocative tone: 'An establishment frequented by kids of all colours, bone-idle and disruptive... Oh sorry, we don't say that anymore... Kids who are often, too often, performing poorly at school. That's the expression we're allowed to use' (1998: 9). Alternatively, she uses her characters to express acutely xenophobic views: 'Wow, it really stinks, it smells of Negroes. It's unbelievable. Well, not that unbelievable, given that the factory workers are all black' (1991: 115).

Thus, Sarraute portrays France as a socially and culturally disparate country; a complex, kaleidoscopic totality in which different nationalities may interact harmoniously, or clash starkly. Ultimately, the picture which she paints is one of an indeterminate cultural space; French society appears fragmented and decentred. Although the tone of Sarraute's texts is largely amusing, she confirms that she uses this humour in order to comment more profoundly on the nature of society. Moreover, on occasions she uses a deliberately serious tone in order to express both this fragmentation and the notion of social transition: 'As in all periods of transition – this one goes from mononuclear to multidimensional – you get lost, for lack of reference points, you grope around, you experiment, you procrastinate as you wait for the right moment, irresistibly carried along by what is fashionable at the time' (1995: 171).

In her journalistic and literary writings, Sarraute gives detailed consideration to both French and foreign people. In the socially and culturally hybrid country which she depicts, the identity of all individuals appears open, that is, receptive to the influence of others, both intra- and interculturally. Sarraute's use of multiple tones in her writings adds a further dimension to her discussion of social, cultural, and political phenomena both in France and abroad. Indeed, such frequent shifts between the serious and the humorous destabilize these writings, reflecting the very nature of society at large and reinforcing Sarraute's subversive treatment of it.

Time and Space

If Sarraute often allows the notions of time and space to develop logically in her texts – a technique which creates an impression of consistency in her narrative – she also frequently plays with them, interrupting the flow and progression of her writing. These textual features are most apparent in her novels; the shorter length of her articles provides less scope for any development, or destruction, of both temporal linearity and spatial continuity. Nonetheless, as time and space are important aspects of all of Sarraute's works, their roles in both her journalistic and novelistic writings merit analysis.

In terms of their temporality, Sarraute's narratives are predominantly linear and display a logical sense of progression ('We'll have a little flashback. After which we'll deal with the present. Before considering the future. Where we've come from, where we are, where we're going' [1996: 9]), but they are frequently interrupted. Individually, her journalistic articles are set in very different time frames. Some occur in the present and others in the past, incorporating events which occurred that day, earlier that week, or several decades previously. A number of references are also made to the future. This said, the story told in each individual article is set in one particular time frame – in the past, present, or future. The narrative consequently remains consistent and progressive.

It is in Sarraute's novels, set mainly in the present tense, that shifts in time produce a greater effect. In the present, the author alternates scenes abruptly. She draws attention to this as she discusses with her readers the success of the 'dissolves' between her scenes (1989: 111). At moments she turns to the past, again making this explicit to her readers. However, on occasion, Sarraute naturalizes certain time-shifts in her novels, using these to explain her characters' past. She also increases the pace of her narrative when she fastforwards time. Thus, through such manipulation of the notion of time, Sarraute alters the rhythm of her narratives and causes a sense of disjointedness and flux within these.

A further point of interest regarding time is Sarraute's tendency to digress briefly from the story which she is telling. Throughout her texts she refers both to events in her own life and to occurrences and trends in society at large. Many of her articles, for instance, either centre on personal anecdotes from her present life and on her past experiences and encounters, or discuss social phenomena relevant to the past, present, or future. However, due to their nature and length, each of Sarraute's articles tends to refer to, or focus on, one particular time frame. It is only when such anecdotes and social comments are interspersed at stages throughout her novelistic texts that they may be seen to interfere with a principal narrative thread. Sarraute peppers her novels with personal tales and information regarding her past and her present, and incorporates much general and social information from the past, present and future, as will be witnessed in Chapter 5. Thus, a clear distinction can be made between Sarraute's use of the notion of time in her journalistic and novelistic writing. In brief, time frames fluctuate and are constructed between individual articles, but within her novels. It is therefore in the latter genre that shifts in time cause a sense of disunity. Nevertheless, by contrasting different times both within and outside her narratives, Sarraute ensures that the time in which her texts are set is presented in relation to other time frames. Time is always a relative concept.

Similar treatment is given to the notion of space in Sarraute's writings. For the most part, space is presented as constant and stable, but it is also disrupted regularly. Many of Sarraute's articles are set in Paris and cite particular roads, landmarks, and *arrondissements* [districts] in the city. Some, however, focus on a different region of France, and others are set yet further afield in England, Europe, Israel and America. Nevertheless, as individual articles tend to concentrate on one particular area or country, the space within each is consistent. Rather, it is the fluctuation and abrupt change of space within Sarraute's novels which cause instability. These novels are largely based in Paris and Ile-de-France, but do send their characters on journeys around France – on weekend breaks and to holiday homes – and on foreign holidays. Consequently, there is a frequent sense of movement and change within the narrative. Uses of spatial settings are altered between individual articles but within novels. This results in the latter's appearing disjointed, but does not affect the former. At all times, Sarraute's contrasting of places within and between her texts presents space as thoroughly relational.

If time and space in Sarraute's journalistic and literary works have been considered independently of each other, they can equally be studied together, that is, in relation to each other and as complete units which position and frame her writings. When both time and space remain steady and constant in Sarraute's writings, a sense of stability is maintained in her work. If, however, there is an abrupt change in one of them, the story is disturbed and may subsequently take an unexpected turn. Consequently, a simultaneous change in, or shift of, both time and space, which typically arises when characters embark upon a journey, unfailingly results in a heightened sense of fragmentation and disruption in the text. In her articles, Sarraute uses the theme of journeys by public transport to convey her criticism of the public services, young people's disrespect of the elderly and women's objection, and response to sexual harassment (see Extract 3). In her novels, simultaneous time-space shifts which are conveyed by a journey may be accompanied by strained relationships between characters and, in such circumstances, serve to reinforce any sense of disturbance in the narrative. In short, Sarraute uses and manipulates the notions of time and space both individually and jointly either to provide continuity and consistency, or to create an impression of fragmentation in her texts. In their depiction of time and space, Sarraute's writings therefore share clear similarities with more mainstream fiction (Lodge 1992: 74–9; Rimmon-Kenan 1983/1997: 45–6).

Given the complexities of Claude Sarraute's writings, at the levels of the 'The Text', 'The Participants', 'Social, Cultural, and Political Issues' and 'Time and Space', it is abundantly clear that particular challenges arise when reading and analysing her work and, to an even greater extent, when attempting to rerender it in English.

Dialogism and the Polyphonic Text

When seeking a paradigm which can assist in theorizing writings as complex and dynamic as those of Claude Sarraute, the most prominent point of reference in mid- to late twentieth-century literary analysis is the work of the Russian philosopher, Mikhail Bakhtin, and the Circle of thinkers to which he belonged. Bakhtin was born in Orel, south of Moscow, in 1895.[1] He was raised to be bilingual in Russian and German and was schooled in Vilnius and Odessa, two multilingual and multicultural Russian cities. In 1918 he joined a group of thinkers who were inspired by the study of German philosophers, and it was in this group that he met his contemporaries, Pavel Medvedev (1892–1938) and Valentin Voloshinov (1895–1936), who were later to become key figures in a distinct group: the Bakhtin Circle. Until the early 1920s Bakhtin and his fellow thinkers studied Kant's thought on the interaction of the mind and the World, and Einstein's theories of relativity. These questions, in particular the concept of relativity, were to prove highly influential to many of the Circle's later works.

In the 1920s Bakhtin wrote a series of methodological and critical writings which focused on anthropological and sociological issues (Todorov 1939/1995: 12).[2] From 1929 to 1935 he concentrated on language and literary criticism and later began to reinterpret literary history, paying much attention to the roles of folk humour and carnival in literature. In the last phase of his writing, until his death in 1975, he revisited some of the major issues raised in the 1920s.

---

[1]   The biographical information contained in this chapter was obtained from two principal sources: Lodge (1990: 1–4) and Todorov (1939/1995: 3–13).

[2]   All specific references to works by the Bakhtin Circle are followed by two dates; that of the original publication in Russian, and that of the translation from which the given citation is taken.

These later essays supplement his original works, clarifying some of his earlier ideas. The authorship of certain works, written in the 1920s and signed by other members of the Bakhtin Circle, was disputed at the time of their publication: some believed Bakhtin to have written these but to have signed them 'Medvedev' or 'Voloshinov' due to their polemical nature and their potential repercussions in the then turbulent political climate in the Soviet Union. Nevertheless, a retrospective consideration of the body of texts published by the Circle displays their great thematic unity (Holquist 1990: 11; Todorov 1939/1995: 8). It suggests that, if Bakhtin was not the sole author of these texts, he did at least work in close collaboration with Medvedev and Voloshinov in order to produce them.

Much of Bakhtin's work was only published posthumously in Russia, was little known in the Soviet Union until the late 1970s, and was virtually unheard of abroad. This situation was nevertheless to change in the 1980s when, following the opening up of the Soviet Union, a number of the Bakhtin Circle's works were translated, resulting in a resurgence in their popularity. Since then, Bakhtin's international reputation has continued to grow, critics have become increasingly familiar with his thought, and over the past thirty years some of his terminology has become firmly established in critical vocabulary. Indeed, Bakhtin has been, and continues to be used variously by linguists and philologists, literary critics, anthropologists, social and cultural theorists, and political scientists alike (Lodge 1990: 89).[3] The Circle's work is unified by the concept of *dialogism*, which draws on the notions of dialogue, interactivity and interrelatedness (ibid.: 5). If properly analysed and subsequently extended, this concept can assist in accounting for the range of qualities which characterize Sarraute's writings in the four principal areas identified in the previous chapter: 'The Text', 'The Participants', 'Social, Cultural, and Political Issues', and 'Time and Space'.[4]

3   Despite this increased awareness of Bakhtin, application of his theory is never straight-
     forward; his ideas are rarely finalized and his terminology is in no way hermetic.
     He writes: 'Hence a certain *internal* open-endedness of many of my ideas. [...] My
     love for variations and for a diversity of terms for a single phenomenon' (Bakhtin
     1970–1/1986: 155).
4   Given the 'open-ended' nature of Bakhtin's ideas and terminology, it is, at times,
     difficult to fully categorize his thought. Nevertheless, this study attempts to organize

Spoken Language, the Written Text, and the Novelistic Genre

The concept of dialogue, which has its roots in the Circle's interests in Kant and Einstein, first emerges in Voloshinov's (1929) treatment of spoken language in *Marxism and the Philosophy of Language*. Beginning with the word, Voloshinov (1929/1973: 86) conveys the interactive, responsive character of this unit of language:

> Orientation of the word toward the addressee has an extremely high significance. In point of fact, *word is a two-sided act*. It is determined equally by *whose* word it is and *for whom* it is meant. As word, it is precisely *the product of the reciprocal relationship between speaker and listener, addresser and addressee*. Each and every word expresses the 'one' in relation to the 'other'. I give myself verbal shape from another's point of view, ultimately, from the point of view of the community to which I belong. A word is a bridge thrown between myself and another. If one end of the bridge depends on me, then the other depends on my addressee. A word is a territory shared by both addresser and addressee, by the speaker and his interlocutor.

The interrelational nature of the word may be more or less explicit. As words have been used by other speakers in the past and are continually reused by different speakers, each use effectively exists in relationships with previous uses. Further, each use of each word anticipates future uses of that word. In these two respects, words are implicitly interrelated and embedded in a context of dialogue. Equally, words clearly enter into more explicit dialogue with different words in order to form sentences, or utterances. As Bakhtin (1979/1986) explains, words spoken in context constitute utterances and, as such, render communication possible. This demonstrates his growing certainty of the importance of the context of language:

> The *real unit* of speech communication: the utterance. For speech can exist in reality only in the form of concrete utterances of individual speaking people, speech

---

elements of the Bakhtin Circle's work systematically, as the above-described quadripartite approach provides a particularly appropriate framework in which to read, analyse and translate Sarraute.

subjects. Speech is always cast in the form of an utterance belonging to a particular
speaking subject, and outside this form it cannot exist. (ibid.: 71)

In order to formulate their own utterances and to understand those of their
interlocutors, speakers draw on vast linguistic resources, that is, on their
knowledge of entire systems of language. At the level of entire languages,
Bakhtin displays similar originality of thought in his distinction between
any one national language and its 'sub-languages'. This phenomenon, termed
'heteroglossia', is defined concisely as 'internal differentiation, the stratifica-
tion characteristic of any national language' (1940/1981: 67). In the same
essay, Bakhtin (ibid.) evokes the struggle between two tendencies in the
languages of European peoples: one a centralizing, unifying tendency, the
other a decentralizing tendency which stratifies languages. These internal
strata may take the form of various registers and codes within one national
language, or any subversive or incorrect use of that language. As such, they
represent social variety. Furthermore, as Bakhtin (ibid: 62) suggests, the
coexistence of such strata within a national language enables speakers to
view their own language use objectively, and therefore self-consciously:

> It is possible to view one's own particular language, its internal form, the peculi-
> arities of its world view, its specific linguistic habitus, only in the light of another
> language belonging to someone else, which is almost as much 'one's own' as one's
> native language.

If such linguistic variety occurs within national languages, it may also be
seen to exist beyond these. Where two or more 'pure' languages are present
simultaneously and exist in relationships with one another, this concept is
captured in the term 'polyglossia'. Such juxtaposition of national languages
increases awareness both of alterity in language and of language as a whole,
and therefore once again makes individuals conscious of the nature of their
mother tongue.

> The [...] opposition of *pure languages* in a novel, when taken together with hybridi-
> zation, is a powerful means of creating images of languages. The [...] contrast of
> *languages* [...] delineates the boundaries of languages, creates a feeling for these
> boundaries, compels one to sense physically the plastic forms of different languages.
> (1934–5/1981: 364)

By identifying heteroglossia and referring to a struggle between 'centrifugal forces' in language (ibid.: 364), and by highlighting the coexistence of pure languages, Bakhtin questions the notion that any one unified, authoritative, national language can exist. In contemporary society, these phenomena are equally apparent. Each national language is composed of various registers, codes, and dialects and, in most countries, the national language exists alongside, and interacts with, other foreign languages. Indeed, within a democratic society there exists a plurality of distinct, independent voices. Bakhtin's thinking thus seems both to reflect a desire for democracy in society and to work against the principles of a totalitarian government which are, conversely, founded on the concept of absolute monologue.

At this juncture, it is important to distinguish between the above-discussed notions of dialogue and interactivity, and the Bakhtin Circle's use of the term 'dialogic'. While clearly founded on the these notions, the Circle's dialogic theory considers specifically the nature of relationships both between and within individual voices (Pearce 1994: 50). This method of linguistic analysis is, then, concerned with the positioning of individuals, and the power dynamics which operate, in language:

> Dialogic relationships are possible not only among whole (relatively whole) utterances; a dialogic approach is possible toward any signifying part of an utterance, even toward an individual word, if that word is perceived not as the impersonal word of language but as a sign of someone else's semantic position, as the representative of another person's utterance; that is, if we hear it in someone else's voice. Thus dialogic relationships can permeate inside the utterance, even inside the individual word, as long as two voices collide within it dialogically. (Bakhtin 1929/1984: 184)

Thus far, discussion of dialogue and interactivity has focused exclusively on the analysis of spoken language. However, in *Marxism*, Voloshinov (1929/1973: 95) pursues this issue and proceeds to establish that dialogue in fact permeates all language activity, both spoken and written:

> Dialogue, in the narrow sense of the word, is, of course, only one of the forms – a very important form, to be sure – of verbal interaction. But dialogue can also be understood in a broader sense, meaning not only direct, face-to-face vocalized verbal communication between persons, but also verbal communication of any type whatsoever. A book, i.e., a *verbal performance in print*, is also an element of verbal communication.

It is in Bakhtin's *Problems of Dostoevsky's Poetics*, written in the same year, that the concepts of dialogue and dialogism are introduced officially at both oral and written levels. Through detailed analysis of this Russian novelist's work, Bakhtin reveals an innovative way of studying language in everyday life and in literature, considering the presence of multiple voices and the interrelationships which exist between these. When this spoken language features in the written work, it is not used as spontaneously as it would be in an everyday, extra-literary context (1979/1986: 62). Rather, the author selects it with greater care, and represents it in various, often contrasting, styles. In *Dostoevsky* (1929), Bakhtin provides a detailed account of the different ways in which language appears in the novel. These range from the direct speech of the author, through the represented speech of characters, to doubly oriented, or doubly voiced speech, which includes all other speech acts by all other addressees (1929/1984: 199). In the following, Lodge (1990: 59–60) provides a comprehensive summary of the distinct types of dialogic language which occur in novelistic texts:

> I *The direct speech of the author.* This means, of course, the author as encoded in the text, in an 'objective, reliable, narrative voice'.
> II *The represented speech of the characters.* This may be represented by direct speech ('dialogue' in the non-Bakhtinian sense) or by the convention of soliloquy or interior monologue, or in those elements of reported speech which belong to the language of the character rather than the narrator in free indirect style.
> III *Double-oriented or double-voiced speech.* This category was Bakhtin's most original and valuable contribution to stylistic analysis. It includes all speech which not only refers to something in the world but which also refers to another speech act by another addresser. It is divided into several sub-categories, of which the most important are stylization, *skaz*, parody and hidden polemic.

Bakhtin (in Pearce 1994: 51) further sub-divided this latter category:

> I Unidirectional double-voiced discourse (represented chiefly by *stylization* and *skaz*).
> II Varidirectional double-voiced discourse (represented chiefly by *parody*).
> III The active type (represented by variations of *dialogue, hidden dialogue* and *hidden internal polemic.*

Some further definition of these terms is required. According to Lodge (1929/1984: 189), 'Stylization occurs when the writer borrows another's discourse and uses it for his own purposes – with the same general intention as the original, but in the process "casting a slight shadow of objectification over it"'. *Skaz* traditionally resembles oral discourse and, as Bakhtin (1929/1984: 191) explains, 'is above all an orientation toward *someone else's speech* and only then, as a consequence toward oral speech'. *Parody* 'introduces [...] a semiotic intention that is directly opposed to the original one' (ibid.: 193) and, as regards *hidden polemic*, 'the other's words *actively influence the author's speech*, forcing it to alter itself accordingly under their influence and initiative' (ibid.: 197).

In his *Discourse in the Novel*, Bakhtin (1934–5/1981: 261) discusses further the plurality of languages and the corresponding multiplicity of styles which characterize the novel as a genre:

> he novel as a whole is a phenomenon multiform in style and variform in speech and voice. In it the investigator is confronted with several heterogeneous stylistic unities, often located on different linguistic levels and subject to different stylistic controls.

In *Epic and Novel* (1941/1981), the self-reflexive, dynamic quality of the novel is also stressed. Bakhtin defines the novel as a constantly evolving genre and contrasts it with the complete, finite nature of the epic. He acknowledges that the novel is consequently uncanonical by definition since it reacts against past literary traditions and more conventional works of literature: '[The novel] is, by its very nature, not canonic. It is plasticity itself. It is a genre that is ever questioning, ever examining itself and subjecting its established forms to review' (ibid.: 39).

The Human Subject

As it is people, or subjects, who make all speech and writing possible, it is important to assess the concepts of dialogue and interactivity in relation to individuals. Anthropological concerns, including the origins of man and the formation of subjectivity, were central to discussions within the Bakhtin Circle in the early days of its existence. These issues emerge clearly in the 1927 book, *Freudianism: A Critical Sketch*, in which Voloshinov calls into question approaches in psychology as they fail to recognize the importance of cultural and historical context, society, and language in the formation and development of the human consciousness. According to Voloshinov (1927/1976: 10), Freud believed the human consciousness to be determined by a person's 'biological being' rather than by 'his place and role in history – the class, nation, historical period to which he belongs'. He therefore omitted to look beyond the individual subject when considering its formation. Moreover, Voloshinov takes Freud to task for ignoring the roles of language and ideology in the formation of the human mind. Following his disagreement with Freud's reasoning, he proposes a more interactive theory of subject formation. Recalling the Marxist view that 'human psychology must be socialized', Voloshinov (ibid.: 22) believes that subjects are never formed alone, but that they are social constructs. As such, they are formed in dialogic relationships with others. He restates this idea in *Marxism*, explaining that:

> The structure of the conscious, individual personality is just as social a structure as is the collective type of experience. It is a particular type of interpretation, projected into the individual soul, of a complex and sustained socioeconomic situation. (Voloshinov 1929/1973: 89)

This particular concept is revisited much later by Bakhtin (1961/1984: 287) in *Toward a Reworking of the Dostoevsky Book*:

> I am conscious of myself and become myself only while revealing myself for another, through another, and with the help of another. The most important acts constituting self-consciousness are determined by a relationship toward another consciousness (toward a *thou*). Separation, dissociation, and enclosure within the self are the main reasons for the loss of one's self.

In this connection, a further issue is noteworthy. As subjects are believed to be constructed in society, within relationships, and as each individual will normally continue to have social encounters throughout his life, Bakhtin (ibid.: 291) suggests that no subject can ever be complete and writes that: 'The dialogic relationship [is] the only form of relationship toward the human-being personality preserving its freedom and open-endedness'.

Thus, human beings exist and operate within communities, and as most interaction within these communities occurs through language, the Circle also pays particular attention to the role of language and dialogue in subject formation. It claims that, as language is always addressed to someone (when 'inner monologue' occurs, one is actually addressing language to oneself), all utterances are social. Indeed, Bakhtin (1929/1984: 252) reveals that it is through the use of dialogue that the subject not only makes himself known to others, but also actually becomes himself:

> Dialogue [...] is not a means for revealing, for bringing to the surface the already ready-made character of a person; no, in dialogue a person not only shows himself outwardly, but he becomes for the first time that which he is – and, we repeat, not only for others but for himself as well. To be means to communicate dialogically. When dialogue ends, everything ends.

In the opinion of the Bakhtin Circle, all language is ideological; it reflects the opinions or 'world views' of those who use it. As Bakhtin (1934–5/1981: 291) explains: 'All languages of heteroglossia, whatever the principle underlying them and making each unique, are specific points of view on the world, forms for conceptualizing the world in words, specific world views, each characterized by its own objects, meanings, values'. Therefore, if subjects are created through the act of addressing language to others[5] and if all language is inherently ideological, in communicative situations, people

---

5   Moreover, as all language is inescapably social, the language which an individual uses is, according to Voloshinov (1929/1973: 85), always determined by the nature of his relationship with his addressee: 'Utterance, as we know, is constructed between two socially organized persons [...]. The *word is oriented towards an addressee*, toward *who* that addressee might be: a fellow member or not of the same social group, of higher or lower standing (the addressee's hierarchical status), someone connected to the speaker by close social ties (father, brother, husband, and so on) or not'. Thus, in all instances of linguistic exchange, individuals are positioned discursively. Each

not only become aware of their own and of others' existence, but they also learn of others' world views and are able to make their own views known to others. In sum, the concepts of dialogue and interactivity emerge very clearly in the Bakhtin Circle's treatment of the human consciousness and subjectivity. The Circle considers human beings to be socially constructed; determined by context, social situations, language use, ideology and relationships. Thus, through repeated human contact, the human subject is continually renewed and is therefore not a fixed, finite entity.

In view of the above, a number of post-Bakhtinian scholars have also projected the Circle's dialogic theory onto models of subjectivity and methods of analyzing the human subject (Pearce 1994; Todorov 1983; Youzi 2006). However, there are clearly problems involved in doing so. The Circle's dialogic theory of text and language displays a clear awareness of the power-inscribed relationships at play in text and language and is not merely used to theorize that which is interrelational. Failure to recognize this could lead to distortion of the Circle's original work. In this vein, Pearce (1994: 99) warns of the postmodern 'tendency to divest the dialogic model of a power dynamic [and] a blindness to the problems of grafting a notion of the dialogic on to universalist models of subjectivity'. Thus, she recommends that:

> The next step is for readers and critics to go beyond an interpretation of the dialogic as a model of amicable exchange and reciprocity, and to explore subjectivity in relation to the political / social / historical constraints and expectations present in Bakhtin's accounts of spoken and written dialogue. (ibid: 100)

These considerations have greatly influenced the extent to which I employ the term 'dialogic' in the present work. Throughout *Preserving Polyphonies*, other less contentious adjectives, such as 'interrelated' or 'interconnected', are deemed more suitable.

Bakhtin builds on the idea of socially constructed beings in his treatment of the characters in novels. In his study of Dostoevsky, he contrasts

---

act of communication is revelatory of the relationship and power dynamic which exist between interlocutors.

the interplay of characters' voices in the works of this Russian novelist with the subordination of characters to the author's monologic voice in the novels of Leo Tolstoy. In Dostoevsky's novels, several different voices and consciousnesses interact on relatively equal terms; author and characters have equivalent authority:

> A *plurality of independent and unmerged voices and consciousnesses, a genuine polyphony of fully valid voices is in fact the chief characteristic of Dostoevsky's novels.* What unfolds in his works is not a multitude of characters and fates in a single objective world, illuminated by a single authorial consciousness; rather a *plurality of consciousnesses, with equal rights and each with its own world* combine but are not merged in the unity of the event. Dostoevsky's major heroes are, by the very nature of his creative design, *not only objects of authorial discourse but also subjects of their own directly signifying discourse.* (Bakhtin 1929/1984: 6–7)[6]

Discussing the notions of dialogism and polyphony, Lodge (1990: 90) clarifies that:

> The discourse of the novel [...] is an orchestration of diverse discourses culled from heterogeneous sources, oral and written, conveying different ideological positions which are put in play without ever being subjected to totalizing judgement or interpretation.

Thus, in the polyphonic novel, characters exist in relationships both with one another and with the author, and the author functions quite differently from authors such as Tolstoy. At times, Bakhtin (1929/1984: 67) presents this new authorial position in a very positive light:

---

6   Although Bakhtin (1929/1984: 91) does not at first consider Dostoevsky's journalistic articles to be polyphonic, he later modifies his position, admitting that these do have marked dialogic qualities. The term 'polyphonic' is not, then, specific to the novel. As Bakhtin (ibid.: 93) clarifies: 'This striving of Dostoevsky to perceive each thought as an integrated personal position, to think in voices, is clearly evidenced [...] in the compositional structure of his journalistic articles. His manner of developing a thought is everywhere the same: he develops it dialogically, not in a dry, lyrical dialogue, but by juxtaposing whole, profoundly individualized voices. Even in his polemical articles he does not really persuade but rather organizes voices, yokes together semantic orientations, most often in the form of some imagined dialogue'.

Here it is [...] appropriate to emphasize the *positive and active quality* of the new
authorial position in a polyphonic novel. It would be absurd to think that the author's
consciousness is nowhere expressed in Dostoevsky's novels. The consciousness of a
creator of a polyphonic novel is constantly and everywhere present in the novel, and
is active in it to the highest degree.

If the author is omnipresent and enjoys a position of authority, he can use
the characters' voices to his own advantage, treating these individuals as
additional mouthpieces through which to express his own ideas. In this
vein, Bakhtin (1934–5/1981: 315) explains that: 'Each character's speech
possesses its own belief system, thus it may also refract authorial intentions
and consequently may, to a certain degree, constitute a second language
for the author'. Moreover, in this essay Bakhtin makes an explicit distinction between the author and the narrator. In the following, the author is
depicted as the supreme authority in the work who wields considerable
power. He chooses his narrator, the teller of his story, and all languages to
be contained in the text, and has an overriding ability to use and manipulate all individual voices and their languages as he so pleases:

> The author is not to be found in the language of the narrator, nor in the normal
> literary language to which the story opposes itself [...] but rather the author utilizes
> now one language, now another, in order to avoid giving himself up wholly to either
> of them. (ibid.: 314)

This positive treatment notwithstanding, Bakhtin's opinion of the author
of the polyphonic novel becomes ambiguous. On a number of occasions he
explains that the author's role is problematic, and his power limited. This
emerges clearly in *Problems of Dostoevsky's Poetics* and becomes a recurrent
theme throughout Bakhtin's (1929/1984: 67–8) work:

> The function of [the] consciousness [of the author of the polyphonic novel] and
> the forms of its activity are different than in the monologic novel: the author's con-
> sciousness does not transform others' consciousnesses (that is, the consciousnesses
> of the characters) into objects, and does not give them second-hand and finalizing
> definitions. Alongside and in front of itself it senses others' equally valid conscious-
> nesses, just as infinite and open-ended as itself.

As the author of the polyphonic novel exists on an equal plane to his characters, it also appears that he has no real language of his own:

> The author does not speak in a given language (from which he distances himself to a greater or lesser degree), but he speaks, as it were, *through* language, a language that has somehow more or less materialized, become objectivized, that he merely ventriloquates. (1934–5/1981: 299)

In addition to this, in some of his later 'Notes', Bakhtin acknowledges that, as the author uses a wide range of styles in the polyphonic novel, he has no personal style or 'setting', and is therefore obliged to imitate other genres. He states that: 'The writer is deprived of style and setting; literature has been completely secularized. The novel, deprived of style and setting, is essentially not a genre; it must imitate (rehearse) some extraartistic genre' (1970–1/1986: 133).

As the creator of a work, the author is traditionally regarded as a figure of authority within that work, exercising a certain amount of control over it. However, in the polyphonic novel many subjects coexist, each of whom has an individual consciousness, and characters enjoy freedom of thought and opinion. Moreover, as these subjects are social constructs, they are neither moulded nor repressed by a single, higher authority; author and characters exist as equals. Within society, recognition of the existence of many different, equal people evidently opposes any notion of a single ruling class or culture, and thus prevents any possibility of political hegemony. These notions, which are present in the work of the Bakhtin Circle, were undoubtedly inspired by the climate of Revolution and Civil War in which it worked, and by the Circle's disapproval of the political repression and terror which existed in the Soviet Union under the reigns of Lenin (1918–24) and Stalin (1922–53). By advocating freedom of opinion and equality, the Bakhtin Circle's work encourages the implementation of such principles within society.

It is evident that Bakhtin's interests in subjects, or people, within the written text centre primarily on the roles of the characters and author. Nevertheless, in two of his essays which constitute *The Dialogic Imagination*, he begins to acknowledge in clear terms that relationships in fact exist beyond the text and he extends this concept to consider the role of the reader. He writes of a text's 'subsequent life' and of 'a continual renewing of the work through the creative perception of listeners and readers' (1938/1981: 254). He also explains that: 'Great novelistic images continue to grow and develop even after the moment of their creation, they are capable of being creatively transformed in different eras, far distant from the day and hour of their original birth' (1934–5/1981: 422). This issue is returned to in a later essay, where it is now recognized to have quite considerable importance. In his 'The Problems of Speech Genres', Bakhtin (1979/1986: 75) states that: 'The work, like the rejoinder in dialogue, is oriented toward the response of the other (others), toward his active responsive understanding'. Moreover, it is in this essay that he introduces the notion of a 'super-addressee'; a hypothetical presence who, due to his 'various understandings of the world', comprehends fully all aspects of the author's text:

> In addition to this addressee [the reader] (the second party), the author of the utterance, with a greater or lesser awareness, presupposes a higher superaddressee (third), whose absolutely just responsive understanding is presumed, either in some metaphysical distance or in distant historical time [...]. In various ages and with various understandings of the world, this superaddressee and his ideally true responsive understanding assume various ideological expressions [...]. Each dialogue takes place as if against the background of the responsive understanding of an invisibly present third party who stands above all the participants in the dialogue (partners). (ibid.: 126)

So far, the essence of Bakhtin's (1929; 1979) concept of polyphony has been identified in the dynamic, interactive nature of the voices of all subjects within and beyond the text. However, at a later stage in his study of Dostoevsky, Bakhtin adds a further dimension to his definition of the polyphonic. He explains that dialogue does not merely occur within the conversations and between the voices of textual subjects; rather, it extends to multiple levels of the novelistic work. In the light of this second definition, it is apt to consider other significant fields in which Bakhtin's (1929/1984: 40) work can help to account for the presence of dialogue, interactivity, interrelationships and, at times, dialogism proper, in both extra-literary and literary contexts:

Indeed, the essential dialogicality of Dostoevsky is in no way exhausted by the external, compositionally expressed dialogues carried on by the characters. *The polyphonic novel is dialogic through and through.* Dialogic relationships exist among all elements of novelistic structure, that is, they are juxtaposed contrapuntally. And this is so because dialogic relationships are a much broader phenomenon than mere rejoinders in a dialogue, laid out compositionally in the text; they are an almost universal phenomenon, permeating all speech and all relationships and manifestations of human life in general, everything that has meaning and significance.

Society, Culture, and Politics

As the Bakhtin Circle argued, individuals, or subjects, are formed in relation to other people, particularly through the language which they use in order to communicate with these others, and it is during such interaction that people become aware of their own existence. If such relationships make the individual aware of what he is, by comparison with what he is not ('I' versus 'you', *je* versus *tu*), this distinction must, by necessity, also make the individual conscious of what is other. Once individuals are aware of their own essence, of the social relationships which exist between themselves and others, and of their belonging to a collectivity, it can be said that they operate in societies. It is widely acknowledged that, on a larger scale, societies are systems of human organizations which generate distinctive cultural patterns; the concept of culture is formed within societies. Culture has been defined as 'the total of the inherited ideas, beliefs, values and knowledge which constitute the shared basis of social action' (Collins 1994: 387). As strong links therefore exist between language, society, and culture, Voloshinov's (1929/1973) use of the term 'dialogue' is again noteworthy. He states that: 'Dialogue can be understood in a broader sense, meaning not only direct, face-to-face, vocalized verbal communication between persons, but also verbal communication of any type whatsoever' (ibid.: 4). This is interpreted perceptively by Voloshinov's translators, Matejka and Titunik, who explain that he 'implies that actually every cultural pattern can be derived from the conceptual framework of human dialogue; hence dialogue assumes the character of a primordial source of social creativity in general' (ibid.). Thus, the Bakhtin Circle saw dialogue to be at play not only within oral and written communication, human relations, and the formation of subjects, but also throughout entire societies and cultures.

First, relationships can occur between people who speak the same language, or variety of language, and by extension, between those who belong to the same society and culture, or strata of a society and culture. It is in his work on Rabelais that Bakhtin focuses explicitly on linguistic, social, and cultural interrelationships within a given community. In his treatment of Rabelais he examines 'folk humour', an oral tradition born in the Middle Ages, of which one important form is the 'Ritual Spectacle' or 'Carnival' (1965/1984: 5), and considers the ways in which Rabelais incorporated folk humour into literature. The usual setting for the carnival is the marketplace, and this occasion is exceptional in that it gathers together people from all walks of life. It is an event in which many people, speaking different varieties of language and belonging to very diverse strata of society, can temporarily coexist. The following extract from *Rabelais and his World* captures the notions of linguistic and social hybridity and equality:

> The suspension of all hierarchical precedence during carnival time was of particular significance. Rank was especially evident during official feasts... It was a consecration of inequality. On the contrary, all were considered equal during carnival. Here, in the town square, a special form of free and familiar contact reigned among people who were usually divided by the barriers of caste, property, profession and age... People were, so to speak, reborn from new, purely human relations [...]. This temporary suspension, both real and ideal, of hierarchical rank created during carnival time a special type of communication impossible in everyday life. This led to the creation of special kinds of marketplace speech and gesture, frank and free, permitting no distance between those who came into contact with each other and liberating from norms of etiquette and decency imposed at other times. A special carnivalesque, marketplace style of expression was formed which we find abundantly represented in Rabelais's novel [*Gargantua* and *Pantagruel*]. (ibid.: 10)

Second, if relationships exist amongst people belonging to the same or to different strata of one's own society or culture, they also occur beyond any one linguistic, social, or cultural group. Although the earlier works of the

Bakhtin Circle appear to concentrate on relationships within a national culture or civilization, which manifest themselves in language through the presence of heteroglossia (Bakhtin 1940/1981: 67), they nevertheless contain some suggestion that these may be extended. A first instance of this can be witnessed in Bakhtin's (1934–5/1981: 364) discussion of polyglossia; the coexistence and juxtaposition of two or more national languages. In a much later essay, Bakhtin returns to this issue, stating more explicitly the importance of both the other and the foreign other. These can heighten, or indeed foster, an awareness of the self:

> In order to understand, it is immensely important for the person who understands to be *located outside* the object of his or her creative understanding – in time, in space, in culture. For one cannot even really see one's own exterior and comprehend it as a whole, and no mirrors or photographs can help; our real exterior can be seen and understood only by other people because they are located outside us in space and because they are others. In the realm of culture, outsideness is a most powerful factor in understanding. It is only in the eyes of another culture that foreign culture reveals itself fully and profoundly (but not maximally fully, because there will be cultures that see and understand even more). (Bakhtin 1979/1986: 7)

Bakhtin's treatment of relationships within and between societies and cultures is, it has been seen, grounded in the study of real-life carnivalesque tradition and this tradition was reflected in certain works of literature. It is in his analysis of the carnival that Bakhtin (1929; 1965) traces humour and laughter in literature back to its roots. However, it is not until much later in his 'Notes' that he blatantly juxtaposes these amusing, comical tones with the 'serious'. He writes: 'The inadmissibility of mono-tony (of serious monotony). The sphere of serious tone. Irony as a form of silence. Irony (and laughter) as means for transcending a situation, rising above it' (1970–1/1986: 134). These notes contain an explicit sense of dialogue and the interrelational. What is humorous exists in relation to what is not. Humour derides what is serious and therefore could not exist as it does if it was not seen in relation to the seriousness against which it reacts. In the following extract from *Problems of Dostoevsky's Poetics*, Bakhtin (1929/1984: 5) lists three major types of folk humour, all of which oppose something more solemn:

I *Ritual Spectacles*: carnival pageants, comic shows of the marketplace.
II *Comic Verbal Compositions*: parodies both oral and written, in Latin and the vernacular.
III *Various genres of Billingsgate*: ['Billingsgate' means 'abuse and violate invective': the term has its etymological origins in the fishwomen of Billingsgate market, London]: curses, oaths, popular blazons.

Festive and jovial 'spectacles' in the marketplace contrast with the everyday activities which occur within one's usual 'class' or 'rank'. 'Oral and written parodies', later to be incorporated into literature, challenge the standards and norms of traditional, canonized literary genres, and 'Billingsgate' effectively disregards polite and generally acceptable language use. These forms of humour all react against what is conventional and widely acceptable and are thus intended to shock and to provoke laughter. Bakhtin (1965/1984: 12) later outlines the complexities of carnival laughter:

> Let us say a few words about the complex nature of carnival laughter. It is, first of all, a festive laughter, therefore it is not an individual reaction to some isolated 'comic' event. Carnival laughter is the laughter of all the people. Second, it is universal in scope; it is directed to all and everyone, including the carnival's participants. The entire world is seen in its droll aspect, in its gay relativity. Third, this laughter is ambivalent: it is gay, triumphant, and at the same time, mocking, deriding. It asserts and denies, it buries and revives. Such is the laughter of carnival.

In view of this, Bakhtin believes humour to have an essential (and indeed dialogic) function in the process of social change in that it serves to undermine authority. He explains that 'carnivalistic laughter is directed toward something higher – toward a shift of authorities and truths, a shift of world orders' (ibid.: 127). In his 'Notes' he reinforces this idea, suggesting that laughter assists in destroying certain hegemonic attitudes. He claims that 'only dogmatic and authoritarian cultures are one-sidedly serious' (1970–1/1986: 134). Once again, this rejection of the notion of any single, ruling authority, a principle which is also played out in Rabelais's literature, both reflects Bakhtin's disapproval of the monolithic political system which was in place in the Soviet Union during the twentieth century, and encourages a reversal of this.

Time and Space

The Bakhtin Circle's treatment of the issues of time and space is concentrated in 'Forms of Time and of the Chronotope in the Novel' (1938). In this essay, Bakhtin employs the term *chronotope* to refer to the ways in which time and space are represented in literary fiction. As he clarifies: 'We will give the name *chronotope* (literally "time space") to the intrinsic connectedness of temporal and spatial relationships that are artistically expressed in literature' (1938/1981: 84). Bakhtin (ibid.: 252) believes chronotopes to be 'the organizing centers for the fundamental narrative events of the novel'. Inspired by past theorists he refers explicitly, in his opening paragraph, to Einstein's theory of relativity which viewed time and space as inseparable. Bakhtin does, however, differentiate himself from this scientist, as his own study of time and space is specifically 'borrowed for literary criticism' (ibid.: 84). Other explicit dialogue takes place between Bakhtin and the many writers and novelists to whose chronotopic works he refers, from the Ancient Greeks to Rabelais. This most in-depth discussion of past writers, whose assimilation of 'an actual historical chronotope in literature has been complicated and erratic' (ibid.: 85), provides Bakhtin's essay with a distinctly historical dimension.

In his overview of the novel, Bakhtin identifies a number of generic types of chronotope. Amongst these are: the biographical novel, in which characters progress through and discover their own lives; the folkloric, realist tradition, which again traces the development of individuals; chronotopes of the fool, clown and rogue – comical individuals who are inherently reactive and who inhabit separate, individual chronotopes –[7] and the Rabelaisian novel. Bakhtin (ibid.: 242) explains that: 'In his novel

---

7   In his study of these comical figures, Bakhtin (1938/1981: 159) recognizes that it is possible that several literary chronotopes may co-exist: 'The rogue, the clown and the fool create around themselves their own special little world, their own chronotope'. Moreover, in such 'polychronotopic' texts (Pearce 1994: 71–2), the author and readers of the text can witness a 'dialogue' between chronotopes (Bakhtin 1938/1981: 252).

Rabelais unfolds before us, as it were, the completely unrestricted, universal chronotope of human life. And this was fully in accord with the approaching era of great geographical and astronomical discoveries.

Sub-categories of the chronotope include those of the encounter and the road. Despite the fact that 'the road is always one that passes through *familiar territory*, and not through some exotic *alien world*' (ibid.: 245), the paths of characters from very different social spaces may intersect in this chronotope. Further sub-categories which Bakhtin (ibid.: 246–7) identifies are the threshold, in which crisis points occur, and the 'parlour' or 'salon', in which elements of social and private lives are intermingled:

> In the parlour and salons of the Restoration and July Monarchy is found the barom-
> eter of political and business life; political, business, social, literary reputations are
> made and destroyed [...]. Most important of all this is the weaving of historical and
> socio-public events together with the personal and even deeply private side of life,
> with the secrets of the boudoir; the interweaving of petty, private intrigues with
> political and financial intrigues, the interpenetration of state with boudoir secrets,
> of historical sequences with the everyday and biographical sequences.

Of particular significance in this essay is the attention which Bakhtin (ibid.: 250) gives to the chronotope's power to structure, or organize, literary texts:

> What is the significance of all these chronotopes? What is most obvious in their
> meaning for *narrative*? They are the organizing centers for the fundamental narra-
> tive events of the novel. The chronotope is the place where the knots of narrative
> are tied and untied. It can be said without qualification that to them belongs the
> meaning that shapes narrative.

and to the (dialogic) ability of one chronotope to 'dominate' or control others:

> Within the limits of a single work and within the total literary output of a single
> author we may notice a number of different chronotopes and complex interactions
> of them, specific to the given work or author; it is common moreover for one of
> these chronotopes to envelope or dominate the others. (ibid.: 252)

The chronotope does, then, clearly have a powerful role in the literary work. Due to the close proximity of the concepts of time and space in literature, if either of these remains constant, a sense of stability can be maintained in the narrative. In his discussion of the idyll, Bakhtin (ibid.: 225) states that: 'This blurring of all the temporal boundaries [is] made possible by a unity of place'. By extension, as this time-space dyad is so powerful in the literary work, if these two concepts are disrupted simultaneously this will inevitably result in instability and fragmentation in the novel.

The key tenets of the work of Mikhail Bakhtin and the Bakhtin Circle therefore constitute a paradigm which can convincingly be brought to bear on the writings of Claude Sarraute. The Circle's diverse work is unified by the concept of dialogism (Pearce 1994; Todorov 1939/1995), which was originally founded on the conviction that all language, both spoken and written, is dynamic and interactive, consists of interrelationships, and is inevitably power-inscribed. If extended, it can be used to suggest that everything exists as part of a greater whole. Entire languages and texts, societies and cultures, time frames and spaces are thus susceptible to mutual influences and are, indeed, products of these. Holquist (1990: 41) explains succinctly that: 'Dialogism's fundamental a priori [is] that nothing *is* in itself'. As this chapter has illustrated, dialogue, interactivity and, in specific cases, dialogism, occur in four principal areas of the Circle's work, which correspond to the four major areas of interest previously identified in Sarraute's writings: 'The Text', 'The Participants', 'Social, Cultural, and Political Issues' and 'Time and Space'. When presented according to these categories, the work of the Bakhtin Circle can, then, be used both to inform the reading and analysis of Claude Sarraute, and to later guide the translation of these writings. As will be discussed in Chapters 4 and 5, it will be deemed that, if my target texts (TTs) manage to preserve in the TL the range of qualities present in Sarraute's polyphonic writings, they will have been successful.

The Translator as Interlocutor: An Eclectic Approach to Reading and Translating Claude Sarraute

Owing to their peculiar character and multiple layers of complexity, Sarraute's writings clearly lend themselves, in many respects, to a Bakhtinian analysis. At the level of the 'Text', these writings are medleys of intra- and intergeneric references, generic imitations and parodies and seemingly transcribed conversations containing colloquial language. The 'Participants' in these texts are equally complex and unstable. Authors, characters, and readers are acutely self-conscious, their self-views fluctuate and their roles are often reversed.

'Social, Cultural, and Political Issues' form the core of Sarraute's subject matter and, in her work, issues pertaining both to France and to other peoples and cultures are described. In her portrayal of France as a culturally disparate, kaleidoscopic totality, Sarraute has frequent recourse to ironic and subversive tones. Her texts are, moreover, underpinned by the notions of 'Time and Space' and her deliberate manipulation of these creates further disjointedness and flux within her work.

Thus, each of Sarraute's writings proves a challenging, and at times puzzling, read for an SL audience. In addition to their dynamism and various complexities, these texts have a tendency to position their readers inconsistently. Sarraute, who constantly interacts with her audience, confides in her readers, advises and guides them and encourages their participation in her work, yet also reproaches them. Her reader's own identity is, then, inherently unstable. As a consequence, Sarraute's writings have, over the years, elicited very diverse responses. Many of these have been positive. Nevertheless, other readers have regarded her work much less favourably. Describing *un éreintement épouvantable* [terrible slating] which she once received in the newspaper, *Libération*, she explained: 'They said that [...] when your mother was the queen of French literature, you could get away with writing like me!' (ICS).

In order to enable each individual reader to arrive at a consistent and coherent interpretation of Sarraute's complex writings, this chapter therefore first reviews rapidly and concisely a diverse range of theories of textual and stylistic analysis and reader-response criticism, before returning to each of these and suggesting their relative applicability to the reading and analysis of Sarraute. Using this brief overview in order to suggest that, when considered collectively, the fundamentally distinct work of Bakhtin and Derrida offers a more fruitful framework in which to approach Sarraute, the chapter then turns to the issue of translating these writings. It again reviews a range of theoretical approaches in the field, before demonstrating their applicability to the rerendering of Sarraute's polyphonies. It concludes by arguing that the work of Bakhtin and Derrida can, once more, greatly assist this task as it encourages the translator to be open, dynamic, and eclectic in their approach.

Theories of Textual and Stylistic Analysis

Rooted in a tradition of German thought which originated in the work of Friedrich Schleiermacher (1768–1834) and Wilhelm Dilthey (1833–1911) and extended to that of Martin Heidegger (1889–1976) and Hans-Georg Gadamer (1900–2002), hermeneutics, as a theory of interpretation, concentrates on the problems of understanding the meanings of texts. Hermeneuticians are concerned with the identification of recurring textual features which, when identified by the reader, enable them to discover both the meaning of the work as a whole and, through this, the author's true intention. Their approach to textual interpretation – the 'hermeneutic circle', which requires that the reader move repeatedly from the 'work's parts' to 'the work as a whole', and vice versa – is explained succinctly by Baldick (1990: 97):

> [The] hermeneutic circle [is] a model of the process of interpretation which begins from the problem of relating a work's parts to the work as a whole: since the parts

cannot be understood without some preliminary understanding of the whole, and the whole cannot be understood without comprehending its parts, our understanding of a work must involve an anticipation of the whole that informs our view of the parts while simultaneously being modified by them.

In a philological, hermeneutic spirit, Spitzer (1962: 135) recommended establishing the 'etymon' of a given text – that is, a particular stylistic feature of the text which is salient on a first reading and whose prominence is confirmed by its recurrence throughout the work – in order to penetrate to the heart of the text and to the 'soul of the author'. In his analysis of Diderot's 1796 *La Religieuse* Spitzer (ibid.: 151) explains: 'In linguistics the concrete precedes the abstract: the "etymology" of a stylistic pattern must be found in that situation which is closest to concrete, to sensuous reality'.

In the early twentieth century, Russian Formalism emerged as a reaction to widespread criticism of the previous vagueness of literature and poetics. Members of this school of literary theory and analysis aimed to adopt a scientific approach to the study of literature. They concentrated on analysing systematically the linguistic features of literary texts and focused on defining 'literariness', that is, those features of literary language which distinguish it from the non-literary. Essentially, the formalists believed that, in order to fully understand literature as an art, the analyst must focus on its form (Eichenbaum 1926).

The formalist tradition paved the way for structuralism, an intellectual movement prevalent in France in the 1960s. According to Baldick (1990: 213–14):

> Structuralism [...] analyses cultural phenomena according to principles derived from linguistics, emphasizing the systematic interrelationships among the elements of any human activity, and thus the abstract codes and conventions governing the social production of meanings. Building on the linguistic concept of the phoneme – a unit of meaningful sound defined purely by its differences from other phonemes rather than by any inherent features – structuralism argues that the elements composing any cultural phenomenon [...] are similarly 'relational': that is, they have meaning only by virtue of their contrasts with other elements of the system, especially in binary oppositions of paired opposites. Their meanings can be established not by referring each element to any supposed equivalent in natural reality, but only by analyzing its function within a self-contained cultural code.

In the field of literary analysis, structuralism seeks to explain those rules, or 'codes and conventions', which exist within a given text in order to create meaning. Like their formalist predecessors, structuralist critics sought to provide objective, scientific analyses of the features of literary texts and to do so by employing linguistic principles. The structuralist literary analyses of Barthes are particularly noteworthy. In his *S/Z*, Barthes (1970) carries out a detailed analysis of Balzac's 1836 *Sarrasine*, exposing recurring patterns of narrative, and the relationships between Balzac's text and those previous works which inspired it. Genette's approach to literary analysis is also firmly situated in the structuralist tradition. In his study of narrative 'levels' and 'voices', Genette (1972/1988: 255–6) introduces such concepts as the 'extradiegetic narrator' (one who is superior to the story which he narrates), the 'intradiegetic narrator' (a figure who is also a character in the narrative told by the 'extradiegetic narrator'), the 'heterodiegetic narrator' (one who does not participate in the story) and the 'homodiegetic narrator' (one who does participate).

Subsequently there was a departure from these relatively static methods of literary analysis and a consequent move towards a theory of language and literature which centred on the notion of language function. While still accounting for the syntactic structure of language, functionalism concentrates primarily on what language does, and how it does so. Halliday's (1964/1970: 70) work provides an important illustration of this approach when he writes: 'If a text is to be described at all, then it should be described properly; and this means by the theories and methods developed in linguistics, the subject whose task is precisely to show how language works'. Adopting this approach, he applies linguistic theory in order to explain features of language contained in Yeats's poem, 'Leda and Swann', and in three passages of prose fiction. In the former, it is demonstrated that uses of the word 'the' occur differently from the ways in which they do in non-literary language, and that Yeats shifts certain verbs functionally so that they become other parts of speech. In his studies of prose, Halliday focuses on the patterns in which nouns occur, on lexical sets, and on textual cohesion.

Halliday's 'systemic functional grammar', a notoriously complex model with which to analyse language, became a key concept in discourse analysis. This analytical method views language as an act of communication and, in the analysis of written texts, relates the writer's choices to the sociological context in which they operate (Munday 2001: 90–1). It studies the relationships between sentences in spoken and written discourse:

> In modern cultural theory, especially in the post-structuralism associated with [...] Michel Foucault, the term has been used to denote any coherent body of statements that produces a self-confirming account of reality by defining an object of attention and generating concepts with which to analyse it (e.g. medical discourse, legal discourse, aesthetic discourse). (Baldick 1990: 59)

In his *L'Archéologie du savoir* (1969) and *L'Ordre du discours* (1971), Foucault posits that there are certain rules determining the structure of language which are closely linked to the ways in which societies are regulated, that is, how these societies are controlled by power. He argues that the rules governing language provide the foundations for 'discursive functions', or the conventions which determine both a speaker's or writer's choice of topic and the means by which they express this.

Foucault pursues the political nature of these functions and suggests that power relations in society define all knowledge and condition the ways in which individuals present this. Discourse is therefore crucial in the construction of power relations within communities, and texts are consequently depersonalized products of political society. Thus, according to this school of thought, language and texts do not merely reflect reality. As was established in the Introduction to *Preserving Polyphonies*, they are also socio-political instruments which have the power to influence, and indeed construct, social and political ideologies. Theories of discourse, based on Halliday's systemic functional grammar, now describe the interactive relationship between the spoken and written word and the social and contextual influences which condition both of these (Chouliaraki & Fairclough 1999; Fairclough 1995; Van Dijk 1995).

The Role of the Reader

Having concentrated principally on the analysis of written works as an objective process, it is now apt to consider the varying degrees of importance which each of the above-discussed approaches to textual and stylistic analysis attaches to the reader. The reader clearly has a central role in the hermeneutic model of interpretation; he relies on his own instinct in order to identify the 'etymon' of a given text and subsequently arrive at a thorough understanding of the work as a whole. Indeed, according to the 'hermeneutic circle', the reader is a dynamic, interactive participant in the reading process. The formalists focused less on the reader himself than on the importance of determining, and analysing systematically, significant features of the literary work. The role of the reader is nevertheless implicit in these processes of identification and analysis. In a similar vein, proponents of a structuralist approach to the analysis of literature were primarily interested in the description of structures within the text. However, as Hawkes (1977: 17) points out, theorists operating in this tradition were beginning to acknowledge the role of the reader/ analyst in both the 'perception' and the 'description' of these structures:

> Structuralism is fundamentally a way of thinking about the world which is predominantly concerned with the perception and description of structures [...] it is the result of a momentous historic shift in the nature of perception [...]. The 'new' perception involve[s] the realization that despite appearances to the contrary the world does not consist of independently existing objects, whose concrete features can be perceived clearly and individually, and whose nature can be classified accordingly. In fact, every perceiver's *method* of perceiving can be shown to contain an inherent bias which affects what is perceived to a significant degree. A wholly objective perception of individual entities is therefore not possible: any observer is bound to *create* something of what he observes. Accordingly the *relationship* between observer and observed achieves a kind of primacy. [...] the true nature of things may be said to lie not in things themselves, but in the relationships which we construct, and then perceive, *between* them.[1]

---

1   Culler (1975/1989: 17–18) argues that it is only by recognizing narrative structures and literary conventions that the reader can understand the text, or have 'literary competence': 'To read a text as literature is not to make one's mind a *tabula rasa* and

The work of Riffaterre represented a significant attempt to combine such structural and reader-centred approaches. Riffaterre was keen to carry out systematic stylistic analyses of literary works. In his 'Describing Poetic Structures: Two Approaches to Baudelaire's "Les Chats"' (1966) he does, however, criticize Jakobson and Lévi-Strauss's structuralist readings of this poem as they concentrate on phonetic and grammatical patterns which its reader may be unable to identify. These two theorists therefore fail to take account of the reader's active participation in the text. The alternative method of analysis which Riffaterre proposes involves identifying those significant linguistic features of the poem which come to the reader's attention during his reading of the text. Thus: 'The pertinent segmentation of the poem must [...] be based on [...] responses [from the reader]: they pinpoint in the verbal sequence the location of the devices that trigger them' (ibid.: 37). Riffaterre ensures that his results are thorough by considering the responses of a 'superreader'; a hypothetical presence which encompasses other poets, critics and translators of the poem, dictionaries and notes in other text books. He writes: 'This "superreader" in no way distorts the special act of communication under study: It simply performs it more thoroughly by performing it over and over again' (ibid.: 38). In short, Riffaterre's approach to literary and stylistic analysis is at once systemic and rigorous, dynamic and fully conscious of the reader.

If Fish also married careful analytical strategies with a constant consideration of the role of the reader, in many respects his work represented a radical break with that of his predecessors. Fish (1970: 70) believed in 'the explanatory power of a method of analysis which takes the reader, as an actively mediating presence, fully into account [and which] has as its focus the "psychological effects" of the utterance'. However, he explains that his approach 'involves an analysis of the developing responses of the reader in relation to the words as they succeed one another in time. The analysis must be of the developing responses to distinguish it from the atomism of much stylistic criticism' (ibid.: 73). Indeed, for Fish, the reader's importance is such that he becomes the producer of the text's meaning.

---

approach it without preconceptions; one must bring to it an implicit understanding of the operations of literary discourse which tells one what to look for'.

Thus, Fish (ibid.: 72) destroys the traditional divide between reader and text and, by suggesting that there is no pre-existing text to which the reader responds, he also challenges the role of the author:[2]

> The sentence [...] is no longer an object, a thing-in-itself, but an *event*, something that *happens* to, and with the participation of, the reader. And it is this event, this happening [...] that is, I would argue, the *meaning* of the sentence.

In his study of stylistics, Fish attaches equal importance to the affective role of the reader. Nonetheless, unlike his predecessors he suggests that, due to the reader's subjectivity, it is impossible to be entirely objective and scientific when carrying out stylistic analyses. As every stylistic analysis is an act of interpretation, Fish argues, style, like meaning, cannot be an inherent property of the text. Instead, it is a series of dynamic effects produced by the reader: 'I would argue that [stylistic patterns] do not lie innocently in the world but are themselves constituted by an interpretative act' (Fish 1976: 177). For Fish, meaning and stylistic effect are, then, dynamic, unfixed, and unstable. As Weber (1996: 3) clarifies:

> [They] have to be seen as a potential which is actualized in a (real) reader's mind, the product of a dialogic interaction between author, the author's context of production, the text, the reader and the reader's context of reception, where context includes all sorts of sociohistorical, cultural and intertextual factors.

The issues of reader and context have remained important in the schools of functionalism and discourse analysis. In the former, identification of textual and stylistic features is only considered important where the function of these features is relevant to the reader's interpretation of the written work. In the latter, the reader/critic's act of analysis is itself subject to scrutiny. As all individuals exist within a certain milieu, which has its own system of values (Medvedev 1928), no one interpretation nor method of analysis chosen can ever be value-free. Thus, the reader/analyst is obliged to recognize their own position and to acknowledge this as having a potentially

---

2   A number of deconstructionists also question the very existence of the author (Barthes 1968; Foucault 1970).

political role in society. Moreover, as a respondent to a given text, the reader/analyst is now increasingly aware of the relationship which exists between that text and their own analysis. Their own text is an intertext, contiguous with that which they have read; the processes of reading and analysis are therefore inherently recursive.

Applicability of Theories to the Reading and Analysis of Sarraute

From this eclectic overview of literary, stylistic, and reader-response theories, it emerges that, while none of the approaches discussed is entirely suited to the reading and analysis of Sarraute, elements of each of these may assist the present study.

The hermeneuticians assumed that the written text has a definite 'core' and an authorial figure whose intention is clearly defined. However, Sarraute's writings are self-ironizing and contain extended instances of *mise-en-abyme* which prevent them from having a true core. *Maman coq* (1989) ends with a scene in which Sarraute is insulted by her editor, Françoise Verny. Verny dismisses Sarraute's latest manuscript and instead praises the work of JJ, a character in *Maman coq*: 'People couldn't care less about you. Nobody's interested in you anymore, my poor pet. It's the next JJ who'll be a sensation' (1989: 228). Furthermore, Sarraute's intentions and opinions are invariably ambiguous, owing to her frequent use of humour and irony. 'That's what's funny about humour', she told me, 'you can say loads of things in dozens of amusing ways' (ICS). Nevertheless, given that the hermeneutic circle, as adopted by such theorists as Spitzer, recommends careful identification of significant, recurring textual features – Sarraute's writings frequently contain dialogic language and subversive, idiosyncratic features, as demonstrated throughout Chapter 1 –, reference to this interactive model of interpretation can usefully assist the reading and analysis of Sarraute.

Similarly, it would clearly be impossible to fully apply to Sarraute those methods of analysis advocated by the Russian formalists. The formalists adopted a highly scientific and rigid approach to the study of purely literary works and concentrated on the analysis of their form. As has been witnessed, Sarraute's writings are thoroughly dynamic and consequently unstable and cannot be considered to be purely literary as they constantly hybridize distinct written genres. Given the extent to which these writings are all deeply embedded in the TL culture, it would also be too restrictive to merely analyse them according to their form. In spite of this, aspects of the formalist approach may be helpful in he analysis of Sarraute. The formalists recommended close, objective analyses of the features of (literary) texts; Sarraute's writings display many striking features at the levels of 'The Text', 'The Participants', 'Social, Cultural, and Political Issues', and 'Time and Space'. Moreover, these theorists advocated an analytical approach which combines literary and linguistic analysis (Eichenbaum 1926). Given the extent to which Sarraute's written works incorporate the spoken word – entire newspaper articles are written as reported conversations, author and characters chat freely and colloquially –, an in-depth consideration of the linguistic minutiae of these writings is essential.

The structuralists focused on the rules, codes, and conventions which operate within the written work in order to create meaning within that text; an approach which appears inadequate when applied to Sarraute. As has been established, exact patterns do not recur in Sarraute[3] and she deliberately seeks to flout literary codes and conventions. This is particularly manifest throughout *Des hommes en general et des femmes en particulier* in which Sarraute (1996) rapidly covers a range of loosely related topics. Besides this, a study which concentrates purely on the narrative structure of these writings would be far too simplistic because Sarraute's work is complex and dynamic in many respects. This said, her narratives do contain core components; there is always a woman, and often a man, present, and the protagonists invariably disagree on a social issue, which

---

3   This is particularly manifest throughout *Des hommes en général et des femmes en particulier* in which Sarraute (1996) rapidly covers a range of loosely related topics.

is presented amusingly and ironically. A structuralist analysis of Sarraute's writings could, then, enhance the reader/analyst's understanding of the internal dynamics of these texts.

On initial inspection, the functionalist approach also appears poorly suited to the reading and analysis of Sarraute. Halliday believes that the reader can gain a detailed understanding of a written text by determining the specific function of language in that text. However, as Sarraute's use of language is often polysemic and therefore equivocal – it contains numerous wordplays and double-entendres – its multiple functions are difficult to determine (see Chapter 5).

Nonetheless, as knowledge of the ways in which specific items of language function within a text can provide the reader with a greater appreciation of the text as a whole, it could be beneficial for the analyst of Sarraute to study certain elements of these writings from a functionalist perspective.

Last, context-based and critical methods are built on Halliday's complex linguistic model and may therefore be difficult to apply to unstable, fluctuating polyphonic writings such as Sarraute's. Elements of these approaches can, nevertheless, greatly enhance the reading and stylistic analysis of her writings. They encourage close, detailed textual analysis and, by taking account of the society- and culture-bound character of language and text (Kramsch 2000), foster greater awareness of Sarraute's motivations, her writings, and their context of production. Simultaneously, this school of thought encourages the individual to acknowledge the value-laden nature of his own reading and analysis of Sarraute will, albeit unintentionally, always be subjective.

Therefore, if some elements of each of the five theoretical traditions discussed are unhelpful, others are certainly of relevance. In addition, it has been established that the role of the reader, to which theorists have attached varying degrees of importance, is an essential consideration in the study of the process of reading Sarraute, and that Riffaterre and Fish offer methods of reading and analysis which may be particularly well suited to this task. Riffaterre's approach can assist identification of a broad range of the significant features of Sarraute's writings, and his insistence on variation of reader response can help to account for the individual reader's interpretation of these multidimensional texts. Equally useful is Fish's attention to the role of the reader in literary and stylistic analysis. By suggesting that meaning, style, and text are never fixed, but are dynamic, defined subjectively, and inescapably context-bound, Fish offers an approach which can usefully be applied to the processes of reading and analysing Sarraute's writings.

Reading and Analysing Sarraute within a Bakhtinian–Derridean Frame

As many of the theories examined above only partially assist the reading and analysis of Sarraute it is, at this juncture, appropriate to consider the approaches to reading and textual analysis commended by Bakhtin and Derrida. These can offer a more fruitful framework in which to consider texts as diverse and variegated in character as those of Sarraute.[4] Although Bakhtin wrote some of his major works in the early twentieth century, these were not translated, and therefore not available to a European audience, until the 1970s and 1980s. It is, then, interesting to consider how Bakhtin's approaches to literary and stylistic analysis and to the reading process compare with those of the above-discussed theorists.

The concept of dialogue, with which Bakhtin was fascinated, is fundamental to the process of reading (polyphonic) texts, and Bakhtin (1970–1/1986: 75) clearly acknowledged the importance of the reader as respondent to the written work. Nevertheless, this theorist's work was

---

4   If Bakhtin and Derrida are now brought together as complementary models for analysing Sarraute, fundamental differences nevertheless exist in their approaches to language and meaning production. In a Saussurean spirit, Bakhtin believed all differences in language to be interrelated; these differences therefore create meaning and enable communication. Bakhtin's reader was not, then, himself responsible for the production of a text's meaning. By contrast, as is later explained in detail, Derrida thought such differences in language to 'defer' any real meaning. Consequently, he considered the meaning of any (written) text to be indeterminate and viewed the reader as the creator of that meaning.

quite distinct from the hermeneutic approach. At no point did Bakhtin attempt to identify a single 'etymon' in the polyphonic work; a text which, on the contrary, is thoroughly dynamic, multivoiced, and multidimensional. Similarly, Bakhtin (1941/1981: 8) explicitly stated the inadequacy of formalist and structuralist literary theory in the analysis of the (polyphonic) novel:

> The utter inadequacy of literary theory is exposed when it is forced to deal with the novel. In the case of other genres, literary theory works confidently and precisely, since there is a finished and already formed object, definite and clear [...]. Everything works as long as there is no mention of the novel. But the existence of novelized genres already leads theory into a blind alley. Faced with the problem of the novel, genre theory must submit to a radical restructuring.

Bakhtin believed that all written works exist in dialogue both with other texts and with their readers, and therefore that they are part of the wider fabric of society. Indeed, he stressed that stylistics should be fully aware of the 'social context of discourse'. In this respect, Bakhtin (1934–5/1981: 300) anticipated the work of, and was resuscitated by discourse analysts who, in the aftermath of Foucault, have focused on the interrelationships between texts and (power) relations in society:

> Any stylistics capable of dealing with the distinctiveness of the novel as a genre must be a *sociological* stylistics. The internal sociological dialogism of novelistic discourse requires the concrete social context of discourse to be exposed; to be revealed as the force that determines its entire stylistic structure, [...], for indeed, social dialogue reverberates in all aspects of discourse.

Bakhtin's late arrival in Europe coincided with the advent of Derrida, whose work, although distinct from that of Bakhtin, is of equal relevance in this study. Derrida (1968) invented the neologism *différance* in order to demonstrate that the nature of words makes any full representation of coherent meaning in language impossible. He devised this term by combining the spellings of *différence*, the French noun, and that of *différant*, the present participle of the verb *différer*. He also merged the two meanings of this verb – 'to differ' and 'to defer', and argued that, if words are to have meaning they must 'differ' from each other, and this 'difference' consequently postpones, or 'defers', any definite meaning in words. As *différance* is always at play within language, language is intrinsically unstable. If no language is stable, no text can, then, have any fixed meaning.[5] Rather, all texts lend themselves to limitless possibilities of interpretation. Indeed, in his interpretation of the text, the reader 'supplements' the written work, both 'enriching' and 'completing' it.[6] Deconstructionist philosophy is also grounded in the concept of *différance*. Derrida believes Western thought to have established its principles on an intrinsically unstable system of language, building on binary oppositions which wrongly privilege one term over another – nature over culture, male over female, speech over writing. He therefore aims to destroy or 'deconstruct' such hierarchies, believing that inferior or marginalized terms are always of crucial importance, as so-called 'privileged' terms must exist in relation to their marginalized counterpart (1967a).

In this work, application of Derrida's *différance* encourages the reader to form a dynamic, interactive relationship with Sarraute's writings, reading these subjectively and *openly* and supplementing them with new meaning. At the same time, implementation of Derrida's deconstructionist method enables *close* stylistic analysis of polyphonic works. If, as Derrida suggests, language and texts are unstable and there can therefore be no privileged understanding of these, no one individual can claim total authority in their analysis of a given text. Nevertheless, if the reader/analyst is thorough in their own approach to the ST, breaking it down into its smallest components, deconstructing and interrogating it, they can maximize their own understanding of Sarraute and, in doing so, become a well-informed,

5   Derrida was also influenced by Saussure's work. According to Saussure (1916), every linguistic sign has two fundamental elements; the *signifiant* [signifier] (its physical form, such as a sound or printed word) and the *signifié* [signified] (the meaning or idea which the signifier expresses). Furthermore, the relationship between these two components is 'arbitrary', as there is no logical relationship between them. However, in his *De la Grammatologie*, Derrida (1967a) attacks Saussure and moves beyond his work, suggesting that language is inherently dynamic, and that meaning itself is thus unstable.

6   Derrida (1967a) first used this concept in his discussion of the way in which writing 'supplements' speech. He identified that *le supplément* has two inseparable functions; one of enriching that which is already there, and one of compensating for that which is not.

competent (Culler 1975) interlocutor of her writings. Therefore, while the deconstruction movement has widely been considered unproductive and negative, this study places a clear emphasis on its positive qualities.

Translation Theory

Clearly, the notions of dialogue or interlocution, and supplementation or completion, are as central to the translation of a given text as they are to the reading of it.[7] Once the translator/interlocutor has entered into dialogue with the polyphonic ST, arrived at their own understanding of its complexity, and supplemented it with their own interpretation, they then articulate their subjective response to the ST in the TL. As Hatim and Mason (1990: 224) write: 'The translator uses as input to the translation process information which would normally be output, and therefore the end of, the reading process'. Thus, the translator further extends, or supplements, the text and, in doing so, effectively contributes to an on-going process of dialogue.

If the translator/interlocutor is to preserve convincingly the qualities of the polyphonic ST in the TL, it will be beneficial for them to engage with elements of translation theory, as these can provide them with a number of

---

7   Over the years, translation has been described variously as 'dialectical and communicative' (Mounin 1963: 276), 'a balance between I and Thou' (Kelly 1979: 214), and 'embodied dialogue' (Robinson 1991: 257). The work of Robinson is of particular significance in the present study. Robinson (1991: rear cover) draws on Bakhtin substantially in his formulation of a dialogic theory of translation: 'He argues that translation is *somatic* – that it is primarily not mental but physical: grounded in feelings, intuitions, and a gut-level sense of the "right" word or phrase. It is also *dialogic* – a variable, unpredictable interaction of the translator with the source-language writer and the target-language reader'. Indeed, this work adopts a similar stance. It argues that dialogue and interactivity permeate all levels of the source and target texts and affect their respective participants. Furthermore, the translator, the mediator between the ST and TT, is indeed a thoroughly interactive being.

practical instruments and valuable insights. Initially, it may seem that they should adopt a predominantly free and adaptive approach to the rerendering of polyphonic writings, which are inherently multivoiced, unstable, and playful. Indeed, this was the approach which Sarraute herself recommended when I broached with her the subject of translating her work into English. 'You shouldn't translate it, you should rewrite it', she insisted. 'It should be completely transposed, you understand?' (ICS). However, examination of a number of key concepts from some of the major phases of translation theory[8] suggests that it may in fact be more appropriate to implement a broader range of strategies in order to fully recapture such polyphonic STs in translation. Important concepts from each of these theoretical phases are now reviewed concisely in order that their applicability to the translation of Sarraute can be determined.

Much early theorizing of the linguistic transferral of written texts centred on the issue of translating the Bible. As a formal record of the word of God, this text was sacred. Consequently, it was believed that any translation of it should be totally faithful to the original. In order to maximize such fidelity, translators often adopted close strategies when rerendering the Bible in the TL. Nonetheless, the shortcomings of 'literal', or 'word-for-word' translation were also widely acknowledged. As literal methods tended to generate rigid, stilted, and nonsensical TTs, many translators instead opted for freer strategies. Of his own approach to the translation of the Greek Old Testament, St Jerome (395 CE / 1997: 25) writes: 'I not only admit but freely announce that in translating from the Greek – except of course in the case of the Holy Scripture, where even the syntax contains a mystery – I render not word for word, but sense for sense'. Several centuries later, the German Protestant theologian, Luther, adopted a similar stance and furthered this freer approach to Bible translation. He not only favoured non-literal strategies, but also used everyday language in his translation of the Bible, with a view to making this text accessible to a wider public. Thus, despite its alarming the hierarchy, Luther's (1522–34) work also made an important contribution to the development of German literature in the vernacular.

8   As is the case of literature, literary theory, and stylistics, translation theory also reflects the cultural ethos of a given period (Lefevere 1992a, 1992b).

This progress notwithstanding, similar debates recurred in the nineteenth century when determining appropriate strategies for translating both religious and non-religious texts. Whereas Matthew Arnold, the English poet and essayist, preferred close methods of translation, producing TTs for scholastic and instructional purposes and supplying his TL audience with ample additional explanation (1861, in Bassnett 1980), his fellow poet, Edward Fitzgerald (1857, in Lefevere 1992a: 80), was clearly much freer in his translation of foreign works: 'It is an amusement for me to take what liberties I like with these Persians, who (as I think) are not Poets enough to frighten one from such excursions, and who really do want a little Art to shape them'.

Inspired by past attempts to discover the true meaning of the ST, hermeneutic approaches to the study of translation thrived in the twentieth century. Based on the individual translator's subjective understanding of the ST and the ST author's intentions, hermeneutic theories were grounded in the work of Schleiermacher. Insisting on the importance of bringing author and reader together, Schleiermacher (1813, in Lefevere 1992a: 41–2)[9] recommends that the translator pursue one of two distinct 'roads':

> Either the translator leaves the author in peace, as much as possible, and moves the reader toward him. Or he leaves the reader in peace, as much as possible, and moves the author toward him. The two roads are so completely separate that the translator must follow one or the other as assiduously as possible, and any mixture of the two would produce a highly undesirable result.

Encouraging translators to follow the first road, Schleiermacher (ibid.: 43) advocates 'alienating', rather than 'naturalizing' strategies, which would allow the foreign qualities of the ST to be preserved in translation.

9   When Schleiermacher (1813 in Lefevere 1992a: 42) first defined these two categories of translation, he insisted that 'the two roads [were] completely separate'. Subsequent thinkers who use these concepts are not so extreme. For instance, Venuti (1995: 29) favours 'foreignization', but acknowledges that this is a relative term. 'Foreignization' must always involve some degree of 'domestication'; when a ST is translated, the TT must be conscious of usual target culture values in order to be able to differ from these and use 'foreignizing' strategies' (ibid.).

Schleiermacher's hermeneutic approach has been highly influential to future generations of theorists. In 'Die Aufgabe des Übersetzers' (1923), translated as 'The Task of the Translator' (1969/1973), which originally served as the introduction to his own translation of Baudelaire's *Les Tableaux Parisiens*, Benjamin suggests that the translator can penetrate to the core of the ST, exposing its 'pure' language. He explains: 'A real translation is transparent; it does not cover the original, does not block its light, but allows the pure language, as though reinforced by its own medium, to shine upon the original all the more fully' (ibid.: 79). Thus, the translator 'releases' in the TL the pure language contained in the ST author's text: 'It is the task of the translator to release in his own language that pure language which is under the spell of another, to liberate the language imprisoned in a work in his re-creation of that work' (ibid.: 80). By 're-creating the ST, the translation therefore allows this text to survive; it gives it "continued life"' (ibid.: 71). Furthermore, Benjamin (ibid.: 80–1) revives Schleiermacher's distinction between 'alienating' and 'naturalizing' strategies and, in the manner of his predecessor, expresses a preference for the former:

> Our translators have a far greater reverence for the usage of their own language than for the spirit of the foreign works [...] The basic error of the translator is that he preserves the state in which his own language happens to be instead of allowing his language to be powerfully affected by the foreign tongue.

Steiner (1975/1998) made a further significant contribution to hermeneutic theories of translation. In this work, Steiner considers first the psychological and intellectual processes which the translator undergoes, and later the concepts of meaning and understanding. He describes the 'hermeneutic approach' as 'the investigation of what it means to "understand" a piece of oral or written speech, and the attempt to diagnose this process in terms of a general model of meaning' (ibid.: 249). Translation is believed to be hermeneutic as it involves 'the act of elicitation and appropriative transfer of meaning' (ibid.: 312). The central tenets of this philosophy are contained in Steiner's fifth chapter, 'The Hermeneutic Motion', in which he sees this 'act' as a movement through four stages. First, 'initiative trust'; the translator believes and trusts that the ST means something and can be translated. Second, 'aggression', which is 'incursive' and 'extractive' (ibid.: 313). Referring to Hegel and Heidegger, Steiner considers the aggressive and penetrative nature of all understanding and the translator's deliberate intention to 'extract' something from the ST. Third, 'incorporation'; the translator brings the meaning which he extracted in the second movement to the TL and 'assimilates' it. Steiner labels this a 'dialectic of embodiment', explaining that it may affect the translator positively or negatively: 'Acts of translation add to our means; we come to incarnate alternative energies and resources of feeling. But we may be mastered and made lame by what we have imported' (ibid.: 315). The fourth stage, 'compensation', is an attempt to counteract any negative tendencies and losses in the translation process. Steiner believes that the ST is 'enhanced' when it is translated as it is extended to another culture. In his view, it is a combination of 'resistance' to, and 'affinity' with, the ST and the resulting tension in the TT which constitute a 'good translation' (ibid.: 413). At a later stage in the chapter, a selection of literary translations is analysed and Steiner builds on the notions of 'acceptance' and 'rejection': 'The relations of the translator to what is 'near' are inherently ambiguous and dialectical. The determining condition is simultaneously one of elective affinity and resistant difference' (ibid.: 381).

In response to those approaches which had characterized translation theory until the mid-twentieth century and indeed beyond, many of which were vague and subjective and were increasingly being deemed inadequate, theorists operating in the 1950s and 1960s identified a need to produce and analyse translations in a much more scientific and systematic manner. During these two decades, numerous attempts were therefore made to categorize translation processes and to provide conclusive taxonomies of prescriptive rules, intended to guide practising translators. Gentzler (2001: 1) explains that: 'Modern translation theory, like current literary theory, begins with structuralism and reflects the proliferation of the age'. Central to these developments were the concepts of 'meaning' and 'equivalence', detailed by Jakobson (1959/2000). It is in his discussion of 'interlingual translation', or 'translation proper', that Jakobson analyses the relationship between linguistic meaning and equivalence. Returning to Saussure's definitions of the 'signifier' and the 'signified', Jakobson reinforces the arbitrary nature of the sign. As regards meaning, he argues that, interlingually, there is often no full equivalence between 'code units'. For instance, in every language the word 'cheese' has a different semantic field. According to Jakobson, this does not however prevent total communication from taking place, as individual 'code units' with no direct equivalent in the TL can be rerendered by entire messages. He therefore claims that it is through acknowledgement of difference that some degree of equivalence can be arrived at: 'Equivalence in difference is the cardinal problem of language and the pivotal concern of linguistics' (ibid.: 114).

Building on the concepts of meaning and equivalence and discussing translatability, or the extent to which translation is possible, Eugene Nida, who was especially concerned with Bible translation, attempted to incorporate linguistic principles into the study of translation in order to approach this task more scientifically. Drawing on Chomsky's 'generative transformational grammar',[10] Nida also stressed the importance of context in the creation of linguistic meaning and thus raised awareness of the need to translate on a pragmatic level. In his attempt to formally define equivalence, Nida (1964) employs the terms 'formal' and 'dynamic' equivalence or equivalence of 'message' and 'effect'.[11] The former can be achieved by maintaining, as far as possible, the 'form' and 'content' of the ST message, and the latter by ensuring that 'the relationship between receptor and message [is] substantially the same as that which existed between the original receptors and the message' (ibid.: 159).

Linguistic and scientific approaches to translation and the issue of equivalence, which dominated translation theory in Europe in the 1950s and 1960s, continued to be keenly discussed throughout the 1970s and beyond. Vinay and Darbelnet's (1958/1995) *Une Stylistique Comparée du français et de l'anglais*, a lengthy manual which provides detailed descriptions of the differences between French and English and proposes a range

10   This grammar describes a language in terms of a set of logical rules which are formulated in order to generate the infinite number of possible sentences of that language and provide an accurate structural description of these.

11   The concept of translation 'effect' had already been identified and discussed many years previously by Arnold (1861, in Lefevere 1992a: 68–9).

of translation techniques, became an international guide for translators and has continued to be successful over the decades. If the work is lengthy and appears complex, its core tenets are nevertheless explained relatively concisely in its 'methodology' for translation. Each of the seven key procedures which constitute this methodology operates at the levels of lexis, structure, and message:

Table 1 Vinay and Darbelnet's Translation Methodology

Direct Translation (~ literal)		
Borrowing	*Calque*	*Literal*
Use of SL word or expression in TT	TL borrows a SL expression but translates it literally	Direct transfer from SL to TL
Oblique Translation (~ free) (When literal is not possible)			
Transposition	*Modulation*	*Equivalence*	*Adaptation*
Change of part of speech required	Change of point of view	Transfer of SL to TL requires different styles or structures (e.g. proverbs)	Change of cultural reference. Creation of situational equivalence

In the 1970s and 1980s there was a departure both from interpretative approaches which viewed the SL as a means of accessing the core of the ST and of discovering the ST author's intentions, and from exclusively scientific approaches to translation, based on static models and highly categorized methods. Rather, functionalist and communicative approaches to translation, which originated in Germany in the 1970s, began to regard translation as both a linguistic activity and an act of intercultural communication. The work of Reiss uses the principle of equivalence, not on the linguistic levels of the word or sentence, but on that of the text. Reiss (1981/2000: 161) advocates the production of 'a functionally equivalent TT' which communicates on the same level as the ST and must be based on 'a detailed semantic, syntactic, and pragmatic analysis of the ST'. In order to recommend a suitable translation method, she identifies a number of 'text types' (*Textesorte*) and their respective functions: informative (which communicate facts), expressive (or creative), operative (which intend to elicit a response), and audio-visual (such as films) (1977/1989: 108–9, in Munday 2001: 73). Recognizing that, as all STs have specific functions their corresponding TTs will also be judged according to their function in the TL culture, Reiss argues that the type of ST with which the translator is dealing will always dictate translation strategy. For instance, an informative text should, above all, achieve semantic equivalence in the TL.

Reiss's study of a translation's function lay foundations for further work on the purpose of translation: 'skopos theory'. The term *skopos* was first used by Vermeer (1989/2000) to refer to the purpose of both a translation (TT) and the act of translating. According to this theory, it is crucial to establish the purpose of a TT if one is to determine which translation methods must be used to produce a text which is functionally equivalent to a given ST:

> The skopos theory is part of a theory of translational action [...]. Translation is seen as the particular variety of translational action which is based on a source text [...]. Any action has an aim, a purpose [...]. The word *skopos*, then, is the technical term for the aim or purpose of a translation [...]. Further: an action leads to a result, a new situation or event, and possibly to a 'new' object. Translational action leads to a 'target text' [...]; translation leads to a *translatum* (i.e. the resulting translated text), as a particular variety of target text. (ibid: 221)

As the way in which a ST is translated depends upon the *skopos* of the TT (ibid.: 230), any one ST may be translated in numerous different ways. As Vermeer (ibid.: 228) explains:

> What the skopos states is that one must translate, consciously and consistently, in accordance with some principle respecting the target text. The theory does not state what the principle is: this must be decided separately in each specific case.

In a similar vein, Even-Zohar's (1970) 'polysystems theory' viewed translation not as a merely linguistic process, but as a culturally situated activity. Drawing on the work of the Russian formalists and their interest in literary historiography, Even-Zohar uses the term 'polysystem' to refer to the full range of literary systems, from canonical texts to marginal, lesser known ones, which exist within a given culture, and studies the interrelationships between these individual systems. He also considers translated literature to form a significant and integral part of any one polysystem:

> It is necessary to include *translated literature* in the polysystem. This is rarely done, but no observer of the history of any literature can avoid recognizing as an important fact the impact of translations and their role in the synchrony and diachrony of a certain literature. (in Gentzler 2001: 116)

For Even-Zohar (1978/2000: 192–7), the position of translated texts within the polysystem of the target culture must be established in order to determine both the translation strategy most appropriate to that particular text and the 'norms' or 'laws' which influence the translator's choices and decisions.

Over the years, a plethora of distinct approaches to translation therefore developed. In the 1980s, with the introduction of Translation Studies as a discipline in its own right, attempts were, however, made to consolidate the different areas of research which had previously been carried out. As Translation Studies has evolved it has become an increasingly heterogeneous field, incorporating not only linguistic and literary, but also cultural, ideological, and political considerations. The major preoccupation of theorists in the 1980s was undeniably the relationship between translation and culture. Due to increasing acknowledgement that texts themselves are culture-bound (Mounin 1963), that is, deeply imbued with cultural values, and therefore emblematic of the society which has generated them, purely linguistic theories of translation were believed inadequate. The papers compiled by Bassnett and Lefevere (1990) commonly focus on the interaction between translation and culture, on the challenges of the intercultural transferral of texts, and on the importance of context, history, and literary conventions in this process. In her contribution to this collection, Snell-Hornby (1990: 79–85) introduces the concept of a 'Cultural Turn' in Translation Studies, in which translation has moved beyond the level of the written text to encompass broader cultural concerns. The *rapprochement* [coming together] of the studies of translation and culture has remained an important issue and is pursued by Bassnett and Lefevere (1998: 138–9):

> What we can see from both Cultural Studies and Translation Studies today is that the moment of the isolated academic sitting in an ivory tower is over, and indeed in these multifaceted disciplines, isolation is counterproductive. Translation is, after all, dialogic in its very nature, involving as it does more than one voice. The study of translation, like the study of culture, needs a plurality of voices.

This reference to plurality is noteworthy. Bassnett stresses the need for Translation Studies to be a multifaceted discipline if it is to account for the many complexities of the translation process. Moreover, recent theorists' discussion of the 'dialogic' nature of translation is not restricted to a linguistic, intercultural level. On the contrary, in the above works dialogism and plurality are recognized both intralingually and intraculturally. Tabakowska's (1990) paper discusses the challenges which the presence of linguistic polyphony in the SL poses for the translator. She rightly states that senders of linguistic messages are often presumed to be monovocal (ibid.: 71), but that, if Bakhtinian thought is applied, all words are individually dialogic. Therefore the exact meaning of words must often be determined by the attitudes with which, and the contexts in which, they are uttered. The translator must pay particular attention to the 'linguistic minutiae' of the ST (ibid.: 77) in order to maximize accurate interpretation of all inescapably dialogic language.

In the same collection, Zlateva (1990: 36–7) considers the notion of 'acceptability' in translation, noting that TTs are sometimes deemed unacceptable when the translator fails to acknowledge the multidimensional nature, or 'substrata', of the languages, people, and therefore the culture into which they are working:

> Some of the 'noise' in the communication channel results from the lack of what we take for granted in our native language: knowledge of the norms of its substrata, in all its spheres of application and in different situations involving different people.

Clearly, the translator is faced with a complex task; not one of transferring a monovocal text from one monovocal audience to another, but rather one of transferring one plurivocal work from one complex and multidimensional culture to another. The issue is further complicated when the questions of 'multilingualism' and 'multiculturalism' occur within both the SL and TL environments. Bassnett (1998: 133) highlights the importance of Cultural Studies in heightening the translator's awareness of these phenomena:

> In short, Cultural Studies has moved from its very English beginnings towards increased internationalism and has discovered the comparative dimension necessary for what we might call 'intercultural analysis'. Translation Studies has moved away from an anthropological notion of culture (albeit a very fuzzy one) and towards a notion of cultures in the plural. [...] The processes that both of these interdisciplinary fields have been passing through over the past two or three decades have been remarkably similar and have led in the same direction, towards a greater awareness of the international context and the need to balance local with global discourses.

In view of the existence of linguistic and cultural plurality in texts and the individuality of all human subjects, theorists have acknowledged the impossibility of achieving complete equivalence in translation and have identified that a process of 'rewriting' is often necessary. In their detailed considerations of the translator, Bassnett and Lefevere repeatedly discuss the ideological and political nature of this role. It is widely recognized that no translation can be free from interpretation (Bassnett 1997: 2; Lefevere 1992b: 13; Robinson 1991: 260). It has, moreover, been suggested that, as the translator exists in a dynamic and dialectic relationship with the ST, applying to this their own reading and ideologies (Hatim & Mason 1997), they may be seen as a co-creator of the original work when it is translated.[12] This said, the translator's interpretation of the ST and production of a TT are not entirely personal. Lefevere (1992b) argues that translators operate according to, and are constrained by, poetical and cultural factors in the TL environment. Whoever is the 'driving force' behind the TT (translator,

---

12 Certain culturally oriented translation theorists seek to demonstrate how the translator can use his or her power and voice to specific effect, particularly to reaffirm the role of women (Simon 1996; Spivak 2000) or colonized peoples (Niranjana 1992). Cronin (1996) argues that such postcolonial power relations also operate in Europe. Viewing translation as a cultural, and inescapably political, act, he considers the role which English has played throughout history in both subjugating and promoting Irish language and culture. <http://www.dcu.ie/news/press/2002/p0102c.shtml>.

literary establishment, or other patron), all translations have the potential
to manipulate their audience and, in so doing, to act as shaping forces:[13]

> Translation is, of course, a rewriting of an original text. All rewritings, whatever their
> intention, reflect a certain ideology and a poetics and as such manipulate literature
> to function in a given society in a given way. Rewriting is manipulation, undertaken
> in the service of power. (ibid.: xi)

In a similar vein, Venuti acknowledges the presence of constraints which
influence translation strategies and the translator's personal freedom to
choose whether to fulfil or react against prevailing cultural expectations.
According to Venuti, no translator is obliged to translate according to such
expectations or norms.

Although translators may passively accept these, they may, alternatively, use more interventionist and proactive strategies. Thus, Venuti (1995)
distinguishes between two types of translator. The first is 'invisible'; they
attempt to imitate fully the ST author and text and give no indication
of their own presence. By contrast, the second type of translator makes
themselves 'visible' by choosing a text and particular translation methods
which draw attention to the fact that their work is not an original, but is
derivative. This may be achieved by making the text sound foreign (closely
adhering to the syntax of the ST, using such linguistic devices as 'emprunts'
or 'calques', juxtaposing archaisms and colloquialisms), writing a preface, or
including explanatory notes. In this respect, translations can be 'studied or
practised as a locus of difference' (ibid.: 41–2). The translator is, then, at
liberty to determine the translation approach which they adopt. Inspired
by Schleiermacher, Venuti (1998: 240) outlines the 'domesticating' strategy of the invisible translator, and the contrasting 'foreignizing' strategy
of the visible translator:

---

13   Lefevere (1992b) explains that pre-twentieth-century debates in translation theory
      also focused on the questions of power, poetics, universe of discourse, language, and
      education. Since these times, translation theory has 'occupied a central position in
      the shaping of European literatures and cultures' (ibid.: xi–xii).

Some [strategies in translation] are deliberately domesticating in their handling of the foreign text, while others can be described as foreignizing, motivated by an impulse to preserve linguistic and cultural differences by deviating from prevailing domestic values.

Summarizing his own work, Venuti (2000: 341)[14] expresses his preference for the latter approach:

> This line of thinking revives Schleiermacher and Berman, German Romantic translation and one of its late twentieth-century avatars. But following poststructuralist Philip E. Lewis [...], it goes beyond literalism to advocate an experimentalism: innovative translating that samples the dialects, registers and style already available in the translating language to create a discursive heterogeneity which is defamiliarizing but intelligible to different constituencies in the translating culture.

Other contemporary theorists study translation as a political act by drawing on principles of discourse analysis. As previously discussed, critical discourse analysis (CDA) analyses the semantic, social, and political functions of language, that is, the ways in which language communicates not only meaning but also social and power relations. Of particular influence was Halliday's model, centred on the principle of systemic functional grammar, which regards language as essentially communicative. According to this approach, the particular words of which a text is composed convey specific meanings, and the author's utterances are always related to their socio-cultural setting. Throughout the 1990s this reputedly complex model

---

14   Venuti was influenced by Berman (1984), who criticizes those translation strategies which conceal the foreign identity of the ST. He rejects 'naturalizing' methods of translation and instead advocates making the foreign qualities of the ST visible in the TT (in Venuti 2000: 285–6). Interestingly, Berman considers the complexities of translating novels, and argues that the translation of novels, which contain 'a proliferation of languages', is rarely successful. In his eyes, this almost always results in the production of homogenized, or linguistically flat, discourse in the TT: 'The Babelian proliferation of languages in novels poses specific difficulties for translation. If one of the principal problems of poetic translation is to respect the polysemy of the poem (cf. Shakespeare's *Sonnets*), then the principal problem of translating the novel is to respect its *shapeless polylogic* and avoid an arbitrary homogenization' (ibid.: 287, Berman's emphasis).

was adopted by a number of translation theorists, including Hatim and Mason (1990; 1997). Hatim and Mason (1997: vii) consider all translations to be 'acts of communication' and employ a range of concepts from pragmatics and sociolinguistics which can assist both the analysis of STs and the production and analysis of translations. Furthermore, not only do they study how texts are constructed in order to communicate sociocultural messages, they also examine the ways in which social and power relations emerge within discourse communities and subsequently in the process of translation. The translator is, then, in a position of power. Although they can, and arguably should, transpose the ideologies contained within the ST, they may choose to impose their own personal ideologies during this process of interlingual and intercultural transfer.

Both ST and TT can, then, be examined in terms of their structure, use of discourse, and ideology, including the author's particular ideology or their intention. Thus, translators are involved in a constant process of exchange (ibid.: 14) as they mediate between the source and target worlds, receiving and processing the ST and subsequently producing the TT. Hatim and Mason acknowledge that this process can be particularly complex; language, whether spoken or written, is not always static, but often dynamic. The resulting linguistic heterogeneity, or multiplicity of idiolects in the ST, therefore affects the translator's decisions, or textual strategy, when producing the TT:

> [There are] *static* and *dynamic* uses of language. While the static provides the translator with a stable world in which text conventions can be learned and applied, the dynamic poses a greater challenge to the translator's concern to retrieve and relay intended meanings. (Hatim and Mason 1997: viii)

Now that the key concepts from some of the major phases of translation theory have been outlined, attempts can be made to determine how they can be applied to the translation of Sarraute.

Applicability of Theories to the Translation of Sarraute

If it appears that none of the above-discussed theories alone can fully account for, nor assist, the translation of Sarraute, elements of each of these can nevertheless provide useful insights into this process and equip the translator with some valuable practical instruments. The translation of Sarraute can evidently not be approached in the same manner as that of the Bible. Sarraute's writings are neither sacred nor authoritative. On the contrary, as was witnessed in Chapter 1, they are iconoclastic and, at times, anti-religious, contain ambiguities, and are in a constant state of flux. At first glance, it may thus seem impossible to translate these texts closely, and indeed more appropriate to rerender them in the playful spirit in which Sarraute originally wrote them. However, on closer inspection, it becomes apparent that Sarraute's writings lend themselves to both close and freer translation strategies. In a typically carnivalesque and irreverent article written for *Le Monde* (See Extract 2, Chapter 5), Sarraute compiles a list of terms which politicians can use to insult one another. Whereas some of these can be rerendered closely – *grande gueule* [big gob], *gros patapouf* [big fatso] –, others, which incorporate cultural references and play with acronyms (*espèce d'I.V.G. pour V.G.E.*), require more inventive solutions (see Chapter 5). Similarly, when rerendering a passage from Sarraute's (1987) *Allô Lolotte, c'est Coco*, in which Sarraute and one of her characters are acutely self-conscious, it is necessary to implement close methods of translation in order to fully convey in the TT an intercultural reference contained in the ST, but to adopt a freer approach so as to recapture a SL pun in the TL (see Extract 4, Chapter 5). Thus, although Sarraute's writings are not sacred but irreverent, and may therefore appear to require a dynamic and playful approach to their rerendering, it in fact seems necessary to employ a blend of close and free strategies, both of which existed at the time of the earliest recordings of thinking on translation, if the unique qualities of these writings are to be preserved in the TL.

Elements of the hermeneutic approach are also unhelpful in the process of rerendering Sarraute. If Schleiermacher (1813/1992) argues that alienating and naturalizing translation strategies can never be employed in combination with one another, Chapter 5 of *Preserving Polyphonies* suggests otherwise. Indeed, when translating individual extracts from Sarraute's writings, both of these strategies can often be used in close proximity to each other (Extracts 2 and 8). Furthermore, adoption of exclusively alienating translation methods could potentially result in obscure and stilted rerenderings of Sarraute and are therefore equally inappropriate. Nevertheless, Schleiermacher's attention to the role of the reader and his acknowledgement of the importance of rerendering the foreign qualities of the ST in the TT are highly applicable to the translation of Sarraute's writings. These texts are conscious of the different interpretations and opinions of their readers, are often explicitly intercultural, and are, at times, highly polyglossic (see Chapter 5).

As regards the work of Benjamin (1969/1973), adoption of solely alienating strategies would again be inappropriate when rerendering Sarraute as these tend to generate linguistically awkward TTs. This said, some reference to this theorist's work may be valuable in the present study. Benjamin acknowledges the dynamic, dialogic role of the translator, while also stressing the creative, regenerative character of the translation process. When faced with certain excerpts from Sarraute, the translator can often rerender these inventively, 'recreating' them in the TL (see Extract 9).

Last, Steiner's (1975) hermeneutic motion presumes that all STs have a definite core or meaning which can be extracted and, by extension, that it is possible to fully identify the ST author's intentions. As has been established, neither of these is clearly identifiable in Sarraute. However, as Steiner considers the translation process to be thoroughly dialectical and to allow various interpretations, and as he views diversity and difference as sources of vitality, his work can provide important insights into the process of translating Sarraute.

In short, if certain elements of the hermeneutic approach to translation are of limited use when rerendering Sarraute – their advocation of 'alienating' methods of translation can produce stilted TTs and they assume too readily that all STs have a definite core –, other aspects of this approach can assist the translation of Sarraute's work. The hermeneutic principle acknowledges the importance of the reader, the inevitable variety of textual interpretation, and the thoroughly dynamic role of the translator. In addition to this, by favouring alienating, or inventive, translation methods, it considers translation as a process of survival, in which the fundamental differences between the SL and TL are seen to be positive and regenerative.

Given that Jakobson (1959) focuses primarily on the linguistic aspects of text transferral, his structuralist-inspired, scientific work may at first seem poorly suited to the translation of Sarraute. Sarraute's writings are deeply rooted in the French culture in which they were produced and contain many other foreign influences and references. Rerendering of these therefore entails far more than a process of interlingual transferral (Bassnett 1980: 49; Lefevere 1992a: 59). This said, some of Jakobson's terminology is directly applicable to Sarraute's work. Many of the code units which occur in her *Papa qui?* (1995) do not have exact TL equivalents: *Il y a un bon docu sur* Arte [There's a good documentary on Arte], *Elle a été aussitôt recrutée par les P.T.T.* [She was recruited immediately by P.T.T.], *Tu vas pas manger un Kim-Cône maintenant, on va passer à table* [You're not going to eat a Kim-Kône now. We're about to sit at the table]. By drawing attention to these elements of language, Jakobson encourages the translator to give careful consideration to their rerendering in the TL. Furthermore, by stressing such interlingual differences, he also highlights intercultural difference. In this respect, his work raises issues which will be crucial when translating Sarraute's writings from French into English and transposing these into the TL culture.

Direct application of Nida's thought to the translation of Sarraute may also be problematic. Nida's (1964) approach is principally language oriented. Owing both to the structural differences between French and English and to Sarraute's rich and varied uses of language (Chapter 1), it is clearly unrealistic to attempt to achieve complete formal equivalence between these writings and their translations. This concept is clearly incompatible with a view of language as dialogic and linguistic meaning as indeterminate. Moreover, due to the subjective nature of dynamic equivalence, it is impossible to measure the original effect of these STs on the ST audience and thus to accurately reproduce this effect on the target readership. Nevertheless, Nida's dynamic principle confirms a move away from the search for strict word-for-word equivalence and acknowledges the importance of reader experience. Indeed, Sarraute's writings should always cause laughter in both the SL and TL cultures. Furthermore, this principle recognizes that different readings of a given text are possible, a particularly important consideration when rerendering Sarraute in another language. Sarraute herself is acutely aware of the potential effect of her writings on her own readership: *'Oui, oui, c'est Lolotte, c'est JJ! Ça vous en bouche un coin, hein! Vous ne vous attendiez pas à les voir dans ces rôles-là.'* (1989: 9) [Yes, yes, it's Lolotte and JJ! You're amazed, aren't you? You weren't expecting to see them in those roles].[15]

Again, elements of Vinay and Darbelnet's (1958) methodology suggest that their work is not particularly well suited to the translation of Sarraute. Their model is based on the beliefs that linguistic meaning is determinate and is essentially static; its concept of equivalence is founded on highly categorized linguistic criteria which fail to consider the communicative function of language. This said, *Une stylistique comparée* does constitute a thorough and highly systematic approach to translation and, as has previously been established, the combination of close and freer practical techniques which it outlines is especially useful in the translation of contemporary texts. Whereas aspects of Sarraute can be translated directly, snippets from her *Dis voir, Maminette* (2003), which contains rich, idiomatic use of language, suggest the on-going validity of Vinay and Darbelnet's 'oblique translation': *Mais, bon, c'est un sujet qui me tient à coeur. Non, c'est vrai, j'en ai gros sur la patate* (2003: 11) [But, well, it's a subject which is close to my heart. No, it's true, there's something really upsetting me].

Thus, structuralist-inspired, scientific approaches to translation do, in certain respects, seem inappropriate when rerendering Claude Sarraute. They focus on the linguistic transferral of texts, may ignore linguistic context, and are based on the belief that linguistic meaning is determinate and on static models of language which are often highly categorized. These

---

15   In the 1980s Newmark substituted Nida's two concepts for 'semantic' and 'communicative' approaches to translation. The former intends to recreate the contextual meaning of the ST, and the latter ensures that the TT reproduces the effect of the ST, provided that both languages and texts are set in the same time frames and spaces (Newmark 1981: 39; 1988: 46–7).

approaches should not, however, be dismissed entirely. They begin to acknowledge the importance of both the reader and the cultural context of language and, at the same time, offer a number of techniques which can be of practical application in the translation of works as multidimensional and complex as those of Sarraute.

Although my earlier explanation of Reiss's (1988/2000) work was simplified, the translation models and methods which this theorist proposes are indeed complex and much too systemic to be fully applicable to Sarraute. Reiss's approach begins by distinguishing between distinct text types, yet it is impossible to fully classify Sarraute's writings as these are generically hybrid (Chapter 1). Moreover, by suggesting that the *Textesorte* of the ST determines translation strategy, Reiss does not take account of the subjective nature of the translator's decisions. Nonetheless, her emphasis on the communicative function of translation is further evidence of the need to move beyond purely language oriented strategies, which is clearly essential when rerendering Sarraute's culture-bound writings (Chapter 1). Reiss's attention to the different choices and strategies of the translator and the diverse audiences in the receiving culture also highlights the importance, and reinforces the subjective, multidimensional quality of textual participants at all levels of the translation process. Elements of Reiss's work can, then, assist in defining an appropriate approach to the rerendering of Sarraute's polyphonic writings.

Vermeer's (1989/2000) functionalist approach, inspired by Reiss, does not seem fully applicable to the translation of Sarraute either. Vermeer does not pay sufficient attention to the linguistic minutiae of the ST in his devising of a translation method. Sarraute's writings, however, teem with instances of linguistic variety and dialogism and these must be carefully reproduced if her STs are to be recaptured convincingly in the TL. This said, aspects of Vermeer's theory provide a helpful dimension to the rerendering of Sarraute. Although Sarraute's own purpose is frequently unclear in her work, an attempt to determine the function of her STs in their original environment can assist in clarifying the *skopos* of their corresponding TTs and the way in which these may be received in the target environment. On one occasion, Sarraute colludes with her readers and, by gently mocking higher ranks of French society, aims to entertain her audience. Thus, if the translator identifies, and recaptures in their TT the purpose of Sarraute's text, they can provide their audience with an accurate insight into certain behaviour in France and common attitudes towards it. Of additional interest in the present study is Vermeer's (1989: 228) insistence that many different translations of any one ST are possible. Through his acknowledgement of this, he recognizes differences in the purpose and interpretation of individual translators and, by implication, the inherently subjective nature of the translating subject.

Similarly, polysystems theory is not entirely suited to the process of translating Sarraute. First, the exact position of Sarraute's writings within the SL culture is indeterminate. At times, Sarraute appears to ridicule her own work thereby suggesting its relatively low status. At other times, however, she blatantly defends and valorizes her novels. By implication, it may be equally difficult, or indeed impossible, to establish the exact position of translations of Sarraute's writings in the polysystem of the TL culture (see Chapter 5). Moreover, the 'laws' which this school of thought sets out to establish are general, abstract, and universal. As Hermans (1999: 117) confirms, the translator's decision-making process is subjective, not objective, and therefore cannot be universalized. However, as Sarraute's writings are always deeply embedded in the social historical/political and literary environments in which they are produced, a translation approach such as polysystems theory, which cultivates a developed awareness of the social, historical, and literary context in which the TT will operate, can provide valuable insights into the process of rerendering Sarraute.

Functionalist and systems-based approaches to translation are often centred on complex models which pay insufficient attention to the language of the ST, attempt to generate objective laws, and sometimes do not acknowledge the subjective nature of the translator's decisions. Furthermore, they often fail to account for the difficulty of positioning in the TL culture texts which are unstable and fluctuating in the SL environment. In these respects, such approaches do not assist the translator of Sarraute. However, as they move beyond purely linguistic translation strategies and insist on the importance of determining the purpose of the TT in the target culture, these theories can raise some pertinent issues in the mind of Sarraute's translator.

Developments in Translation Studies which focus on linguistic and cultural plurality on both intra- and intercultural levels, in both the source and target languages and their respective environments (Bassnett & Lefevere 1990), provide highly relevant insights into the process of translating the polyphonic ST. In Sarraute's writings, instances of linguistic and cultural plurality abound and all participants (author, characters, and readers) are thoroughly multivocal, interactive, and interrelational beings. In addition, the translator, as dynamic, intercultural respondent to the ST, adds a further dimension to this dialogue, acting as mediator between the source and target environments. The concept of rewriting also supplies the translator with important insights into the task of rerendering Sarraute. Indeed, it may not be the translator's intention to manipulate or shape their readership. However, by recognizing that their TTs are inevitably conditioned by not solely personal but also social ideologies, the translator can ensure that they rerender and re-present Sarraute as neutrally, objectively, and fairly as possible.

An awareness of Venuti (1995) can also equip the translator with a greater understanding of their own role, alerting them to the freedom which they exercise in their choice of translation strategies, and, at the same time, can provide them with certain practical translation instruments such as foreignizing and domesticating strategies. Furthermore, if Venuti advocates predominantly foreignizing translation techniques which can result in distortion of the ST, his acknowledgement of the linguistic diversity of contemporary STs and his insistence on the importance of preserving such variety in the TL are nevertheless highly relevant to the translation of Sarraute. Amongst the many interesting linguistic features contained in Sarraute's writings are plentiful instances of heteroglossia and polyglossia (Chapters 1, 2 and 5).

As regards models of discourse analysis, if these are, at times, criticized for their degree of complexity, certain discourse-based theories of translation can, however, enhance the translator's approach to Sarraute. Hatim and Mason's (1990; 1997) work accounts for the presence of dynamism in linguistic, social, and ideological spheres of both the ST (Chapter 1) and the TT (Chapter 3), and for the equally dynamic and varied ideologies, and corresponding linguistic strategies, of the ST author (Chapter 1) and the translator (Chapter 3).

It has been suggested that elements of culturally and politically oriented translation approaches are not particularly well suited to the process of rerendering Sarraute's polyphonic writings. Certain proponents of these theories argue that all TTs are manipulative, advocate that dynamic STs be completely foreignized in the TL, and draw on complex models of discourse which cannot be fully applied to Sarraute. Nonetheless, it has also been witnessed that other aspects of these approaches have much to contribute to understanding the process of rerendering such writings. They recognize that the translator cannot be entirely neutral in their work, acknowledge the translation difficulties posed by the presence of multidimensionality and heteroglossia in the ST, and stress that instances of linguistic and cultural plurality are manifest within the ST and the TT.

Translating Sarraute within a Bakhtinian–Derridean Frame

Although distinct from one another, the majority of those translation approaches considered above are united by their reliance on the notion of equivalence (between SL and TL, ST and TT), and by their assumption that the process of translation consists of rerendering in the TL a stable, original text, written by an autonomous ST author. With the emergence of deconstruction, the fundamental principles on which translation had formerly been founded were called into question (Gentzler 2001: 145). As previously discussed, Derrida seeks to challenge the very essence of language by invalidating Saussure's distinction between the 'signifier' and the 'signified' and by focusing on *différance*. He rejects the stability of the linguistic sign and, in doing so, interrogates the primacy of meaning contained in words. In his *Des Tours de Babel*, Derrida (1985a) considers the implications of the unstable nature of language for the translation process. At the core of his thesis lies the conviction that, as words can have multiple meanings, which is demonstrated by the wordplays contained in the title of this book, no language can be easily translated and therefore no theory can presume that equivalence, or literal translation, of languages is possible. In this work, Derrida reads and comments on Benjamin's (1923/1969) 'The Task of the Translator'. He deconstructs Jakobson's tripartite categorization of translation[16] and claims that his own commentary is merely 'the translation of another text on translation' (1985a: 175). Replacing Benjamin's concept of pure language with the term *différance*, Derrida later blurs any distinction between ST and TT.[17] If no text has a fixed kernel or deep structure, but is merely composed of different chains of interdependent signifiers, the divide between an original ST and a subsequent TT can be destroyed, or deconstructed, and the concept of translation is therefore destabilized. As his argument unfolds, Derrida posits that the TT is not a reproduction of an original text, but that the ST actually translates itself and grows during translation. Thus, the TT contributes to the development and survival of the ST. In a later work, *The Ear of the Other* (1985b: 122), he builds on this idea, describing translation as a process of transformation which modifies both the SL and the TL:

> The translator must assure the survival, which is to say the growth, of the original. Translation augments and modifies the original, which, insofar as it is living on, never ceases to be transformed and to grow. It modifies the original even as it also modifies the translating language. This process – transforming the original as well as the translation – [...] assure[s] a survival, not only of a corpus or a text or an author but of languages.

Given that the deconstructionists seek to destabilize all language, written text, and individual subjects, their philosophy may at first appear destructive, negative, and therefore unhelpful to the translator of Sarraute. However,

---

16 Jakobson (1959, in Venuti 2000: 114) identifies three categories of translation: intralingual, interlingual, and intersemiotic.

17 Although at no point did Bakhtin propose a theory of translation, Emerson (1984: xxxi–ii) rightly states that the concept of translation is a key idea in his work: 'Translation, broadly conceived, was for [Bakhtin] the essence of all human communication. [...] To understand another person at any given moment, therefore, is to come to terms with meaning on the boundary between one's own and another's language: to translate'.

application of deconstructionist thought, especially those elements of it which bear similarities with Bakhtin's work, can actually positively enhance the process of translating Sarraute's writings. This philosophy acknowledges the dynamic, interactive nature of language, texts, and human beings, all of which are prominent in Sarraute (Chapter 1) and can be theorized by referring to the work of the Bakhtin Circle (Chapter 2). Furthermore, as deconstructionists believe that translation can 'assure a survival [...] of languages' (Derrida 1985b: 122), and therefore consider this process to be regenerative and life-giving, they encourage the translator to respond to, and supplement, the ST. Therefore, they effectively invite them to participate in an on-going process of dialogue. Indeed, Emerson's (1984: xxxix). comments on the translation of Bakhtin are fully applicable to the rerendering of Sarraute:

> For Bakhtin, 'the whole' is not a finished entity; it is always a *relationship*. An aesthetic object – or for that matter, any aspect of life – acquires wholeness only when an individual assumes a concrete attitude toward it. Thus, the whole can never be finalized and set aside; when a whole is realized, it is by definition already open to change [...]. To translate Bakhtin, I suggest, is therefore not only to translate the ideas [...] but also to reproduce the sound of the open-ended, self-developing idea. This would be his 'conversation in progress', his dialogue about dialogue, his interlocution with readers who still have to respond.

Thus, although it may at first seem appropriate for the translator to adopt a predominantly free and adaptive approach to the rerendering of multivocal, intertextual, hybrid, unstable, and playful writings, an approach which Sarraute herself advocated, a review of a number of key principles from the major phases of translation theory suggests that this is not entirely so. Given the inherent complexities of such texts, no uniform approach to their rerendering can be implemented. Rather, if they are to preserve in the TL the intricacies and peculiar qualities of Sarraute's writings, the translator may, as an individual, subjective, and intercultural interlocutor of the ST, be better advised to interact with, and apply, a heterogeneous blend of translation approaches which can supply them with a variety of useful insights and instruments. In response to Sarraute's writings, the translator is at liberty to be eclectic (Ellender 2006b: 160–1). This stance, which I adopt and illustrate in detail throughout my translations of Sarraute, is closely in line with current trends which are dominating thinking in Translation Studies, as is demonstrated in Chapter 5. At present, translation theorists are using combinations of analytical methods and are adopting thoroughly interdisciplinary approaches to their work (Bassnett 1998: 138; Gentzler 2001: 187–203; Munday 2001: 181–95; Venuti 2000: 333–4). As Venuti (ibid.) explains, in the 1990s various theoretical translation approaches began to converge:

> The conceptual paradigms that animate translation research [in this decade] are a diverse mix of the theories and methodologies that characterized the previous decade, continuing trends within the discipline [...], but also reflecting developments within linguistics [...] and in literary and cultural theory [...]. The decade sees provocative assessments of the competing paradigms. It also sees productive syntheses where theoretical and methodological differences are shown to be complementary and precise descriptions of translated text and translation processes are linked to cultural and political issues. At the start of the new millennium, translation studies is an international network of scholarly communities who conduct research and debate across conceptual and disciplinary divisions.

In sum, it is by entering into a dialogue with each ST, adopting both an open approach to its reading and a close approach to its stylistic analysis, employing a range of translation strategies, and thus ultimately situating themselves within a contemporary Translation Studies paradigm, that the translator, as Bakhtinian-cum-Derridean interlocutor of Sarraute, can be suitably equipped to rerender her polyphonic writings in the TL.

CHAPTER 4

Polyphonies in Practice

'Theory' should not be just some individual's brain-child: it should arise
from observing practice, analyzing practice, and drawing a few general
conclusions to provide guidance. These conclusions should naturally be
tested in practice. Leading to better guidance; better prescription based
on better description.

— WAGNER, in Chesterman & Wagner 2002: 6[1]

Yes, scholars do talk too much to each other rather than to a wider audience. Yes, we should spend more time studying real translators in real
action. [...] A dialogue between scholars and professional translators can
shed light on both sides.

— CHESTERMAN, in ibid.: 136

Chesterman and Wagner's comments, like those of a number of their contemporaries (Gentzler 2001; Hartley 2004; Munday 2001; Robinson 2012),
are evidence of the increasing recognition that, rather than being separate
and unrelated, translation theory and practice can in fact complement each
other. As regards the rerendering of Sarraute's polyphonic writings, it has
been established that translation theory can both provide the translator
with important insights into this task and supply him with certain useful

---

1   *Can Theory Help Translators? A Dialogue Between the Ivory Tower and the Wordface*
    (2002). Essentially a dialogue between its authors, Chesterman, a theoretical scholar,
    and Wagner, a professional translator, this work begins by expressing the clear divide
    which commonly exists between theory and practice (also Bassnett 2003: 18–19;
    Landers 2001: 49–50). As the dialogue progresses, the authors argue in favour of
    uniting translation theory and practice.

instruments (Chapter 3). However, given the complementarity of theory and practice, the present chapter argues that it is also valuable to consider how the translator of Sarraute can gain from studying past practice and subsequently combine those theoretical and practical lessons which they have learned. In order to do so, the chapter proceeds in three stages. First, it focuses on a collection of polyphonic source texts and their corresponding translations (ST-TT pairs), illustrating the ways in which practitioners have responded to the challenges of translating such writings. It then seeks to explain these findings, before ultimately applying them to Sarraute.

Illustration

The body of texts from which examples are drawn is an eclectic one, comprising some thirty ST-TT pairs. Source texts have been selected from throughout history to provide a wide-ranging view of polyphonic works and a flavour of writers from the 1500s (Erasmus, Rabelais) to the late twentieth and early twenty-first centuries (Fielding, Houellebecq). The choice of TTs has, however, been restricted to versions produced in the 1900s and in this century. This was deemed necessary in order both to limit the present study and to synchronize the present chapter with the latter part of Chapter 3, whose focus was translation theory post-1900. The works are predominantly European novels, originally written in French or English. However, a small number of texts belonging to other cultures (Dostoevsky, Pushkin) and genres (Goscinny's *Astérix*) have been examined, where these ST-TT pairs are particularly instructive to the study of Sarraute.

Within the four categories already used for analytical purposes – 'The Text', 'The Participants', 'Social, Cultural, and Political Issues', and 'Time and Space', significant features of these STs, as identified in the writings of Sarraute and theorized by the Bakhtin Circle, are targeted. A representative sample of the challenges which these pose for the translator is presented, and a range of the strategies which have been employed by practising translators in order to deal with these, are offered.[2] At this stage, the intention is one of illustrating a broad spectrum of possible pragmatic solutions which are available to the translator of the polyphonic text, rather than providing subjective analyses of their relative merits and shortcomings. Those strategies which can assist the rerendering of Claude Sarraute are identified at a later stage in the present chapter and implemented in Chapter 5.

The Text: Literary and Generic Issues

If a text contains plentiful instances of intra- and intergenericity, the translator confronts multiple challenges when transferring these into the TL. Study of a broad range of STs which display such features reveals that translators have responded to these challenges in a variety of ways and by adopting certain broad approaches.

One strategy prevalent among translators entails providing a close translation and supplementing this with varying degrees of explanation for the TT reader. Instances of self-consciousness in the ST lend themselves particularly well to close linguistic transferral. For instance, the entire prologue to Cervantes's *Don Quixote* (1605–15) centres on a discussion of the ways in which the work is constructed. The narrator recalls the humorous advice which he received from a friend and which ensured that his work appeared erudite. Grossman (2004: 5–6) captures this satirical passage in her recent translation:

> First, to solve the question of sonnets, epigrams, or laudatory poems by distinguished and titled people, which you need at the beginning, you must make a certain effort and write them yourself, and then you can baptize them with any name you want, attributing them to Prester John of the Indes or to the emperor of Trezibond, both of whom, I have heard, were famous poets.

2   Examples or passages quoted may sometimes refer to both the ST and the TT. Where this is the case, a double page reference is provided (e.g. Gide 15/7); this relates to pages of the ST and TT respectively.

If, as is the case of *Don Quixote*, the nature of the ST is made explicit in the body of the text itself, this notion can be transferred directly to the TT with no additional explanation for the new readership. However, where the nature of the ST is less apparent and the translator believes that this may be of interest to the TT reader, supplementary information is often provided. Francis Ledoux's 1958 translation of Dickens's *Oliver Twist* (1837–8) is a case in point. Curtis's (1973: 9, my translation) preface to the translation, which is intended for its francophone readers, discusses Dickens's art of storytelling:

> In short, if we examine point by point the way Dickens tells a story, his art of story-telling, these prove to be the exact opposite of modern aestheticism which is full of taboos and which instead recommends a refusal of moralism, psychology, intrigue, absolute primacy of form [...]. [Dickens] tells a story. He proves that it is possible to move by walking.

Translation challenges are clearly multiplied when a ST displays an awareness of other texts. Handling of intertextual references varies considerably between translators.[3] At times, titles are not translated and remain unaltered (Lainé, 60/25) whereas at other times they are translated (Gide, 27/24). They sometimes feature as an integral part of the TT and are left unexplained (Lainé, 60/25), or they are clarified in detail (Erasmus 1982: 56). Allusions to other texts are also dealt with variously. At times they are translated closely but no further explanation is provided (Barbara Wright's 1960 translation of Raymond Queneau's 1938 *Zazie dans le métro*, 90/100), and at other times they are clearly referenced and explained. Grossman (2004: xviii) uses plentiful footers throughout her translation of *Don Quixote* and justifies her decision in this way:

---

3   For the purpose of the present discussion, I employ the term 'intertextuality' in a narrow sense to indicate references and allusions to other written works. The concept can, of course, be used to describe the presence of whole discourses and genres in a given text. I deal with these other issues, and the translation challenges to which they give rise, elsewhere in this chapter.

I debated the question of footnotes with myself and decided I was obliged to put some in, though I had never used them before in a translation. (I did not want the reader to be put off by references that may now be obscure, or to miss the layers of intention and meaning those allusions create).

When attempting to reproduce generic imitation or parody in the TT, the translator faces similar issues. Rabelais's *Gargantua* (1534/1972) contains parodies of scholastic style (chapter 13), and of war stories and battle scenes which resemble those in the *Iliad* (chapters 23 & 25). In his translation of this work, Cohen (1955) succeeds in recapturing the flavour and humour of the original with relatively little recourse to explanatory footnotes. Other translators of parody, however, annotate their TTs in detail. In his preface to Johnston's rerendering of Aleksandr Pushkin's 1833 *Eugene Onegin*, Bayley (2003: xxxi–xxxii) clarifies the contrasting literary modes which are reflected in, and parodied throughout, this Russian narrative poem. Jacques Pons's (1965: 424, my translation) *Voyages de Gulliver* gives similar treatment to instances of parody and pastiche in Swift's original text and offers additional, brief explanation in a number of his endnotes: 'This whole passage is a pastiche of Robinson Crusoe'.

The iconoclasm of these works, that is, the disruption of traditional literary hierarchies which they create by allowing supremely different texts and genres to coexist within one work, is at times made apparent in the ST and closely rerendered in the TT. Grossman (2004: 8) translates the advice received by the narrator of *Don Quixote* as such: 'Keep your eye on the goal of demolishing the ill-found apparatus of these chivalric books'. Where the ST does not make its intention so explicit, this may either be left unexplained in the TT, or clarified at length by the translator, as in the following note attached to *Voyages de Gulliver*: 'This is a broad outline of Swift's underground work, which created a huge stir in the aristocratic circles of the English Court' (Pons 1976: 14, my translation).

In contrast to those who adopt a close approach and provide generous explanation, certain translators demonstrate a clear preference for freer and more adaptive strategies when attempting to recapture instances of inter-genericity. In their translation of the *Astérix* series, Anthea Bell and Derek Hockridge show an admirable ability to retain the essence of Goscinny's

STs while simultaneously adapting these in order to make them accessible to an anglophone readership. Humour pervades these *bandes dessinées* which appeal to readers of all ages. One source of entertainment for the adult ST reader is the presence of literary allusions to, and quotations from, classic works of French literature. Bell and Hockridge rerender these in the TT by using examples from English literature, thus rewriting the ST in order to make it immediately comprehensible and amusing to the TL reader. In a discussion of this process, Bell (1999: 2–3) writes:

> Some [jokes] run to extended literary references, for older children and adults. In *Le Cadeau de César* there is a whole page where Asterix, defending the local innkeeper, slips into the character of Cyrano de Bergerac as he fights a duel with a Roman while composing a ballad. Quotations from Rostand, Cyrano's creator, come thick and fast. The translation replaces them with probably the most famous sword fight in English literature, Hamlet and Laertes, and suitable Shakespearian quotations: the innkeeper's wife begins by advising her husband, 'Act with disdain!', whereupon the belligerent Roman can point out, accurately, 'I am more an antique Roman than a Dane', thus launching the literary sequence.

Instances of intergenericity in *Astérix* are not confined to literary allusions and quotations; these *BD* also incorporate other genres, such as the song. Discussing the translation of the lyrics in songs, Bell (ibid.: 3) explains that: 'Like those of the French originals, they have to be both recognizable and capable of anachronistic distortion'. Thus, song lyrics in *Astérix en Hispanie* (1969) are thoroughly rewritten. The ST reads: *Je suis un petit garçon, fils de Gaulois moyen!... Les sangliers, ça est tellement bon! J'vous eï apporteï des sanglieeeers* [I am a little boy, the son of an average Gaul! Wild boar is so delicious! I've brought you some wild boar!]. Bell and Hockridge rerender this in their *Asterix in Spain* (1971) with the following: 'I'm dreaming of a White Solstice... Wonderful wonderful Durovernum... Rockabye Pépé, on the tree tops'.

Equally adaptive in approach is Barbara Wright's 1958 translation of Raymond Queneau's *Exercices de style* (1947). Queneau's work, which contains ninety-nine versions of one short story, plays with and parodies many styles of writing – from the official letter, to philosophic, modern, and telegraphic styles – and different genres, including five forms of poetry.

Exercices de style is, then, a highly experimental work and recreation of such linguistic and generic variety in the TT requires a similar degree of flexibility and innovation on the part of the translator. The opening lines of Queneau's telegraphic version read: *BUS BONDÉ STOP JNHOMME LONG COU CHAPEAU CERCLE TRESSÉ APOSTROPHE VOYAGEUR INCONNU SANS PRÉTEXTE VALABLE STOP* (p. 95, capitals in the original). These are recaptured by Wright in the following: 'BUS CROWDED STOP YNGMAN LONGNECK PLAITENCIRCLED HAT APOSTROPHISES UNKNOWN PASSENGER UNAPPARENT REASON STOP' (p. 123).

In such texts, juxtaposition and manipulation of distinct styles and genres can blur traditional literary and generic divides and this tendency may, or may not, be motivated by a particular political agenda on the part of the ST author. Bell and Hockridge convey powerfully this hybrid of different literatures and genres in the body of their TTs, but make no additional references, in the form of an introduction or footnotes, to Goscinny's motives. By contrast, Wright (1958: 15) addresses this issue explicitly in her introduction to *Exercises in style*, directly quoting Queneau:

> People have tried to see [*Exercises*] as an attempt to demolish literature – that was not at all my intention. In any case my intention was merely to produce some exercises; the finished product may possibly act as a kind of rust-remover to literature, help to rid it of some of its scabs. If I have been able to contribute a little to this then I am very proud, especially if I have done it without boring the reader too much.

If the translators previously discussed have tended to adopt either predominantly close and explanatory, or free and adaptive, approaches to the transferral of intergenericity, others have employed a combination of the above. The work of Arlette Stroumza (1998), translator of Helen Fielding's (1996) *Bridget Jones's Diary*, provides a clear illustration of this. When dealing with a broad range of intertextual references in the ST, Stroumza translates those which are already available in French translation. *A Midsummer Night's Dream* becomes *Songe d'une nuit d'été*, and *Men are from Mars, Women are from Venus* is translated as *Les hommes viennent de Mars, les femmes viennent de Vénus*. However, where texts have no exact equivalent in the TL culture, references are not translated (*The Sunday Telegraph*) and they are sometimes left unexplained; a strategy which creates a certain degree of exoticism in the TT. This said, Stroumza does supplement her text with explanations of both intergeneric references (*Eastenders, Blind Date*) and allusions to other author's works (Brontë, Dickens) where she considers these to be essential to the TT reader's understanding of the original text. In contrast to this close approach, Stroumza is, at times, much freer in her rerendering of intergeneric and intertextual references, completely eluding these or indeed substituting them with a TL text: 'At last I got to the bottom of Mum and Dad. I was beginning to suspect a post-Portuguese-holiday Shirley-Valentine-style scenario and that I would open the *Sunday People* to see my mother' becomes: *J'ai enfin réussi à comprendre ce qui arrive à mes parents. Je commençais à soupçonner un scénario post-vacances portugaises, du style Marie-Claire. Un de ces jours j'allais ouvrir le magazine et y trouver la photo de ma mère.*

In this respect, Stroumza's balanced approach resembles those of Johnston and Cohen. While Johnston's translation of Pushkin is adaptive and playful, Bayley's (1977/2003: xxxv) preface to it acknowledges the importance of providing the TL reader with additional explanation of the multiple literary references contained in this ST:

> Pushkin's incessant literary 'borrowings' are also part of a process of [...], polemic and imitation through which he takes issue and invites comparison with Russian and European contemporaries and predecessors. As with the grander designs of other 'national poets', such as Dante or Shakespeare, some of this detail is now barely accessible without explanatory footnotes.

Similarly, in the introduction to his translation of *Gargantua et Pantagruel*, Cohen provides detailed explanation of Rabelais's literary inspirations. He does, however, state that a comprehensive knowledge of all instances of intertextuality in the SL is by no means necessary if the twentieth-century reader is to understand and enjoy this work (1955: 18–19).

In Fielding's *Bridget Jones*, other genres are also explicitly referred to, imitated and borrowed. The entire work is written as a diary. Thoughts and events are frequently recorded in note-form, personal pronouns are omitted, and sentences are brief. 'Har har. Just called Sharon' [*Ha ha. Viens d'appeler Sharon*] (42/50); 'Must get weight off before Christmas gorging' [*Maigrir absolument avant le gavage de Noël*] (285/317). E-mails, handwritten letters, and various lists and shopping lists are also incorporated into the body of the ST and are reproduced closely and accurately by Stroumza. Certain cases of generic borrowing do, however, require the translator to adapt and rewrite the original text. When a poem by Wendy Cope features in the ST, Stroumza enables this to rhyme in the TT by altering slightly the semantic content and rhyme scheme of the original in her translation (285/317):

> At Christmas little children sing and merry bells jingle.
> The cold winter air makes our hands and faces tingle.
> And happy families go to church and cheerily they mingle,
> And the whole business is unbelievably dreadful if you're single.

> *À Noël, les enfants chantent et les cloches sonnent.*
> *L'air froid de l'hiver glace nos mains et nos visages.*
> *Les familles heureuses célèbrent les Rois mages.*
> *Et moi, pour partager ces joies, je n'ai personne.*

By incorporating contrasting references to works of high and low literature, and by imitating and juxtaposing distinct styles and genres, Fielding's work challenges traditional literary norms and suggests its own status as a work of popular literature.

The Text: Linguistic Issues

Given that linguistic variation and a resulting sense of cacophony are also prominent features of polyphonic works, these texts give rise to further exclusive translation challenges. In the body of ST-TT pairs studied, a close approach to the transfer of linguistic variety and dialogism has been repeatedly identified. One aspect of the SL which appears to always lend itself to a close rerendering is that of vulgar language. Queneau's *Zazie dans le métro* teems with obscene language, and this is carefully recaptured by Wright in her translation (15/18):

– Zazie, déclare Gabriel en prenant un aire majestueux trouvé sans peine dans
son répertoire, si ça te plaît de voir vraiment les Invalides et le tombeau véritable du
vrai Napoléon, je t'y conduirai.
– Napoléon mon cul, réplique Zazie. Il m'intéresse pas du tout cet enflé, avec
son chapeau à la con.

'Zazie', declares Gabriel, assuming a majestic air which he effortlessly selects from
his repertoire, 'if you'd really like to see the Invalides and the genuine tomb of the
real Napoleon, I'll take you there'. 'Napoleon my arse', retorts Zazie. 'I'm not in the
least interested in that old windbag with his silly bugger's hat'.

In his *Literary Translation: A Practical Guide*, Landers (2001: 151) supports
this approach and stresses the importance of retaining offensive language
in the TT:

> What you cannot do is apply your own standards of decency and morality, or those
> of any hypothetical audience, to the task [...]. A prissy or sanctimonious translator,
> or an unscrupulous one, can totally skew the TL reader's perception of a writer; as
> translators we do not have that right.

Translators whose objective is to provide a highly accurate rendering of the
many levels of the SL often supplement their close translation with an introduction. In this, they may combine a linguistic commentary of the ST with
an outline of their translation strategy, and/or footnotes, which explain
individual instances of linguistic variation and dialogism in the SL. Twain's
Huckleberry Finn (1885) and its translation illustrate just such an approach.
The ST contains several coexisting dialects of spoken American English.
It would be impossible to fully recapture these in the TT; the French language evidently does not have varieties which correspond exactly to these
American dialects. Twain's translator therefore uses a sub-standard register
of French to convey the dialects, and provides a more detailed explanation
of these SL varieties in her introduction and footnotes (Nétillard 1973).
A similar approach is adopted to the translation of Dickens. *Oliver Twist*
contains contrasting registers of eighteenth-century English, juxtaposing
the speech of the upper classes with that of members of the workhouse and
Cockneys. Ledoux rerenders these through use of colloquial and standard
registers of French.

Curtis's preface to this TT includes further explanation of the SL and Leyris's endnotes clarify many English expressions and wordplays which feature in the original work. Explaining the names of two characters in *Oliver*, Leyris (1958: 283, my translation) writes: 'Blathers refers to somebody who talks a lot of nonsense, and Duff, to a good-for-nothing oaf'.

Instances of polyglossia in the ST may be rerendered equally closely in translation. Words and phrases which appear in the original text and which belong to languages other than the principal language of the ST can, for instance, be transferred directly from the ST to the TT, a technique used by Cameron in his 1997 translation of Voltaire's 1759 *Candide*. When the foreign word in the ST belongs to the TL, this word can, again, be transferred directly to the TT. In his translation of Michel Houellebecq's *Platforme* (2001), Wynne (2002) naturalizes uses of English which appear in the French ST. Other translators, however, prefer to convey the foreign resonance which TL words have in the original text, and do so by highlighting this in footnotes. Such is the approach of Bussy (1927: 83) in her translation of Gide's *Les Caves du Vatican* (1914): 'In English in the original'.

When large quantities of spoken language are incorporated into a written work, a tendency which is often apparent in polyphonic texts, the ST author's intention may, or may not, be to reduce the traditional divide which exists between spoken and written discourses. If the ST author's intention is deliberately political, those translators who adopt a close and meticulous approach to transferring the ST may clarify this. In the introduction to his translation of *Gargantua et Pantagruel*, Cohen (1955: 17–31) explains at length Rabelais's decision to integrate into his literary work language which conventionally belongs to an oral tradition.

While equally scrupulous in preserving the linguistic variety and dialogism of the SL, a second group of translators adopt a freer and more adaptive approach to recapturing this in their TTs. These translators thus engage in a process of rewriting; a strategy which they consider necessary where close translation of the multiple languages, or language varieties, in the ST would be impossible. Queneau's *Zazie* contains an abundance of colloquial French language which the author writes, as if to phonetically transcribe his characters' conversations. Furthermore, in this process Queneau frequently merges words; a technique which his translator has labelled 'logosymphysis' (Wright [n.d.]: 3). Amusing examples of these, which Wright (ibid.: 9) creatively rewrites, include 'Dukipudonktan?' (*D'où qu'ils puent donc tant?* [How do they stink so much, then?]), which is rerendered as 'Howcanaystinksotho?', and 'Skeutadittaleur' (*Ce que t'as dit tout à l'heure* [What you said earlier]), which becomes 'Whattusaidjusnow'. Other features of language lend themselves to adaptation and recreation in the TT. In *Astérix*, for instance, certain characters drink heavily and slur their speech. Bell and Hockridge succeed in maintaining this in their translation, rerendering: *CH'EST QUE J'VEUX ETRE SUR QUE CE N'EST PAS D'LA POCHION MAGI... HIPS!... MAGIQUE!* (1966: 23, capitals in the original), as 'JUSHT MAKING SURE IT WASHN'T MAG – HIC – MAGIC POTION! (1973: 23)

A common feature of linguistically dynamic, varied texts is their tendency to play with language. Thus, language is treated as a game and is a rich source of entertainment in the ST. When the SL displays such qualities, the translator's task is particularly complex. As no pun remains the same when literally translated, some degree of rewriting is always inevitable. If the translator is able to remain relatively close to the image and humour of the original pun, rewriting may be minimal. Discussing Christmas presents, Bridget Jones asks her father 'How are the ear-hair clippers?'. 'Oh marvellously – you know – *clippy*', he replies (1996: 12). In her translation, Stroumza (1998: 18) recaptures this humour in her play on the French word *poil*, where *poil* means 'hair' and *au poil*, 'just the ticket': *Et ta pince à tailler les poils dans les oreilles? Oh! Euh... au poil!* More commonly, however, the translator must deviate further from the ST when rerendering a pun in the SL. Bell (1999: 2) discusses her 1976 translation of a play on the Venus de Milo in *Astérix aux Jeux Olympiques* (1968):

> In the French original [...], athletes from all over Greece enter the arena in procession, and the arrival of the team from the island of Melos – or, more commonly, 'Milo' – is announced with the words 'Ceux de Milo sont venus aussi'. This neat play on the Venus of Milo doesn't work in translation. So in English, the words become: 'Some of the competitors from Attica are mysteriously eleusive' – referring to the ancient Greek mysteries of Eleusis.

The names of characters in the ST may present the translator with similar challenges. When names have standard equivalents in the TL, the translator has only to decide whether to leave these in the original, thus providing the TT with a sense of the foreign (Wright's 1983 translation of *Zazie*), or to use the available TL equivalents (Bussy's 1927 translation of *Les Caves*). However, when the names of ST characters contain wordplays, which is the case throughout the *Astérix* series, the translator may decide to be equally playful in their rerendering of these. As Bell (1999: 3) explains:

> For Asterix, references have to be dredged up from elsewhere. There are the names in the French originals, about 400 in all, and only a very few, like Julius Caesar and Vercingetorix, are genuine. The rest are French compound phrases ending –ix for Gauls, –us for Romans, –os for Greeks and so forth, and they need rethinking in English. Asterix and Obelix, luckily, are no problem. But their chieftain Abraracourcix (literally, 'with arms shortened', as in 'ready to pitch in') is Vitalstatistix in English because of his girth.
>
> Obelix's dog, Idéfix, turns into Dogmatix. A couple of minor Roman legionaries become Sendervictorius and Appianglorius. In the most recent book the French name of the high priest of Atlantis is Hyapados (from 'il n'y a pas d'os', or 'there's no snag'). In English he becomes Absolutlifabulos; even if the famous television series fades from memory, the name should still fit, since Atlantis really is a place of fable.

When the SL is spoken by non-natives, further rewriting is often required. In *Astérix chez les Bretons* (1966/1973), the British people's spoken French contains numerous anglicizms. At times, these are highlighted by the French people who are aware of the differences between the two languages (ibid.: 9/9):

Il nous faut de la magique potion pour combattre les romaines armées. Pourquoi parlez-vous à l'envers?	Your magic potion is just what we need to help us fight the Romans, what! What do you keep saying what for?

Indeed, many anglicizms which appear in the ST are rerendered in the TT through exaggerated use of an elevated register of English (ibid.: 6/6):

Bonté gracieuse! Ce spectacle est assez	Goodness gracious! This is a jolly rum
superbe.	thing, eh, what?
Je dis, ça, c'est un morceau de chance.	Oh I say, what a bit of luck.

In *Astérix*, many other nationalities speak French and their native accents shine through. In several of these *BD*, characters are of African origin and characteristically drop the sound 'r' when they communicate in French: *NAVI'A BABO'D! NON! SONT-CE DES 'OMAINS. PA'JUPITE'!* (1966: 5). However, as this is rewritten as: 'SHIP TO PORT CAP'N. NO! ROMAN SHIP TO PORT, BY JUPITER! (1973: 5, capitals in the original), Bell and Hockridge's translation appears to somewhat lose the African resonance which the French words have in the ST.

Some adaptation and rewriting is also considered necessary when transferring instances of polyglossia from the ST to the TT. When the original French version of *Zazie* contains English words or phrases, Wright (1983) replaces these with German words in her TT in order to preserve the impression of linguistic hybridity and exoticism present in the original work:

'– Male bonas horas collocamus si non dicis isti puellae *the reason why this man Charles went away.*
– Mon petit vieux, lui répondit Gabriel, mêle-toi de tes cipolles. *She knows why and she bothers me quite a lot.*' (Queneau 1938/1996: 92)

'Male bonas horas collocamus si non dicis isti puellae *weshalb dieser Mann Karl weggegangen ist.*
'My dear little fellow, replied Gabriel, mind your own Geschäft. *Sie weiss warum und sie* ärgert mich sehr'. (Wright 1983: 101)

Whether or not the SL author's considerable use of oral language in his written text has a political function, translators who are free and adaptive in their rerendering of the ST tend not to provide comment on this in their TT. Nevertheless, in a separate article, Wright discusses Queneau's desire to reform literature by writing radical, playful, and innovative works. She clarifies that, in producing these works, Queneau's intention was to 'create a modern written language which corresponds to the language actually spoken' (Reading Raymond Queneau [n.d.]: 3).

While helpful in classifying many translators' strategies for rerendering linguistic variety and dialogism, the two above-discussed approaches are by no means mutually exclusive. A number of translators draw on a combination of these, at times remaining close to the language(s) of the ST and providing additional explanation for the TT reader, and at other times allowing themselves greater freedom in their re-adaptation and rewriting of the original text. In a detailed preface to her translation of Queneau's *Exercices de style*, Wright 1958/1979: 14) discusses the author's purpose – 'a profound exploration into the possibilities of language' – and justifies her own playful and experimental approach to translating the work:

> Perhaps the book is an exercise in communication patterns, whatever their linguistic sounds. And it seems to me that Queneau's attitude of enquiry and examination can, and perhaps should?, be applied to every language, and that is what I have tried to achieve with the English version. (ibid.: 16)

Wright proceeds to adopt this approach in her translation of the ninety-nine versions of the original short story which form the basis of Queneau's work. Particularly noteworthy is her total rewriting in Cockney of the version of the story which is written in 'vulgar' language in the ST:

> L'était un peu plus dmidi quand j'ai pu monter dans l'esse. Jmonte donc, jpaye ma place comme de bien entendu et voilàtipas qu'alors jremarque un zozo l'air pied, avec un cou qu'on aurait dit un télescope et une sorte de ficelle autour du galurin. (Queneau 1947/2000: 64)

> So A'm stand'n 'n' ahtsoider vis frog bus when A sees vis young Froggy bloke, caw bloimey, A finks, 'f'at ain't ve most funniest look'n' geezer wot ever A claps eyes on. Bleed'n' great neck, jus' loike a tellyscope, strai' up i' was, an 've titfer 'e go' on 'is bonce, caw. (Wright 1958/1979: 88)

In their translation of Anthony Burgess's *A Clockwork Orange* (1962), Belmont and Chabrier (1972) adopt a similarly balanced approach. They write an intoductory note to explain the particularities of the language which pervades Burgess's work; a dialect named *nadsat* which has its roots in slang, Romany, and Russian, and attach a glossary of many key terms to their translation. They explain that this is 'to amuse rather than to clarify' (ibid.: 7, my translation). Subsequently, in the body of their TT, they retain some of the original *nadsat*, but frequently adapt other elements of it. At all times they succeed in preserving not only the foreign and somewhat alienating effect which is experienced by readers of the ST, but also the typically violent undertones of the original:

> And then I cracked this veck who was sitting next to me and well away and burbling, a horrorshow crack on the ooko or earhole, but he didn't feel it and went on with his 'Telephonic hardware and when the farfarculule gets rubadubdub'. He'd feel it all right when he came to, out of the land. (Burgess 1962: 5–6)

> Et puis j'en ai mis un à ce veck qui était assis à côté de moi, complètement décollé et bafouillant, je lui ai mis une bogne tzarrible sur l'ouko, autrement dit le trou de l'oreille, mais il n'a rien senti et il a continué son déconnage: 'Quincaille téléphonique et quand le loinloincululé devient rabadabdab'. Il le sentirait au retour, le choc, quand il atterrirait. (Belmont and Chabrier 1972: 14)

When non-natives speak the SL, thus rendering the ST interculturally heteroglossic, a balance between a close, explanatory translation approach, and a free and adaptive one, can also work successfully. Wright's preface to her translation of Queneau's *Exercices* provides a helpful backdrop to her creative rewriting. She rerenders *Anglicismes* as 'Gallicisms', *Italianismes* as 'Opera English', and *Pour lay Zanglay* as 'For ze Frrensh'. Once again, Wright (1958: 13) both replicates Queneau's playfulness as she herself manipulates language throughout her *Exercises in Style*, and, in her preface, provides clear explanation of Queneau's original intention by directly citing his introduction to *Bâtons, chiffres et lettres*:

> I consider spoken French to be a different language, a very different language from written French. [...] I came to realize that modern written French must free itself from the conventions which still hem it in, (conventions of style, spelling and vocabulary) and then it will soar like a butterfly away from the silk cocoon spun by the grammarians of the 16th century and the poets of the 17th century. It also seemed to me that the first statement of this new language should be made not by describing some popular event in a novel (because people could mistake one's intentions) but, in the same way as the men of the 16th century used the modern languages instead of Latin for writing their theological or philosophical treatises, to put some philosophical dissertation into spoken French.

The Participants: Author

As has previously been established the polyphonic text is not merely a medley of genres and languages; it also contains 'a *plurality of independent and unmerged voices and consciousnesses* [...] which combine [...] in the unity of the event' (Bakhtin 1929/1984: 6–7). The voices of the participants in the polyphonic work, and the translation challenges to which these give rise, can therefore be considered independently of each other. However, as the voices in polyphonic texts do 'combine in the unity of the event' and are therefore intrinsically connected, a degree of overlap between these, and between the translation issues and challenges which they pose, is inevitable.

When the author of a text is socially constructed they are neither a stable nor a monovocal figure. Rather, they are open to many influences and defined in relation to other subjects, towards whom their attitude may vary. At times, they may display a certain self-awareness, but their self-view is often unclear. Furthermore their opinions and ideologies may be contradictory their position in the text may fluctuate, and they may often be multivoiced. Rightly cautious in their handling of texts which are produced by such authors, certain translators adopt a predominantly close approach to the transferral of these STs, frequently supplementing their translation with additional information for the new readership. When the ST makes explicit reference to its own autobiographical content, transferral to the TT is relatively unproblematic (Houellebecq 1994: 14, transl. Hammond 1998: 12). Less explicit references may, nevertheless, be identified in footnotes: 'Cervantes himself had been a captive for some five years and many of the elements in the story may be autobiographical' (Grossman 2004: 334). More detailed biographical information, contained in a preface or introduction, can also draw attention to those influences which have been central to shaping the ST. Bayley (1977: ix–xxviii) adopts this approach in his preface to Johnston's translation of Pushkin.

Where the ST author continues to construct himself in the process of writing, he relates to the other participants in his text and communicates with them through the use of language (see also subsequent sections of this chapter). In the collection of ST-TT pairs examined, there are many instances where such conversations can be rerendered closely, preserving the register, forms of address, attitudes, and tone[4] of the ST author towards others (prologue to *Don Quixote*, pp. 3–9). It is sometimes the narrator of the work (the teller of the story) in a given narrative, rather than the author himself (the writer of the work), who speaks to characters and readers. In their *L'Orange mécanique*, Belmont and Chabrier (1972: 140) recapture accurately the sense of narrator-reader solidarity which prevails in Burgess's ST: *Ce fut un jour atroce et affreux, O mes frères et seuls amis* [It was an atrocious, awful day, O my brothers and only friends]. Adopting this close approach, other translators have also supplemented their TTs with additional explanation of the author's attitude towards these other participants (Bayley 1977: xli).

Similarly, a number of translators remain close to the original text when communicating the ST author's self-view, that is, the way in which he perhaps doubts himself, or expresses concerns about the quality of his work (Grossman 2004: 3–9). The author's self-opinion may be further clarified in an introduction to the TT: 'Pushkin's pride was extreme [...] but as an artist he knew how to make fun of himself' (Bayley 1977: xxi). Moreover, if the author expresses multiple, conflicting opinions in the ST and their world vision is ambivalent, translation may be close and additional explanation may be provided (Bloom's introduction to Grossman's *Don Quixote*, 2004: xxxii). At a linguistic level, the fluctuating position of the ST author may also lend itself to close transferral. Instances of such flux in Lainé's *La Dentellière* (1974) are closely recaptured by Crowther (1976). These include a clear narrative voice, an explicit distinction between author and narrator and multiple occurrences of indirect speech. However, as the author's position in the ST is, in these instances, not fixed, translators often

---

4   Landers (2001: 209) provides the following concise definition of tone: 'A [...] term relating to the overall feeling conveyed by an utterance, a passage, or an entire work, including both conscious and unconscious resonance. Tone can comprise humour, irony, sincerity, earnestness, naïveté, or virtually any sentiment'. He discusses the importance of recapturing the tone of the SL utterance when producing the TT (ibid.: 67–8). The author's tone is an important aspect of his voice.

consider further explanation to be necessary. This can serve to clarify how the author features explicitly in the ST 'At all times, Dickens jumps into his story with both feet and reminds us that he is there, ensuring the enjoyment of our reading experience' (Curtis 1973: 8, my translation), or how they display multiple consciousnesses (Grossman 2004: xxxii) or shifts in identity (Bayley 1977: xliv).[5]

Conversely, where their objective is to preserve in the TT the ST author's instability and multivoicedness, and where a very close transferral of this would clearly be impossible, translators do, of necessity, allow themselves a certain freedom. Queneau's *Zazie* contains an example of a thoroughly multivoiced author-narrator. This individual directly reports conversations between characters, reproducing their colloquialisms, idioms, slang, and use of vulgar language. Interestingly, he continues to write in this register when using free indirect speech and thus renders ambiguous the identity of the voice; character and narrator appear to speak simultaneously. However, at other times, the author-narrator frequently reverts to a clear narrative voice, employing an elevated register and more refined language, including the past historic tense and the imperfect subjunctive. Such linguistic hybridity is illustrated in the following extract:

> Tout faraud, [le ptit type] cria:
> – Tu pues, eh gorille.
> Gabriel soupira. Encore faire appel à la violence. Ça le dégoûtait cette contrainte. Depuis l'hominisation première, ça n'avait jamais arrêté. Mais enfin fallait ce qu'il fallait. C'était pas de sa faute à lui, Gabriel, si c'était toujours les faibles qui emmerdaient le monde. Il allait tout de même laisser une chance au moucheron.

5   In Chapter 3 it was established that, in contemporary Translation Studies, the potential power which the translator wields is being increasingly recognized. They may alter stances or opinions expressed in the ST if they have a particular political agenda. Clearly, this issue raises certain ethical questions. The present study, which focuses on the translation of polyphonic texts, will, however, assume that the objective of the translators of the STs under consideration is to transfer the qualities of the original texts and their authors, as they appear in the ST. This would support a close approach to translation of the ST author's attitude and the opinions and ideologies which they express in their text. This issue is revisited in connection with my translations of Sarraute.

– Répète un peu voir, qu'il dit Gabriel.

Un peu étonné que le costaud répliqât, le ptit type prit le temps de fignoler la réponse que voici:

– Répéter un peu quoi? (Queneau 1938/1996: 10)

Wright (1983: 12) recaptures this medley of voices in the following:

Cock o' the walk, [the little chap] screeched:
'You stink, you gorilla.'
Gabriel sighed. Incitement to violence again. This coercion made him sick.
Since the first hominisation it had never stopped. However, what had to be had to be. Wasn't his fault if it was always the weaklings who gave everybody the balls-ache.
Still, he'd give the gnat a chance.
'Say again', says Gabriel.
A bit surprised that the stalwart should answer back, the little chap took his time, and concocted the following reply:
'Say what again?'

She uses idiomatic alternatives to SL words and vulgar language, omits pronouns in the TL where the negative *ne* is dropped in the SL, and rerenders the colloquial manner of reporting speech in French (*Répète un peu voir, qu'il dit Gabriel*) with the English present tense. As it is impossible to reproduce the French past historic in the TL Wright compensates for this, ensuring that the elevated register is conveyed in translation, and embellishing certain other uses of the SL in the TT. Transferral of this extract has clearly required the translator to adapt, and indeed rewrite, elements of the original work in order to preserve the multivoicedness and the unstable position of the ST author-narrator in the TT.

The Participants: Characters

Similarly, the presence of socially constructed characters in a work presents a range of challenges for the translator. A number of these may be dealt with through use of relatively close translation strategies. In Queneau's *Zazie*,

French characters are engaged in permanent dialogue with one another and their conversations are often revelatory of their self-view and of their position in relation to fellow characters. On one occasion, a character in the novel objects to being addressed informally by another character, as the latter uses the verb *tutoyer*. He protests, asserting that: *D'abord, je vous permets pas de me tutoyer*. As no equivalent verb exists in the TL, Wright (1983: 12) retains the pronoun *tu* in her translation, thus presuming some knowledge of the SL on the part of her TT readership: 'And anyway, who said that you could call me "tu"?'. The particular forms of address used in French, informal *tu* or formal *vous*, either reinforce character solidarity or emphasize any distance between these individuals. Whereas this cannot be recaptured exactly when a French ST is rerendered in English, where the ST is written in English, francophone translators can exploit this feature of their own language. By selecting the appropriate pronoun when translating from English, it is possible to bind characters together (Belmont & Chabrier 1972) or to accentuate any supposed distance between them:

Alors, il m'a enlevé mon verre de champagne de la main, il m'a embrassée et il a dit: Et maintenant, Bridget Jones, je vais vous expliquer ce que pardon veut dire. (Stroumza 1998: 342)	So, he took my glass of champagne from my hand, kissed me and said: And now, Bridget Jones, I'm going to explain to you what *sorry* means. (My translation)

To further reinforce character relationships which are reflected in dialogic uses of language, certain translators draw particular attention to changes in register and attitude: 'When he is extremely angry Don Quixote changes the way he addresses Sancho, moving from the second person singular to the more distant second person plural. [...] He maintains his irate distance until the end of the paragraph' (Grossman 2004: 255).

The independence and self-assertion which is demonstrated by characters in polyphonic works may, however, be challenged by the author. It may be clear in the body of the ST that the author is using one of their characters to a specific end, and this can be closely transferred to the TT. However, at times, the TT reader may require further explanation of the ways in which the ST author uses their characters to express their own voice. For instance, Levi's (1971: 7–14) detailed introduction to Radice's 1982 translation of Erasmus's *Praise of Folly* (1509) offers a detailed commentary of Folly's four voices and defines the stages at which Erasmus uses this character to express himself. As any instance of an author explicitly addressing their characters is extremely rare, no examples of an author's attempt to reproach or dominate their characters in an effort to control them have been identified in the body of texts studied. Nevertheless, where this is an important feature of the ST, the translator could rerender closely the language used by paying attention to the above-discussed considerations and by providing explanatory notes where they deem these to be appropriate. If the independence of characters is at threat and they fight to retain it, this may be evident in the ST itself. However, in certain TTs, author-character relationships may also be outlined in a preface or notes: 'For Pushkin one of the pleasures of writing the poem as he did is that he was greatly taken with his cast of characters and enjoyed feeling that he did not know what they would do' (Bayley 1977: xviii). Once again, as author-character dialogue is rare, no instances of characters who reassert their independence and blatantly argue with their author have been identified in the present study. This may, however, be dealt with by applying a number of the above approaches.

Certain translators have dealt with this specific set of translation challenges in freer and more adaptive ways. It has been established that, when used in the second person, French pronouns are difficult to rerender in English. In *Astérix*, characters who do not know each other and who are therefore not on familiar terms, use the 'tu' form to address people of other nationalities, including those who they consider to be their enemies. In spite of the absence of an equivalent pronoun in English, Bell succeeds in conveying this lack of respect in her TT. She concentrates on the tone of entire sentences rather than attempting to preserve the original use of the informal pronoun. Thus: *Je réfléchirai, Romain, je te ferai savoir ma réponse* (1968: 11) becomes 'I'll think about it, Roman, I'll let you have my answer' (1976: 11). The same principle may be applied to transferral of the French *vous*. In Voltaire's *Candide*, all characters use this form of address, regardless of the nature of their relationship with their addressee. In his 1947 translation, Butt succeeds in conveying this sense of respectful formality by maintaining an elevated register of language elsewhere in the dialogues which take place between characters. Candide speaks to his love interest, Cunégonde: *O ma chère Cunégonde! Faut-il vous abandonner dans le temps que Monsieur le gouverneur va faire vos noces! Cunégonde menée si loin, que deviendrez-vous?* (1759/1990: 97). In the following, the register and tone of the original are fully recaptured by Butt (1947: 61): 'My darling Cunégonde', he exclaimed, 'to have to leave you just when the Governor had promised to come to our wedding! What's to become of you, Cunégonde, now I have brought you so far from home?'.

The Participants: Readers

On an extra-textual level, readers, like authors and characters, are socially and dynamically constructed individuals. Furthermore, they enter into particular forms of dialogue with both the text itself as they read and interpret it and, at times, with the author or narrator of the text.[6] When translating a ST in which there is explicit author-reader dialogue,[7] the translator faces a specific set of translation challenges.

In the body of ST-TT pairs studied, translators adopt an overwhelmingly close approach to the transferral of all author-reader interaction in the ST, making only minor adjustments to the original exchanges rather than entirely rewriting them. Unmistakably, Rabelais's entire prologue to his *Gargantua* is intended for his readers and opens with the following address: *Buveurs très illustres, et vous, Verolez très précieux – car à vous, non à aultres, sont dediez mes escriptz* (1534–8/1972: 11). Rabelais's assumptions

---

6   In order to avoid repetition, the terms 'author' and 'reader' will be used henceforth. However, the present discussion is, of course, relevant to instances of both author-reader and narrator-narratee interaction in the ST and to the translation of these.

7   According to Auerbach (1946: 279), few, if any, authors before Rabelais addressed their readers in an explicit fashion. This tradition, which renders self-conscious the reading process itself, thus has its beginnings in Rabelais's prologue to his *Gargantua*.

about his readers are humorously discourteous. However, his use of the adjectives *illustres* and *précieux* suggests that he does have a certain degree of respect for his audience. Cohen (1955: 37) rerenders this line as: 'Most noble boozers, and you my very esteemed and poxy friends – for to you and you alone are my writings dedicated'. Therefore this translator not only recaptures the ST author's conflicting attitudes towards his readers, but also adds the term 'friends'. He thereby reinforces the existing impression of author-reader solidarity. Such solidarity is a prominent feature of Burgess's *A Clockwork Orange*. At intervals throughout the novel the narrator and principal character, Alex, speaks affectionately to his readers. This is particularly so in the concluding passage of the work:

> A terrible grahzny vonny world, really, O my brothers. And so farewell from your little droog. And to all others in this story profound shooms of lip-music brrrrr. And they can kiss my sharries. But you, O my brothers, remember sometimes thy little Alex that was. Amen. And all that cal. (Burgess 1962/2000: 141)

Burgess's translators recapture the familiar tone of the original by remaining close to the lexis and tone of the ST:

> Terrible, ce monde. Vonneux et grassou à souhait, O mes frères. Sur ce, votre petit droug vous salue bien. Et pour chacun de tous ceux qui sont dans cette histoire, un gros choum pétouilleux des lèvres frouppp frouppp. Et libre à eux de m'embrasser les charrières. Mais vous, O mes frères, souvenez-vous de temps en temps du petit Alex qui était vôtre. Amen. Et tout le gouspin. (Belmont and Chabrier 1972: 214)

When the author of the ST provides his readers with advice, preservation of the register and tone of, and use of tenses in, the original also ensures that the nature of the author-reader relationship is conveyed in the TT. This can be witnessed in the source and target versions of *Gargantua*: *Ha, pour grâce n'emburelucoquez jamais votre esprit de ces vaines pensées, car je vous dis qu'à Dieu rien n'est impossible* (p. 17). This is rerendered by Cohen (1955: 52–3) as: 'For goodness' sake do not obfuscate your brains with such an idle thought. For I say to you that to God nothing is impossible'.

On certain occasions, the ST author may give their readers guidance on how to interpret, and thus actively participate in, the text. Rabelais's (1534–8/1972: 12–13) preface to *Gargantua* contains the following advice:

> Et, posé le cas qu'au sens littéral vous trouvez matières assez joyeuses et bien correspondantes au nom, toutefois pas demeurer là ne faut, comme au chant des sirènes, ains à plus haut sens interpréter ce que par aventure cui-diez dit en gaîté de coeur.

In his translation, Cohen (1955: 38) modifies the lexis of the original, replacing the antiquated vocabulary of the SL with more contemporary TL alternatives, but maintains the elevated register and advisory tone of the ST:

> But even suppose that in the literal meanings you find jolly enough nonsense, in perfect keeping with the title, you must still not be deterred, as by the Sirens' song, but must interpret in a more sublime sense what you may possibly have thought, at first, was uttered in mere light-heartedness.

Thus, by adopting a close approach to the transferral of author-reader dialogue in the ST, including choice of lexis, register, and tone, translators have succeeded in conveying in the TT both the ST author's attitude toward his readers and the positioning of these individuals in relation to each other. Indeed, it may be questioned whether the TT readership can, or should, be addressed in exactly the same way as the SL audience. However, it would appear that, in the texts studied, the overriding objective of translators is to preserve the exact, dialogic nature of the original SL utterances rather than to alter or adapt these for their target readership.

When the ST author addresses their readers and, in doing so, also anticipates their reaction to themselves or to their works, they again make use of certain forms of address, registers, and tones. In the body of ST-TT pairs examined, ST authors have predicted a range of responses from their readers and these have been closely rerendered by translators. Such is the case, for instance, when Rabelais suspects that his readers will view his works negatively and consider them to be frivolous. This passage from *Gargantua* is again closely recaptured by Cohen:

A quel propos, en votre avis, tend ce prélude et coup d'essai? Pour autant que vous, les
bons disciples et quelques autres fols de séjour, lisant les joyeux titres d'aucuns livres
de notre invention, [...], jugez trop facilement n'être au-dedans traité que moquer-
ies, folâtreries et menteries joyeuses: vu que l'enseigne extérieure (c'est le titre), sans
plus avant enquérir, est communément reçue à dérision et gaudisserie.(Rabelais
1534–8/1972: 12)

Now what do you think is the purpose of this preamble, of this preliminary flour-
ish? It is that you, my good disciples and other leisured fools, in reading the pleasant
titles of certain books of our invention, [...], may not too easily conclude that they
treat of nothing but mockery, fooling and pleasant fictions; seeing that their outward
signs – their titles, that is – are commonly greeted, without further investigation,
with smiles of derision. (Cohen 1955: 37)

Therefore, by closely preserving both the semantic content and the respectful tone and register of the ST, translators have succeeded in recapturing
the original author's attitude toward their readers and the ways in which
author and reader exist in relation to each other. The question of whether
or not the translator can presume that the TT reader will react to the text
in the same way as readers of the ST is open to debate. Nonetheless, this
consideration does not seem to have greatly affected the translators of the
body of texts studied. Again, it appears that the objective of these translators has been to preserve the exact nature of the ST, as it was written for its
original readership, rather than to readapt it for, and anticipate alternative
reactions on the part of, TT readers.

The Participants: Gender

When studying the socially constructed nature of human subjects,
Voloshinov (1927) did not consider the issue of gender. However, as this is
central to, and affects, all interpersonal relationships and the construction of
all individual identities, theorists have since suggested that gender is key to
the study of human subjects (Pearce 1994). The transferral of both gendered

interaction and of socially constructed, gendered, and often stereotypical personalities from the ST to the TT, gives rise to certain challenges.

As little author-character interaction has occurred in the texts examined, it has not been possible to identify any distinction between the way in which authors address male and female characters. As regards author-reader communication, audiences of these texts tend to be addressed as a collectivity, which may be composed of both male and female readers; again, only extremely rarely are gender-specific addresses made to male or female readers, for example, in Rabelais's preface to Gargantua. When approaching the translation of STs which contain gendered author-character and author-reader dialogue it is nevertheless instructive to refer to those techniques which have been used to convey gendered interaction between other textual participants (for instance, the characters), and to consider how these have been transferred to the TT. In the body of texts examined, translators have adopted a predominantly close approach to the transferral of ST authors' attitudes towards the genders.[8] In Lainé's *La Dentellière* (1974), misogynous tendencies can be recognized in the principal male character, Aiméry de Beligny, as well as clichés, stereotypes, and an attempt to devalorize women in the portrayal of his female counterpart, Pomme. Depictions of subjugated women are deliberately exaggerated to emphasize their stereotypical status. They accumulate throughout the work, painting a satirical portrait of gendered relationships. At no point, however, does Crowther (1976) consider further explanation of Lainé's intentions to be necessary in the TT. Conversely, in Dickens's *Oliver Twist* (1837–8), the roles of male and female characters, although explicit in the ST and closely transferable to the TT, are given additional commentary in the preface to their French translation (Curtis 1973: 7–16).

---

8   In a consideration of the ethics of translation, Chesterman (2002) discusses the ways in which STs may be adapted by the translator, if he or she wishes to communicate a particular ideological position. When the feminist translator wishes to revalorize women in her TT, she may implement certain translation strategies, strengthening 'female presence in the text by using stronger verbs when the agent is a woman, more expressive adjectives, etc.' (ibid.: 103). No such manipulation of a ST has been identified in this study.

Interaction which occurs between characters of the same and of the opposite sex has also been closely recaptured in the TTs studied. In Twain's *Huckleberry Finn* (1885), Huck's father addresses him in an abrasive, unaffectionate manner and, when the boy replies insolently, he is reprimanded. Preservation of the tones expressed in the original text enables this father-son relationship to be conveyed accurately in the TT:

> Ne fais pas le malin avec moi, tu as compris? Tu es devenu un joli coco depuis mon départ, mais je te rabattrai le caquet avant d'en avoir fini avec toi. (Twain 1885/1994: 27–8)

> Don't get clever with me, do you understand? Since I left, you've become a nice-looking bloke, but I haven't finished with you yet. I'll take you down a peg or two. (Nétillard 1973: 34)

Similarly, *Bridget Jones* contains many instances of gendered interaction. Multiple conversations between women are reported. These often centre on instances of female bonding and communicate feminist attitudes:

> 'We women are only vulnerable because we are a pioneer generation daring to refuse to compromise in love and relying on our own economic power. In twenty years' time men won't even dare start with fuckwittage because we will just *laugh in their faces*', bellowed Sharon. (Fielding 1996: 21)

> Nous, les femmes, nous sommes vulnérables parce que nous sommes une génération de pionnières, qui refusons le compromis, qui nous assumons financièrement. Dans vingt ans, les hommes n'oseront plus se conduire en enfoirés affectifs, parce que nous leur *rirons au nez*, beugla Sharon. (Stroumza 1998: 28)

The work also incorporates dialogue between males and females who are friends, relatives, and lovers. Preservation of the topics of conversation which feature in the ST and the humorous tone of the SL ensures that the male-female relationships described in the ST are thoroughly transferred in the process of translation. Indeed, the humour in Fielding's work is closely and entirely recaptured in Stroumza's translation. As Fielding's text appeals to people of various nationalities, it can be successfully transferred from the SL to the TL culture.

Last, the behaviour of stereotypical, gendered characters does not merely emerge in dialogue, but is often described in detail in the ST. *Huckleberry Finn* focuses on male comradeship and adventure. By contrast, *Bridget Jones* concentrates on female behaviour and rituals and female friendships, yet also considers male-female relationships and the positioning of the sexes in society. The following extract from Fielding's novel, which describes stereotypical female 'date-preparation' and which likens this to an agricultural process, and its subsequent translation by Stoumza, demonstrate how the semantic content and humour of the original can be successfully preserved and communicated to readers of the target culture:

> 6 p.m. Completely exhausted by entire day of date-preparation. Being a woman is worse than being a farmer – there is so much harvesting and crop spraying to be done: legs to be waxed, underarms shaved, eyebrows plucked, feet pumiced, skin exfoliated and moisturized, spots cleansed, roots dyed, eyelashes tinted, nails filed, cellulite massaged, stomach muscles exercised. The whole performance is so highly tuned you only need to neglect it for a few days for the whole thing to go to seed. (Fielding 1996: 30)

> 18:00. Au bord de l'épuisement. Ai passé la journée à me préparer pour ce soir. Femme. C'est pire que paysan – semis, arrosage, arrachage, récolte... on n'en finit jamais. Jambes à épiler, aisselles à raser, sourcils à épiler, pieds à poncer, peau à gommer et à hydrater, points noirs à enlever, racines à décolorer, cils à teindre, ongles à limer, cellulite à masser, abdominaux à exercer. Un programme si rigoureusement exigeant qu'il suffit de se laisser aller quelques jours pour se retrouver en jachère. (Stroumza 1998: 38–9)

Social, Cultural, and Political Issues

When considered collectively, that is, in relationships with one another, all individuals exist within societies. The concept of a collectivity or society is often a central concern within the multivoiced, polyphonic text. Given that those individuals who function within all texts are representatives of a particular society or culture, translators face a multitude of challenges as they attempt to communicate to an audience of another cultural background the particular vision of the SL culture which is presented in the ST. When faced with a text which contains abundant references to the SL culture, a number of translators transfer these references closely. Nétillard (1973) translates cultural products and items of food which feature in Twain's (1885) *Huckleberry Finn* and does not annotate these.[9] Other translators closely rerender aspects of the source culture and provide some degree of additional explanation. In his translation of Rabelais, Cohen (1955) retains references to personalities, places, and events in the source culture and provides only minimal explanation of a small number of these in his footnotes. When a text is as rich in cultural references as are the works of Rabelais, the translator must indeed exercise caution in his provision of additional notes in order for the TT not to become overburdened and consequently impenetrable, even though opinions on this matter vary considerably (Landers 2001). Such assistance may be presented in alternative forms. Nabokov (1964) attaches a detailed introduction to his translation of Pushkin in order to explain the manners, customs, and habits which were common in Russian culture in the early twentieth century. Ledoux's 1997 translation of Dickens contains similar cultural information in its preface. Alternatively, a number of translators provide equally thorough explanation in the form of footnotes. In order to recapture the rich picture of Spanish life which is painted in Cervantes's *Don Quixote*, Grossman (2004) annotates her TT with copious footers which detail all aspects of the source culture.

---

9   If this strategy is adopted, the translator must be certain to fully understand the items in the ST, otherwise instances of mistranslation occur. It is clear that Stoumza is not familiar with certain English products mentioned in Fielding's novel, as she rerenders these incorrectly. 'Custard creams' (biscuits) are, for instance, translated as 'custard'; an error which is not particularly serious. Nevertheless, there are occasions when Stroumza's misunderstanding of the original leads to a more significant mistranslation of the ST. When Jones lists the food which she has consumed one day, she explains that she made the mistake of eating a bar of chocolate because she had had too much to drink: 'Peppermint Aero (pissed)' (Fielding 1996: 74). Stroumza (1998: 86) translates this as: *Peppermint soda (éliminé peu après)* [Peppermint soda (eliminated shortly after)]. Her lack of familiarity with the SL product results in mistranslation of both the product and of the way in which the term 'pissed' is used in the original.

Those translators who prefer not to rely heavily on the use of footnotes adopt freer and more adaptive translation strategies so as to fully rerender aspects of the SL culture. In his translation of Houellebecq's (1994) *Extension du domaine de la lutte*, Hammond (1998) makes some modifications to the ST by translating certain source culture terms obliquely. *Les énarques* is rerendered as 'the graduates of the École Nationale d'Administration' (ibid.: 58), and *un CRS* is also expanded, becoming 'a CRS policeman' (ibid.: 61). Other translators, such as Wright, retain SL terms in their TT but do not explain them: *C'est un cacocalo que jveux* (1938/1996: 18) becomes 'It's a cacocalo I want' (Wright 1960: 21). This strategy again modifies somewhat the ST, as natural and unremarkable references in the original text appear foreign or exotic when they are directly transposed into the TT.

It is not necessarily the case that translators of texts which contain multiple SL references adopt exclusively close or free strategies when producing their text in the TL. For instance, in her translation of *Bridget Jones*, Stroumza (1998) implements a combination of the above approaches. She leaves the names of certain personalities untouched when these are generally more internationally known figures (Mary Poppins; Germaine Greer), but provides explanation of those who may only be familiar to an anglophone readership (Barry Norman). At times, she uses cultural equivalents. 'A passed over *British Rail* sandwich' becomes *un sandwich SNCF périmé*, and 'Dennis Healey eyebrows' is rerendered as *sourcils à la Groucho Marx*. However, at other times, cultural references are omitted and entirely rewritten:

> 11 a.m. Oh God, I can't have them both arriving at the same time. It is too *Brian Rix* for words. Maybe the whole lunch thing is just a parental practical joke brought on by *over-exposure* of my parents *to Noel Edmonds*, popular television and similar. [...]. Maybe Dad will appear hanging upside-down outside the window *dressed as a Morris dancer*, crash in and start hitting Mum over the head with a sheep's bladder. (Fielding 1996: 47)

> 11:00 Seigneur, ils vont me tomber dessus tous les deux à la même heure. *Un vrai vaudeville* à la française. Et si mes parents souffraient *d'une overdose de sitcoms*? Cette histoire de déjeuner est peut-être une mauvaise plaisanterie. [...]. Papa fera peut-être son apparition par la fenêtre, tête en bas, *avec un nez de clown* entrera en cassant les vitres et se mettra à taper sur la tête de maman avec une vessie de mouton. (1998: 56, my emphases)

If, as has been established, a factual or neutral presentation of the SL culture in the ST gives rise to a number of translation challenges, a multi-tonal depiction of this culture will further test the translator. Landers acknowledges that texts may often be multi-tonal, and suggests that fidelity to the tone of the ST can ensure that the author's intention and changes in style are successfully preserved in the TT (Landers 2001: 67–8). Frequently, shifts from a serious to a humorous or subversive tone can be easily detected in the ST and directly recaptured in the TT. However, some translators deem it necessary to further explain instances of irony, satire, and humour which may target many aspects of the source culture, including philosophy and politics (Voltaire), society and the class-system (Dickens), and customs and institutions (Rabelais), and do so in the form of an introduction or preface. In the body of texts examined, additional explanation of multi-tonality in the ST has also been identified in translators' footnotes and in extensive, comprehensive endnotes (Pons 1965: 412–38).

All societies are, then, internally interrelational; they are composed of individuals who belong to the same culture and who exist in relationships with one another. If extended, the concept of interrelatedness can be applied to consideration of foreign or other cultures. Texts which are essentially rooted in the SL culture but refer to other nationalities create specific challenges for the translator. In the body of works examined, there is evidence of considerable intercultural awareness. Many of the STs considered contain stereotypical portrayals of foreign peoples and cultures. Study of their corresponding TTs demonstrates that a smooth and direct transferral of these is possible. The impression of cultural hybridity, achieved through the juxtaposition of different cultures in the ST, can also be recaptured in the TT with relative ease. By re-presenting a plurality of cultures in the TT, the translator can preserve the cultural medley which is apparent in the original. Other TTs, however, provide their readership with further explanation of the foreign peoples referred to in the ST in their preface (Butt 1947: 14–15). Moreover, a number of translators use footnotes in order to explain these peoples' cultural and historical background, their customs, and the foods which they eat (Grossman 2004: 67). By contrast, in her rerenderings of *Astérix*, Bell enables her anglophone readership to understand foreign cultural references which appear in the ST by adopting an alternative approach and thoroughly rewriting these.

Should the ST author present foreign peoples in a humorous, and possibly mocking manner, further translation challenges arise. In certain texts, national stereotypes and cultural traditions are directly transposed from the ST to the TT. In *Astérix*, for instance, preservation in the TT of exaggerated ST portrayals of both the self and others is greatly facilitated by fully replicating the amusing images of the original. Places, food, customs (Goscinny and Uderzo 1969: 35), food, drink, and national sports (Goscinny and Uderzo 1966: 29) are communicated visually in the ST and the TT. Nevertheless, in other STs, derision of foreign peoples occurs in more subtle forms. These are often stated explicitly and clarified by the translator (Radice 1971: 134).

The *bande dessinée* is, of course, a unique genre and, as Bell (1999: 3) acknowledges, 'is about the only [one] that can still make harmless use of politically incorrect, xenophobic attitudes'. Translation of such attitudes, which are conveyed through the images and the language of the original *BD*, can, then, be transposed and appear equally inoffensive in translation. However, in the majority of interculturally aware STs, the portrayal of xenophobic attitudes and the use of racial terms are much more sensitive issues, and appropriate transferral of these to the TT becomes an important consideration for the translator. As Landers (2001: 139) warns: 'Few choices of words can have greater impact than those impacting race and ethnicity. The literary translator must be constantly vigilant to select the term that conveys not only denotation but connotation as well'. Landers thus advocates that the original force of the ST language be preserved, however politically incorrect this may appear. He also stresses that: 'The translator has no right to introduce his or her own notions into the text, above all when such accretion distorts the views of the author or warps the TL reader's perception of the SL culture' (ibid.: 138). Translators of the texts studied have adopted just such an approach, closely preserving and recapturing controversial, racist language which is used in the original: *Un homme à visage couleur de suie* (Voltaire 1759/1990: 189) [A man with a face the colour of soot (Cameron 1997: 87)]; 'Apparently some sort of deal's been done with... with the filthy wop' (Fielding 1996: 282) [*Ils ont négocié avec ce sale métèque* (Stroumza 1998: 312)].

Time and Space

In order to determine the particular issues which the chronotopic ST raises for the translator, it is appropriate to consider separately the two constitutive elements of the chronotope: time and space. Particular translation issues arise when the time in which the narrative is set, and / or the tenses which are used, are either stable and logical, or unstable and therefore in a state of flux. When the time frame is stable and explicit in the body of the ST, transferral from ST to TT does not pose translation difficulties. Goscinny's *Astérix* repeatedly opens with an indication of the time in which the narrative is set and this is preserved by Bell in her TTs. *Nous sommes en 50 avant J-C* becomes 'The year is 50 BC'. Nevertheless, where the precise period is less explicit, or further information on this would assist understanding of the era in which the original text is set, a number of translators provide additional explanation. This may be included at length in an introduction (Cohen 1955; Nabokov 1964), or in the form of supplementary notes. Similarly, STs in which a logical development of time is conveyed grammatically, through the uses of tenses, and lexically, through the use of particular time phrases, can be closely recaptured in the TL. Rabelais's *Gargantua* contains an abundance of such language which is carefully preserved by Cohen (1955: 97) throughout his translation: 'So they went on, wasting, pillaging, and stealing till they arrived at Seuilly, where they robbed men and women alike and took everything they could'.

If approaching a ST in which linear time is frequently disrupted, the translator must remain alert to multiple references to different time frames and to constant switches of tense in the original. Such switching of tenses often reflects deviations from chronological order within narrative writings (Lodge 1992: 75). These features of language may often be closely transposed to the TT by using functional equivalents which exist in the TL. For instance, Lainé's 1974 *La Dentellière* contains a number of shifts in narrative time, one of which occurs in the transition between chapters one and two. These are carefully preserved by Crowther (1976) in his translation and no further explanation is required by the new readership. In

Houellebecq (1994), the narrator recalls events from an earlier stage in the novel and anticipates future events. Once again, these references are transferred from ST to TT and no additional explanation is necessary. However, where references to other times are heterodiegetic (Genette 1972/1988), the translation process may become more complex. A number of texts include references to the ST author's life (Houellebecq 1994; 2001), or to past trends in society (Burgess 1962). Where the language of the original may be closely preserved and the content of the original is self-explanatory, no particular difficulties arise. However, where the ST contains references to time frames which are distant from the principal era in which the TT is set, certain translators deem it necessary to explain such movements or shifts in the form of an introduction or footnotes: 'Dickens takes his reader at least ten years back in time, because, at the time of *Oliver Twist*, night watchmen had already been replaced by policemen' (Ledoux 1958: 529, my translation).

Equally, all STs in which the notion of space features prominently, be this in a predominantly fixed and stable, or a fluctuating and disruptive manner, present the translator with a range of challenges. A ST set in one particular area of the SL country may contain a number of references to local places and landmarks. Queneau's 1938 *Zazie dans le métro* mentions a number of the principal sights in Paris, and these are retained by Wright (1938: 11) in her translation. By preserving the original location of the ST, Wright creates a certain authenticity and exoticism in her text, reminding the TT reader of the foreign context of the original work. A number of translators adopt a similar approach. Nevertheless, while Wright provides no additional explanation of the Parisian monuments which feature in *Zazie*, other translators presume less knowledge on the part of their new audience. For instance, in his translation of Céline (1934), Manheim (1983) retains place names which are contained in the ST, explaining a number of these in a glossary. At times, he also highlights the inaccuracy of some geographical details which appear in the ST (ibid.: 438–40).

In stark contrast to this close approach, other translators prefer to be freer and more adaptive in their rerendering of the relatively stable ST location; they transpose entirely the context of the ST from the SL to the TL culture by effectively rewriting the ST. In a pertinent article, Bassnett

(2003) praises the work of Adriana Hunter. Describing Hunter's translation of Beighbeder, Bassnett (ibid.: 18–19) explains 'the translator's skill in domesticating a French work'; an extreme and risky strategy which, in this instance, nevertheless succeeds:

> Hunter transposed every Parisian reference to London, [...] tracked down the trendiest restaurants, boutiques and wine-bars in London and substituted every French reference. She effectively erased the French context in which the novel was set, and yet the narrative [...] worked in its new context. This was an incredibly risky strategy for a translator, but one we couldn't help admiring. (ibid.: 19)

All translators do not necessarily adhere exclusively to one or the other of the above approaches; certain use a combination of close and adaptive techniques. The quintessentially British flavour of Fielding's *Bridget Jones* is indeed enhanced by references to certain areas of London. Stroumza's 1998 translation directly transfers some of these. 'The *Marble Arch* Marks and Spencers' becomes *[le] Marks et Spencer de Marble Arch*. At times, however, Stroumza translates place names obliquely, thereby rewriting the original references. 'Perpetua had been happily looking for lamps with porcelain cats as bases around the Fulham Road' is rerendered as *Perpetua chinait chez les brocanteurs pour dénicher un pied de lampe en forme de chat.*

A similar variety of approaches may be adopted to the rerendering of greater shifts in space which occur in the ST. In such STs, characters may travel between a variety of locations in the SL country or to foreign destinations. In many translations these multiple place names are left untouched, and no further explanation is provided. Thus, both the variety apparent in the ST and the resulting impression of disruption and disorientation experienced by the ST reader can be entirely preserved in the TT. Moreover, by retaining the contrived German names of the places which the characters in Voltaire's 1759 *Candide* visit on their travels ('Thunder-ten-Tronckh'), Butt (1947) and Cameron (1997) succeed in maintaining not only the foreignizing effect but also the humour of Voltaire's text in their respective TTs. While adopting an equally close approach to the rerendering of place names in the SL country and abroad, other translators also provide explanation of these in an introduction (Nabokov 1964), footnotes (Grossman 2004; Nétillard 1973), or endnotes (Pons 1965).

Therefore, where there is movement in the ST, both in France and, to a greater extent abroad, a combination of close and adaptive approaches may be adopted when rerendering this in the TT. Such is the approach of Anthea Bell in her translation of the *Astérix* series. Bell leaves unaltered the names of certain places in France and translates explanatory footnotes which are provided in the original. *Burdigala* remains the same in the TT, and is also translated as 'Bordeaux' in a footnote for the twentieth-century TT reader. Other references to places in France are, however, rewritten and transposed into an English context. *Ce terrain se trouvant du côté de Carnac, cela nous permet de supposer que là, est l'explication d'un mystère historique, au sujet duquel on dit beaucoup de bêtises* (Goscinny & Uderzo 1969: 23) is rewritten as 'The fact that Unhygienix's property was located on Salisbury plain suggests a solution to the ideological problems that may have mystified so many scholars' (Bell & Hockridge 1971: 23). In the same vein, Bell translates certain foreign place names closely – Greek sights and monuments are left unaltered but rewrites others. Amusingly, the name of an English pub, *Chez l'ami Bidax* (1966: 36) is rerendered as 'The Dog and Dux' (1973: 36).

Explanation

Examination of a body of polyphonic STs and their corresponding TTs has demonstrated not only that such texts pose a vast array of translation challenges within the categories of 'The Text', 'The Participants', 'Social, Cultural, and Political Issues', and 'Time and Space', but also that it is possible to adopt a range of approaches to the rerendering of each of the particular qualities of such texts. It has been witnessed that choice of translation strategy varies both between translators, as they recapture these qualities in the ST, and in the work of certain individual translators who draw on a dialogue of approaches, or a combination of techniques, when producing their TTs (Grossman 2004; Stroumza 1998). In each of the four above-mentioned categories, translation challenges can be dealt with by implementing predominantly close or free strategies, or by employing a combination of these.

In the collection of ST-TT pairs examined, all translations selected are texts which have been published, are widely available, and have sold well in the TL country or countries; these translations are all acceptable. Thus, despite the evident variety in approach to the rerendering of polyphonic works, there is no one correct way to translate such texts. Rather, it would appear that choice of translation strategy is shaped and conditioned by a number of factors at each stage of the dialogic, interactive process of translation and on different levels. Evidence has been gathered to suggest that the dialogic, interactive nature of the translation process is being increasingly acknowledged by translation theorists (Chapter 3), and has also influenced practising translators of polyphonic texts (Chapter 4).

Like all individuals, the ST author is a socially constructed subject. They are affected by their interaction with other people and by a variety of other factors, including the era in which they live, their upbringing, and education. These may first inspire their decision to write and subsequently determine the genre to which their text belongs, the language in which it is written, the content of the work, and the ideologies which are expressed in it. The social, interactive nature of all subjects, including the author, was discussed by the Bakhtin Circle (Chapter 2). In the field of literary criticism, attention has been given to the ways in which the influences to which an author has been exposed can have a bearing on their work. An awareness of these considerations has been demonstrated in certain editions of the STs examined. Prefaces and introductions suggest how an understanding of the author's social relationships, background, and education can enhance understanding of the original work (Rabelais).

Interactivity manifests itself in a variety of ways in the polyphonic ST. For the most part, these are explicit. However, in some of the STs examined, detailed commentary is also provided on the peculiar character of the text (Burgess, Dickens, Voltaire).

The potential audience is a key consideration in the production of any text. While the author may attempt to target their text at a particular readership (male or female, young or old, scholar or layman), it is impossible to predict or define the precise nature of one's readership. All audiences are potentially composed of a large number of individuals, each of whom is of a different background, has different interests, knowledge and sense of humour, and will thus interpret the text in a unique way. The ST audience is, then, thoroughly multidimensional. Bakhtin's treatment of the reader was discussed (Chapter 2), as was his position in relation to other theorists of reading (Chapter 3). Theories of interpretation and of reader-response acknowledge that each person is unique and that texts will therefore unfailingly elicit a broad spectrum of responses. While it would be impossible for a ST to be tailored to each of its potential readers, a number of those texts examined clearly target a particular audience. These may contain copious annotation for the educated and interested adult reader (Burgess, Dickens), or close commentary and study prompts for the student or scholar (Rabelais, Voltaire).

The time and place in which texts are received are often equally varied. Texts may be read by persons who live in different centuries and in very different places or countries. Bakhtinian theories of the notions of relational time and space in (source) texts have been discussed (Chapter 2). These considerations have also influenced the ways in which the STs examined have been presented. First, editions of individual texts differ over time. Where the ST is set in the present time, no further explanation is required. However, where it is framed in the distant past, greater assistance is necessary for the reader. Second, editions of individual texts may vary according to the country in which the intended audience lives. Where the ST is set in the SL country, the SL audience is quite familiar with this context. Nevertheless, should the text take its audience on a journey much further afield, additional explanation and maps may, for instance, be provided (Voltaire).

The presence of dialogue, interactivity, interrelationships, and dialogism in all of the above areas are important considerations for the translator. Furthermore, all of these features of the ST are interpreted subjectively by this individual who has been socially constructed and is therefore equally interactive in nature. They have been shaped and conditioned by their relationships with others, the era in which they translate (Lefevere 1992a; 1992b) their background and education. Understandably, such factors will impact on their choice of ST, and on the ways in which they interpret this text and rerender it in the TL. This process will involve choice of translation strategy, use of language (the translator's particular idiolect) and any ideologies which they may wish to communicate in their TT. In Chapter 3 it was demonstrated that, since Benjamin, translation theory has given increased recognition to the subjective nature of the translator who, as interlocutor of the ST, interprets the given text and rerenders it in the TL (Álvarez & Vidal 1996; Hermans 1999). This, of course, explains how multiple translations of any one ST may exist (Bassnett 1997). Indeed, as interlocutor of the ST, the translator is at liberty to translate this text as they deem appropriate. Similarly, practitioners have recognized the individuality and subjectivity of each translator (Motteux 1975; Landers 2001). This is clearly reflected in the variety of translation strategies which are adopted, the language and idiolect in which texts are rerendered, and the ideologies which they convey. Such variation is apparent not only in the translation of different STs, but between translations of one particular ST; certain works have been translated many times and in a number of different ways (Rabelais, Voltaire).

If the interactive, subjective translator is to rerender convincingly the polyphonic ST, they must preserve multiple features of this text within the categories of the 'The Text', 'The Participants', 'Social, Cultural, and Political Issues', and 'Time and Space'. Through an examination of key phases of translation theory, Chapter 3 suggested how theorists are increasingly acknowledging and accounting for the challenges involved in recapturing these STs. Furthrmore, a detailed examination of the ways in which dialogue, interactivity, and variety have been rerendered by practising translators (Chapter 4) demonstrated that practitioners are also paying considerable attention to the difficulties posed by this type of ST, and that they employ a broad range of strategies in order to deal with these.

In their rerendering of the polyphonic text, the translator must also take account of the fact that their potential TT audience will be as complex as the readers of the original text. Once again, it would be impossible to predict the exact nature of the new audience. It will be composed of many individuals, each of whom will have a particular background, different interests and levels of knowledge, and an individual sense of humour, and will therefore interpret the TT in a unique way. In Chapter 3 it was demonstrated that translation theorists widely acknowledge the importance of considering the TT reader. Certain scholars have developed this line of thought, recognizing the 'thoroughly heterogeneous' nature of the TL audience (Venuti 2000: 477). Clearly, then, the TT may be interpreted in a multitude of ways by its readership. The above examination of polyphonic TTs suggests that practising translators also acknowledge the inevitably varied nature of their audience. While it would evidently not be possible to tailor any TT to each of its potential readers, many of the TTs studied do target a particular readership; the adult, educated reader or the scholar (Cervantes, Erasmus, Rabelais), or the child (Finn), for whom simplified explanations and illustrations are provided.

A final consideration is the temporal and spatial framework in which the TT is received. Like their corresponding STs, TTs may be read in many different times and places. Although some TTs remain unaltered and are republished in exactly the same format over many decades (Dickens, Sterne), theorists and practitioners widely acknowledge that reader interpretation also varies according to time and space (Chesterman & Wagner 2002; Motteux 1975).

Clearly, there is no single, uniform strategy which must be adopted when translating polyphonic writings. The translation of such texts is itself a dialogic (Robinson 1991), interactive activity, and choice of translation strategy is influenced by multiple factors which are at play at each level of this process. There is evidence to suggest that this notion is being recognized by theorists and has also influenced practitioners; in this respect, there are marked similarities between theory and practice. Reference to both of these can, then, provide important insights into the process of translating polyphonies.

Application

In view of the above, the translator can maximize their chances of devising an appropriate strategy for rerendering the polyphonic text if they are conscious of the dialogue, interactivity, and variety which are present at each level of the translation process in which they are involved. In order to prepare the ground for translating Claude Sarraute, key instances of these, which occur at each stage of the process of rerendering this author, are recapitulated in Tables 2 and 3. Table 3 provides a useful starting point for approaching the translation of Sarraute. A full *skopos* (Vermeer 1989) and rationale for my translations of ten extracts from Sarraute's writings are provided in my introduction to Chapter 5.

Table 2 The Dialogic Nature of Sarraute's Text Production

ST author	ST	ST audience	Time / place in which ST is produced and received
Claude Sarraute. Socially constructed and interculturally aware person and author (Chapter 2).	Non-canonical texts. Dialogic, interactive, interrelational (literature / language / people / society and culture / humour / time and space). Often polyphonic.	All audiences are multidimensional, yet Sarraute targets the French adult and non-scholar who reads for pleasure. Some knowledge of Europe presumed.	Produced between 1985 and 2005 in France. Received in francophone countries since mid-1980s.

Table 3 The Dialogic Process of Translating Sarraute

Translator	TT	TT audience	Time / place in which TT is produced and received
Myself. An equally socially constructed and interculturally aware person whose reading of Sarraute and choice of translation strategy are necessarily subjective (Chapter 3).	Equally dialogic, interactive, interrelational (polyphonic) texts of non-canonical status which are rerendered in the TL.	This audience will be multidimensional. However, the TT will broadly target the anglophone adult and non-scholar who is reading for pleasure and entertainment. Some knowledge of Europe presumed.	Translations to be produced in the near future and received principally in UK but potentially further afield (in other anglophone countries).

Given the above considerations and the inevitable presence of variables at each level of the translation process, it follows that my translation of any one extract of Sarraute's work will be unique; other translators will, of course, provide equally original versions, since 'every instance of translation is unique' (Bassnett 1997: 2). Consequently, it would be impossible for myself, as interlocutor and translator of Sarraute, to locate a ST-TT pair which would provide an exact model to emulate. It may nonetheless be instructive to refer to a number of other polyphonic ST-TT pairs for guidance and I draw on many of this chapter's findings when preparing my translations of Sarraute (Chapter 5). One extremely appropriate example is Fielding's (1996) *Bridget Jones's Diary* and Stroumza's (1998) corresponding French translation. First, many similarities exist between the nature of the ST authors, Sarraute and Fielding, their texts, intended audiences, and the spatial and temporal settings in which the works exist. Clear comparisons may thus be drawn between Tables 2 and 4.[10]

---

10 Despite these multiple points of comparison, in an instance of explicit intertextuality in one of her novels, Sarraute (2003: 36) discusses *Bridget Jones* (1996) and suggests that her own characters are deliberately different from those of Fielding.

Table 4 The Dialogic Nature of Fielding's Text Production

ST author	ST	ST audience	Time / place in which ST is produced and received
Helen Fielding. Socially constructed and interculturally aware person and author. Like Sarraute, began by writing newspaper column, then progressed to novels.	Non-canonical texts. Dialogic, interactive, interrelational (literature / language / people / society and culture / humour / time and space). Often polyphonic. (Examples throughout Chapter 4).	Multidimensional audience, but ST is broadly targeted at anglophone adult and non-scholar who is reading for pleasure / entertainment and who has some knowledge of other European countries.	Produced in 1996 in Great Britain. Received in GB and further afield in other English-speaking countries.

Second, the translator, her text, audience, and the space and time in which she operates, are of a comparable nature. Similarities therefore exist between Stroumza's circumstances (Table 5) and my own (Table 3).

Table 5 The Dialogic Process of Translating Fielding

Translator	TT	TT audience	Time / place in which TT is produced and received
Socially constructed and interculturally aware individual, whose reading and rewriting of Fielding are subjective.	Equally dialogic, interactive, interrelational, polyphonic and of non-canonical status. Rerendered in the TL.	Multidimensional audience, but texts are targeted at the French adult and non-scholar who is reading for pleasure / entertainment and who has a reasonable knowledge of other European countries.	Produced in 1998 in France. Possibly read in other francophone countries.

As has been suggested throughout the present chapter, Stroumza's TT succeeds admirably not only at recapturing the many intricacies of Fielding's work, but also at preserving the subject matter and the quintessentially British character of the original text. Stroumza's approach is a balanced one. At times she rerenders the ST closely, and at other times she is freer and more adaptive. She explains certain references in the ST, but nevertheless ensures that her TT reads smoothly and is not overburdened with footnotes. Stroumza thus employs a variety of strategies in order to rewrite Fielding's work. My objective will be to achieve a similar result when translating Sarraute. Careful consideration of all levels of Table 5 will, then, assist me in my task as outlined in Table 3.

An appreciation of the issues which arise in the dialogic (Robinson 1991), interactive process of translation will, moreover, help to determine which theoretical approaches I draw on and which practical solutions I apply when rerendering Sarraute. By referring to a selection of translation theories which acknowledge the complexities of rerendering polyphonic texts (Chapter 3) and by using a combination of tried-and-tested practical translation strategies (Chapter 4), that is, by implementing an eclectic blend of theory and practice and thus situating myself in a contemporary Translation Studies paradigm, I, as Sarraute's interlocutor, should be sufficiently well informed, and suitably equipped, to embark upon a translation of her writings.

Rerendering Claude Sarraute

Thus far, the foundations have been laid for reading and analysing texts of a polyphonic nature and for rerendering such works in the TL. At each stage, the writings of Claude Sarraute have been considered and the ways in which these can be read, analysed, and subsequently rerendered have been examined. Building on this work, the present chapter focuses yet more closely on a collection of extracts from Sarraute's writings, which it reads, analyses, and reproduces in English (for full set of ST-TT pairs, see Ellender 2006a). Ten extracts were selected in order to offer a comprehensive coverage of Sarraute's work and to reinforce that, irrespective of the genre to which they belong, the time at which they were written, and the subjects which they discuss, her texts are indisputably polyphonic. Accordingly, the present chapter groups my ten chosen extracts, of approximately four hundred to one thousand words each, according to their genre: article for *Le Monde* (Extracts 1 to 3), novel (Extracts 4 to 7), social critique (Extract 8), column for *Psychologies* (Extracts 9 and 10). It approaches these chronologically, from the 1980s to the twenty-first century, and seeks to encompass a broad range of the subject matter which Sarraute typically covers in her works, from education and politics, through male-female and family relationships, to multiculturalism. Most significantly, this chapter offers a thorough illustration of the particular qualities of Sarraute's writings occurring within the four major defining categories which have served as the leitmotif of *Preserving Polyphonies*, viz.: 'The Text', 'The Participants', 'Social, Cultural, and Political Issues', and 'Time and Space'.

    In the interests of clarity and concision, each of my commentaries, which in a Derridean sense, supplement my translations of Sarraute, considers one of these ten ST-TT pairs and adopts a tripartite approach to it. First, it outlines the theme and content of the given ST and, where relevant, situates the extract within the broader context of the work from which it emanates. Second, it identifies the essential dialogic, interactive, and interrelational qualities of the text. Third, it then examines the ways in which these qualities are reflected at various levels of the ST. This approach intends to deconstruct the individual STs in order that they are understood in depth (Derrida's close approach, Chapter 3). It then pinpoints the translation issues and challenges to which each of these gives rise and explains the individual solutions which have been employed when producing the TT, acknowledging those translation theorists and practitioners who have been especially influential to this process.

Sarraute's polyphonic writings contain a wide range of distinctive features and the translation solutions which I implement in order to rerender these in the TL are correspondingly diverse. In order to present and explain succinctly these features and the translation strategies which I have adopted, I supplement my ten commentaries with four complementary tables (Tables 6–9) which synthesize their salient empirical findings and which correspond to the four above-mentioned categories. Each table provides a systematic taxonomy of the multiple instances of dialogue, interactivity and interrelatedness which have occurred throughout extracts 1 to 10 in the given category. Numbers which appear in brackets in these tables refer to the extracts from Sarraute's writings in which the cited examples occur. Brief explanations and justifications of the approaches adopted in order to rerender these are also supplied, as are the names of all influential theorists and practitioners. The findings recorded in the tables are then expanded upon, and a number of important conclusions are drawn.

In order to rerender a given ST competently, the translator must adopt a methodology which is grounded in a thorough understanding of the purpose of his TT. If the target text is to be acceptable, the TL readership must also be clearly identified. Consideration of these issues can assist the translator in determining their translation strategy, enabling them to produce translations which are consistent in approach and quality and of a publishable standard.

In Chapter 1 it emerged that, in her writing of idiosyncratic, iconoclastic texts, Sarraute's overriding objectives have been to set herself apart from her mother, an established literary figure, and to cause laughter. These aims have directly influenced the *skopos* of my translations. In my rerenderings of Sarraute, I seek to *preserve* the considerable range of dynamic, interactive, reactive and subversive qualities present in these culture-bound French writings and, in doing so, to entertain my readers. In short, my intention is to produce fair, accurate and full representations of my chosen STs in the TL.

Broadly speaking, Sarraute writes for French adults who are reading for pleasure. This said, she is clearly aware of the potential diversity of her audience. At times, individual works may appeal to a range of people (1987; 1991). At other times, however, her articles are intended for specific readerships (1985: 255–6; 1985: 113) and her novels contain comments which refer to the experiences of certain sub-groups of readers (1989: 53). When approaching each of my ten chosen extracts, consideration of the precise nature of the implied SL reader (Iser 1974) has been influential in defining my target audience. While directing my collection of TTs at the general adult reader, I recognize that individual extracts in my collection will appeal variously to different reader groups in the TL culture. The TL audience contains further sub-divisions. While my anglophone readers will undoubtedly have a shared interest in contemporary France, they may not all be speakers of British English (the principal language of my TTs) and will certainly not all have the same knowledge of the French language and culture. These considerations, and that of the *skopos* of my TTs, were central to the shaping of my translation strategy.

In order both to preserve in the TL the peculiar qualities and humour of Sarraute's French STs and to cater for a variety of reader groups in the TL audience, I adopt an eclectic approach to rerendering my ten chosen extracts. Often invisible as translator, I seek to achieve pragmatic equivalence and to create a smooth, enjoyable read in the TL. Nevertheless, I take care not to domesticate Sarraute's writings to the extent that their French character is lost in translation. Thus, I sometimes become visible. Without unsettling my readers unnecessarily, I supplement my TTs with a number of didactic footnotes, providing keener readers of my audience with additional cultural information where I deem this to be relevant.

Preserving Polyphonies has viewed translation as a highly interactive process. Indeed, translation is a transaction, a collaborative enterprise in which the translator communicates not only with the ST author and the various reader groups in the TL culture, but also with their commissioner and publisher. Sarraute's writings belong to a variety of genres and thus occupy various places in France's polysystem. Distinctive, humorous articles written in conventionally oral language are published in a column in the Left-wing newspaper, *Le Monde*, and a number of these are collated in a book (1985). Novels and a social critique are works in their own right, and more recent, socially aware articles feature in the magazine, *Psychologies*. Were my translations of texts belonging to these various genres to be published individually, they could reasonably appear in / as comparable TL publications (*The Guardian*, novels, *Psychologies / Zest*). However, my current multigeneric collection of TTs would be most suitably published as it stands. As such, it would occupy a place as translated literature in the TL polysystem. My ten ensuing commentaries make explicit how the issues of purpose, readership, translation strategy and channel of publication have directly influenced my translations of Claude Sarraute.

Extract 1: '*Dans le taxi*' – article for *Le Monde*, published in *Dites donc!* (1985: 11–12)

Originally written for *Le Monde* in the early 1980s, '*Dans le taxi*' was later republished as part of a collection of Sarraute's (1985) newspaper articles under the heading of *Dites donc!* This particular text centres entirely on a spoken dialogue between Sarraute and a taxi driver of Guadeloupian origin, who is driving her to Roissy airport. Their somewhat acrimonious conversation begins as the driver guesses that Sarraute will be travelling to Tel-Aviv. She is offended by the suggestion that her Jewish identity is obvious and is defensive, until the driver draws her attention to the Star of David necklace which she is wearing. Ironic in his tone, the driver fails to understand how any non-native resident of France would voluntarily display his foreign identity; clearly, he cannot conceal his own. When the driver discusses the differences between Jews and West Indians, Sarraute is surprised at the philosophical nature of his comments. In response, he assumes a strong Créole accent, implying that she believes him to be a stupid and uneducated foreigner. The conversation ends as Sarraute attempts to backtrack, attributing her surprise to the driver's age, rather than to his cultural origin.

'*Dans le taxi*' is, without doubt, a highly dialogized, polyphonic text. It has no controlling narrator and is composed of an interpersonal, power-inscribed dialogue between two people of opposed cultures (Bakhtin 1965). In turn, dialogism and interactivity are reflected variously throughout the ST and give rise to a range of interesting translation issues and challenges. In Bakhtin's (1929/1984: 40) words, the present article qualifies as 'polyphonic' as it is '*dialogic through and through*'. This definition, which was originally used to describe the novelistic genre, is thus also clearly of multigeneric application.

'*Dans le taxi*' is not a conventional newspaper article written in prose, but an apparently transcribed conversation between the author and her driver. Sarraute is the 'real author' of the present article (Baldick 1990: 146; Rimmon-Kenan 1983/1997: 86–7) and a 'homodiegetic' figure (Genette 1972: 255–6) as she participates as a character in it. Given the particular nature of this text, it reacts against an established generic norm.[1] Although it was possible to closely preserve this characteristic of the original text in translation, I considered it appropriate to be freer and more creative when rerendering its title, in order to reinforce in the TL the original context in which the ST appeared (*Le Monde*). I therefore rewrote this title using alliteration to convey explicitly the content of the text and making it humorous by supplementing it with a tabloid quality. Thus: 'Tension in the taxi: Foreigners in France get touchy in transit'.

The conversation between Sarraute and her driver takes place as they are travelling in the taxi. This text can, then, be theorized by reference to Bakhtin's 'Chronotope of the Journey' (1938). Bakhtin believed that the presence of such a chronotope reinforces any sense of tension and instability

---

1   Thus, a primary genre (speech) is incorporated into a secondary one (written text) (Bakhtin 1979/1986: 62). This article provides a clear illustration of Bakhtin's *skaz*. Written language resembles oral discourse and 'is above all an orientation toward *someone else's speech* and only then, as a consequence toward oral speech' (1929/1984: 191).

in a text. Indeed a latent tension, which is grounded in cultural difference, does underpin 'Dans le taxi'. The principal manifestations of dialogue and interactivity in this text occur on a cultural level, and these are communicated variously through the language used in the ST.

In his *Freudianism*, Voloshinov (1927) stressed the socially constructed nature of all individuals. Indeed, the discomfort of both characters with regard to their respective cultural identities has evidently been shaped by their interaction with xenophobic French natives.[2] Furthermore, not only do these characters consider themselves as 'others' in French society, they also see themselves as different from one another: *Excusez-moi, mais juif et Antillais, ce n'est pas pareil* [Sorry, but Jewish and West Indian aren't the same]. Their resulting sensitivity is apparent in their conversation and presents certain issues for the translator. Sarraute, for instance, bristles repeatedly at her driver's comments. Landers (2001) rightly stresses the importance of recapturing accurately the tone of SL utterances in the TT. In line with this view, I rerendered closely Sarraute's defensive retorts in my translation, hence:

Pourquoi? C'est écrit sur ma figure?	Why do you say that? Is it written on my face?
Ah! ben, ça c'est un peu raide.	Well, that's a bit much!
Vous ne croyez pas que vous poussez un peu?	Er, don't you think you're going a bit far?

Similarly, it was possible both to transfer closely some of the driver's ironic remarks and his brusque concluding comment, and to transfer some of his other language, making only small modifications to this in the TL. Application of Vinay and Darbelnet's (1958) transposition thus transforms *Il y a toutes les chances pour que ce soit Tel-Aviv* into 'It's probably Tel-Aviv'.

2   It will be recalled that, in both *Allô Lolotte, c'est Coco* (1987: 90) and in my interview with her, Sarraute speaks explicitly of the difficulty which she has had in accepting her Jewish identity. I included a footnote to this effect in my TT in order to draw attention to the autobiographical quality of this text. By adopting this approach, which is also favoured by Grossman (2004), I become visible as the translator.

Nevertheless, when the driver resorts to imitating a Guadeloupian (Créole) accent in his mockery of European attitudes, translation becomes more challenging. He exclaims:

> *Ah! paske ti neg' pa savoi' pa'lé fwancé... Pa capab' wésoné... Ti neg' pa gwan wabin... Ti neg' pa...*

I decided that, in order to fully preserve this sentence, it was necessary first to transfer its semantic content, and subsequently to transpose a Créole accent onto my translation. After simplifying the TL syntax and replacing all mispronounced 'r's with the sound 'w', I referred to the poetry of Benjamin Zephaniah, whose *City Psalms* (1992) are written in a Jamaican-accented English, and borrowed some of his phonetically-spelled words ('cause' and 'yu') to produce my rewriting: 'Oh! Cause yu Negwo, don't know how speak Fwench... Can't weason... Yu Negwo not chief wabbi... Yu Negwo not...'.

A further dimension to *'Dans le taxi'* which is conveyed through language is the irony of the discrimination to which the two characters have been subjected. Racial tension often occurs when non-natives do not, or cannot, adapt to life in the host country. Due, however, to their excellent mastery of the SL, it is clear that Sarraute and her driver are both thoroughly integrated into the SL culture. Their French is heteroglossic (Bakhtin 1940/1981: 67) – it contains the use of contrasting informal and formal registers – and Sarraute displays linguistic awareness; she distinguishes between banter and her driver's more philosophical comments. The translator's task thus becomes one of preserving the multidimensionality of the SL in the TT. In my attempt to recapture this sense of discursive heterogeneity in my translation, I felt it necessary to remain relatively close to the SL. I rerendered Sarraute's informal and slightly dated *flûte!* with the infrequently used TL exclamation 'drat!'. I sought to preserve the contrast between this and the driver's accurate and formal *Vous ne risqueriez pas de l'oublier* by using the subjunctive in the TL: 'There would be no danger of your forgetting it'. In the same vein, I attempted to maintain this juxtaposition of registers in the following two instances:

| *Évidemment, si vous restez au niveau événementiel […]* | Of course, if you remain on a factual level […] | Literal (Vinay & Darbelnet 1958) |
| *Hou là! Mais, dites donc, c'est de la haute philosophie, ça!* | Whoa! I say, that's highly philosophical, that! | Transposition (Vinay & Darbelnet 1958) |

Last, the characters' mastery of French is also demonstrated by their rich use of idiom. While aiming to closely preserve the meaning of this language, I allowed myself greater freedom in its rerendering, expanding and rewriting certain expressions to recreate a similarly colloquial effect in the TL. Reference to Pilard's *Rude French* (2002) helped me to cultivate an appropriate mind-set for this task and inspired some of my translations, amongst which:

Pourquoi?	Why do you say that?
Enfin... presque.	Well... just about.
Vous, les juifs, vous avez la chance que ça ne se voit pas.	You Jews are lucky that your true identity isn't obvious to all and sundry.
Un jour avec, un jour sans.	Now you see it, now you don't.

Extract 2: '*Eh! Va donc!*' – article for *Le Monde* published in *Dites donc!* (1985: 62–5)

'*Eh! Va donc!*' is the second of my chosen extracts which was first written as an article for *Le Monde* and later included in the collection, *Dites donc!* In this irreverent and humorous piece, which is set during the run-up to a round of local elections in France, Sarraute considers name-calling between politicians during this period. She suggests that the insults which are used are generally dull and dated and that politicians must be more creative when criticizing one another if they are to please the public and win votes. As members of the government appear neither to receive advice on being offensive nor to consult appropriate dictionaries, Sarraute takes it upon herself to compile a collection of punchy and entertaining insults for their use. She mentions a number of these and reflects on her sources of inspiration, which range from works of classical literature and comic books to prehistoric animals and political history. She concludes by warning that these terms are a mere sample from her collection and explains that her regular readers have more treats in store.

'*Eh! Va donc!*' is an amusingly iconoclastic text. When examined from a Bakhtinian perspective, this iconoclasm may be described as relative and dialogic, as it constitutes a reaction against the established political hierarchy in France, and as distinctly carnivalesque, as it appears to encourage chaos and social instability and is clearly intended to provoke laughter (Bakhtin 1929/1984: 12). Interrelationships, dialogism, and humour are not only present in the content of '*Eh! Va donc!*', but are also reflected in its language, style, genre, and tone. Thus, a powerful sense of multidimensionality and instability is felt throughout the text. Given its inherent complexities, this article poses a wealth of translation challenges.

Humour and a sense of cacophony are particularly apparent in the language of '*Eh! Va donc!*'. The article's opening paragraph is heteroglossic and hybrid (Bakhtin 1940/1981: 66); it contains words and expressions which belong to standard and slang registers of contemporary French, and these are juxtaposed with more archaic uses of language. In order to preserve this linguistic medley and to avoid homogenization of the TL, I sought words and expressions in English which have comparable resonances to those of the original SL utterances. I therefore rerendered closely the relatively standard use of *bagarre* with the TL noun 'fight'. In an attempt to maintain the contrast between this and the sub-standard register of the French *ça gueule, ça*, I was slightly more free in my translation, recapturing this with the similarly colloquial expression, 'It's really kicking off out there'. Preceded by such contemporary language, Sarraute's unexpected use of the somewhat dated *madame* appears misplaced, and thus comical.[3] When recapturing

---

3 Tabakowska (1990: 77) argues that all words are individually dialogic and that they are determined, amongst other things, by the context in which they are uttered. In this ST, *madame* is clearly used out of its usual context, hence the jarring effect which it produces.

the expression *dites donc, ça gueule ça, madame*, I therefore decided to exaggerate in the TL these dissonant uses. I drew on both the Cockney 'Cor blimey' and the expression 'oo-er missus', commonly associated with the comedian Frankie Howerd, to produce a comparatively disharmonious hybrid: 'Blimey missus, it's really kicking off out there'.

The self-conscious insults peppered throughout this ST are also heteroglossic; Sarraute opposes those which she believes to be boring and old-fashioned with her playful alternatives. In order to preserve the contrast between dull and inventive terms of abuse, I again drew on a range of translation strategies. While it was appropriate to remain close to the original SL uses when recapturing *grande gueule* [big gob],[4] *gros patapouf* [big Fatso] and even the more entertaining *bachibouzouk* [bashibazouk – a type of brutal Turkish soldier] and *ptérodactyle* [pterodactyl], a looser approach was required to the translation of other words. For instance, the French *con* has many rerenderings in the TL, including 'bastard', 'bloody idiot', 'git', 'bugger' and so forth. I chose the TL 'silly old bugger' which, I felt, retains the derogatory and pitying sense of the original, rather than 'bastard' or 'bloody idiot', which have connotations of nastiness and stupidity respectively. I was also relatively free when rerendering *crétin des Alpes*, in order to inject into my TT the sort of vitality and humour which Sarraute advocates throughout her article Having considered such translations as 'mountain moron' and 'moronic mountain man', I opted for the equally alliterated 'Alpine ass', thus retaining the original geographical reference. I was most free, however, in my rendering of the insult *sagouin*, which is usually translatable as 'filthy pig', 'swine', or 'useless idiot'. As Sarraute associates use of this term with the works of the writer François Mauriac, a name which would be unlikely to have any real significance for a TL reader even if it were explained in a lengthy footnote, I omitted this and rewrote the reference. Thus: *des expressions telles que sagouin, ça prouve qu'on a lu*

---

4   At first, I was tempted to re-render *grande gueule* as 'Mr Gobby', playing on the name of the character, Mr Blobby, in the former television programme, *Noel Edmond's House Party*. However, I later decided that this would be inappropriate, given that Sarraute uses this SL term as an example of a dull and uninventive insult.

Mauriac, ça fait cultivé became 'expressions which prove that you're well-read and which look cultured'. As Cohen (1955: 18–19) suggests in the introduction to his translation of Rabelais's *Gargantua et Pantagruel*, it is not necessary for the TL reader to be familiar with all instances of intertextuality in the ST if they are to understand and enjoy the TT.

Sarraute also parodies various styles of speech and writing in *'Eh! Va donc!'*; a dialogic technique which further reinforces the impression of disharmony in her article (Bakhtin 1940/1981: 60). Recreation of this amalgam of styles in the TT also required implementation of a range of translation strategies. The humorous words of politicians, which resemble those of difficult and argumentative children, *c'est pas ma faute, c'est lui*, could be closely translated as 'it's not my fault, it's his'. However, I was slightly freer when recapturing the advice which members of the government may be given with regard to their image. Sarraute's *T'as pas le look, Coco*, a play on the title of the 1984 single *T'as le Look Coco* by Laroche-Valmont, is exaggeratedly affected and appears to imitate the voice of a stereotypical style guru. As this expression evokes characters from the British comedy, *Absolutely Fabulous* (1992–2012), I rerendered the SL expression with 'You don't look right, Sweetie'.

The written styles which Sarraute pastiches are highly rhetorical, and translation of these also calls for a variety of approaches. Her use of onomatopoeia (*boum, tchac, cling!*), which often features in children's cartoon books, could be translated closely with the TL 'crash, bang, wallop!', as is the case in Bell's translations of *Astérix*. Nevertheless, I diverged from the SL in order to recapture her *ça se dit des vilaines choses, ça se traite de tous les noms* and used alliteration and two similar TL nouns to maintain the original sense of repetition: 'There's all sorts of bitching and backbiting'.

An additional dialogic and humorous device which hybridizes this ST is Sarraute's imitation, or indeed her parody, of other written genres. The final sentence of the first paragraph is written in prose but has an unmistakably poetic quality: *Même quand ils se tapent dessus, nos politiciens, c'est en langue de bois, ça pèse une tonne, et ça ne frappe plus personne* [Even when they hit each other, our politicians, it's with a wooden tongue, it weighs a ton and it no longer strikes anyone]. While preserving the semantic content of the SL, I allowed myself considerable freedom in its rerendering, rewriting the original in order to fully recapture the rhyme and humour which are present in the ST.[5] Hence: 'Even when they do hit out, they never deal a powerful clout. What ineffective old invective'. I subsequently reintegrated this rhyme into the translated passage of prose, as does Sarraute in her ST.[6]

In this text, Sarraute expresses her own clear voice in the first person. Her voice does, however, contain contradictions and is multidimensional. It appears in print but is written as informal, colloquial, and lively speech, it discusses a political subject but does so with humour, and it directly addresses its readers (or narratees) in a variety of tones. Sarraute is the 'real author' of this article and its narrator. In the opening paragraphs she describes a scenario and later enters into the text itself, assuming a homodiegetic role (Genette 1972: 255–6). When recapturing the fluctuating, unstable nature of Sarraute's voice it was, at times, possible to remain relatively close to the language of the ST:[7] *Je croyais qu'ils faisaient un effort* became 'I thought they made an effort'. At other times, it was appropriate to make minor alterations in the TL. *Je ne comprends pas* became 'I just don't understand'; insertion of the word 'just' highlights Sarraute's lack of understanding. In addition to this, modulation was used in the transferral of other phrases. Hence: *Bon, ben alors, il ne me reste qu'à* was rerendered as 'Right, well, I'll just have to'. Similarly, I translated closely some of the comments which Sarraute addresses to her audience: *Ils n'ont pas des conseillers, ces gens-là?* becomes 'Haven't these people got advisers?'. However, at times, greater adaptation was needed. *Ils n'y sont pas?* therefore became 'They don't have a clue?'.

The dialogic, interrelational character of this ST is also emphasized by the instances of intertextuality and intergenericity and the multiple

5   As was witnessed in Chapter 4, a number of translators are free in their rewriting of pastiched genres (Bell 1971; Stroumza 1998; Wright 1958).

6   This coexistence of genres is reminiscent of Queneau's *Exercices de Style* (1947) and of Wright's (1958) rewriting of this work, which incorporates a combination of close and highly inventive translation strategies.

7   Belmont and Chabrier (1972) adopt this relatively close approach when translating the voice of the first person narrator and the narrator-reader addresses in Burgess's *A Clockwork Orange*.

references to important cultural and political figures which it contains. In order to preserve these in the TT, ensuring that they were transposed both accurately and naturally, I employed a range of translation strategies. For instance, the title, *Tintin*, could be dealt with closely and directly transferred to the TT, as Hergé's works are familiar to many members of the TL culture. By contrast, it is unlikely that anglophones would recognize the reference to *Le Bébête Show*, a French television programme popular in France in the 1980s. As a precise knowledge of this would not be vital to the TL audience's appreciation of the text, I replaced the original reference with the name of a similar puppet show in the TL culture, *The Muppet Show*. Thus, I avoided an unnecessary footnote and created a comparable sense of intergenericity in my TT. It was for precisely the same reasons that I replaced the original reference to the political adviser and publicist, Jacques Séguéla, with an approximately equivalent figure in the TL culture, Max Clifford. Nevertheless, as Sarraute's mention of François Mauriac was accompanied by a specific reference to his use of language, and as this would have required greater explanation in the TT, I omitted this name and rewrote the sentence in which it appeared in the ST.

Once again, it was necessary to adopt a similar range of approaches when rerendering Sarraute's references to politicians in the SL culture.[8] I transferred directly those names which I believed would be familiar to TL readers – Barre, Chirac, Fabius, Le Pen and Mitterrand. I also rerendered closely Veuve Mao and Yvette Roudy in the TT. The sentence which preceeds Sarraute's reference to Mao reads: *On peut aussi donner dans la chinoiserie*. This can be translated relatively closely with the TL equivalent, 'You could also get unnecessarily complicated'. Although Sarraute's play on the term *chinois* [Chinese] cannot be retained in translation, I nevertheless preserved the notions of both complication and exoticism with the

---

8   This balanced approach to the rerendering of SL references is exemplified in Stroumza's 1998 translation of Fielding (1996), as discussed in Chapter 4. I did, however, decide that it would at no point be acceptable to provide TL equivalents of the names cited in *'Eh! Va donc!'*. These individuals constitute the core of the ST, which is deeply rooted in the French political scene of the 1980s. Rewriting of these would thus have entailed considerable semantic loss in the TT.

following: 'You could also get unnecessarily complicated and use foreign references: "widow Mao" for Yvette Roudy'. Furthermore, as it is essential to appreciate the similarities between these women if one is to understand Sarraute's playing with their names, I supplemented the two references with an explanatory footnote. However, in order to recapture Sarraute's inventive use of acronyms in the SL – *I.V.G. pour V.G.E.* –, I decided to be equally playful with the TL to produce: 'V.E.D. (Vehicle Excise Duty) for V.G.E. (Valéry Giscard d'Estaing)'. I expanded these in couplets in the TL as, while both acronyms in the SL would be immediately comprehensible to the ST reader, this would not necessarily be the case of those which I use in my TT.

Extract 3: *'Pince-fesses'* – article for *Le Monde* published in *Dites donc!* (1985: 113–14)

The third and final of my chosen articles from *Le Monde*, *'Pince-fesses'* is a part bawdy, part serious treatment of sexual harassment in France. In the opening paragraphs, Sarraute claims that she pinches men's backsides when travelling by *métro*. She then promptly encourages her female readers to do likewise, both to amuse themselves and to avenge the many generations of women who have been harassed by men. In the latter half of the text, Sarraute explains that her decision to deal with this subject was inspired by her recent reading of an article in the magazine, *L'Humanité*. This article recalled the story of a waitress in France who was repeatedly molested by her boss, but whose formal complaint was dismissed by the court. It then described how a group of female militants from the Communist Youth Movement achieved justice by finding this man and pinching him themselves. After comparing the unacceptability of sexual harassment in the workplace in countries such as Sweden and the USA with the way in which this issue is either dismissed or considered to be amusing in France, Sarraute again advocates taking one's own revenge.

As did the previous two articles discussed, *'Pince-fesses'* lends itself fully to a relational, Bakhtinian analysis. This text opposes the sexes and focuses on negative and acrimonious relations between them.[9] By suggesting that sexual harassment of women by men should be reciprocated, it promotes gender equality and would seem to destroy any notion of a male-female dichotomy in which the male is considered superior. Moreover, Sarraute is, herself, highly interrelational in character. She has been subjected to diverse influences and draws on other texts, and on her knowledge of past events and other countries, in order to write this article. Such references to other time frames and spaces render *'Pince-fesses'* chronotopic (Bakhtin 1938). In her text, Sarraute recommends and justifies the sort of audacious and humorously indecent behaviour which would flout common standards of decency in society. This behaviour is again reminiscent of carnival time (Bakhtin 1965) when crudeness and vulgarity were both expected and tolerated. Interestingly, in this relatively short piece, interrelationships, multidimensionality, and a resulting sense of disharmony are also reflected throughout the text in a number of ways. These present the translator with a set of issues and challenges which call for particular solutions.

Throughout *'Pince-fesses'*, Sarraute's voice is multidimensional and often appears unstable. In this particular article, Sarraute describes her actions and their consequences, retells a story which she read in another newspaper, and comments on this. She is a fully homodiegetic narrator. A distinction can be made between the principal voice of the narrator and those instances where Sarraute addresses her – unusually and specifically female – readers (or narratees) explicitly. These will be considered in turn. Sarraute's voice is both multi-tonal[10] and heteroglossic. At first glance,

9   As was witnessed in Chapter 2, Bakhtin did not focus on the study of gender. Nevertheless, some feminist critics believe that the use of Bakhtinian theory can facilitate a relational analysis of gender and therefore enable a better understanding of this subject (Pearce 1994).

10 In his 'Notes', Bakhtin (1970–1/1986: 134) considered mono- and multi-tonality: 'The inadmissibility of mono-tony (of serious monotony). The sphere of serious tone. Irony as a form of silence. Irony (and laughter) as a means for transcending a situation, rising above it'.

juxtaposition of tones and varieties of language is most evident between paragraphs. The tone of the first two paragraphs is predominantly frivolous and amusing, and this is emphasized by Sarraute's uses of colloquial and slang language. By contrast, the third and final paragraphs are more serious and, at times, more ironic in tone, and in this latter part of her article the narrator uses language of a more formal register, including certain legal terminology. However, on closer inspection, it becomes clear that instances of multi-tonality and heteroglossia also occur at inter- and intra-sentential levels throughout the ST. It is at these levels that the translation difficulties which Sarraute's voice poses, and potential solutions to these problems, will be explored.

Sentences written in dissonant tones and registers are a recurrent feature of this text. If the translator is to preserve in the TT the sense of contradiction between sentences in the ST, they must confront a number of issues. The title, 'Pince-fesses', is at once amusing and informal. Not only does it describe accurately the content of Sarraute's article, it also refers to a very specific type of social event: *Pince-fesses: réception où les invités se comportent de façon vulgaire ou relâchée* [reception where the guests behave in a vulgar or lax way, *Le Robert Micro-Poche* 1993: 949, my translation]. In order to fully recapture the tone and register of this term in the TT and to preserve its original message and effect, I rewrote it creatively and produced the following: 'Misbehaving in the *métro*: Pinch his bum and watch him move'. By comparison, the first sentence of the first paragraph is serious in tone and of a relatively standard register. *Je vais vous faire un aveu* could thus be translated with the comparably standard TL equivalent, 'I've got a confession to make'. In subsequent sentences, however, Sarraute reverts to a humorous tone, while still using relatively standard vocabulary.

Juxtaposition of tones and registers between sentences does indeed continue throughout 'Pince-fesses'. In the third paragraph, sentences written in informal and idiomatic language such as *[L'Huma] en a fait tout un plat* (translated with a TL equivalent) are contrasted with more formal ones such as *[Maryse] a porté plainte et elle a été déboutée* (translated closely and using equivalents), and also with some ironic comments which use free indirect speech. While at times applying Vinay and Darbelnet's principle of modulation, I attempted to preserve the blend of formality and irony contained in this sentence with another close translation. Thus: *La cour d'appel de Besançon n'a vu là que les saines manifestations d'une familiarité bien naturelle dans les relations de travail!* became 'The Court of Appeal in Besançon simply saw the man's behaviour as a healthy expression of the sort of familiarity which is completely natural between work colleagues!'. Similarly, the serious intercultural comparison which Sarraute makes in her fourth paragraph clashes with the humorous tone and vulgar language of the final sentence of the paragraph which is again written in free indirect speech. I translated this cultural comparison closely, with the exception of the legal term, *droit de cuissage*, which I expanded, as its literal translation, *droit de seigneur*, appeared unnatural. I then preserved the humorous tone of the last sentence, but was more adaptive in my rendering of impolite language. In order to transfer to my TT the full force and the nuances of these terms,[11] I expanded each of these. *Celles qui gueulent, qui protestent, ne cherchez pas, c'est des mijorées, des mal baisées, des refoulées* thus became 'Those women who kick up a fuss and protest shouldn't bother. They're full of airs and graces, in need of a good shag and sexually repressed'. I contemplated other translations of *mal baisées*, including 'frustrated' and 'unsatisfied', but thought both to be inadequate. The former suggests that these women have little sex, rather than sex which is of poor quality (*mal baisées*), and the later loses the crudeness of the original SL term. Sarraute maintains this humour in her concluding sentence when she again advocates taking one's own revenge. She plays with the usual SL expression, *à malin, malin et demi* [there's always somebody cleverer than you], creating *à vilain, vilain et demi!* Rather than rerendering this as 'there's always somebody nastier than you', I decided to recapture it more loosely and idiomatically in the TL: 'Don't just give as good as you get, go one better!'.

Dissonant tones and linguistic registers are in even greater proximity within Sarraute's individual sentences. These heighten the sense of cacophony in the ST and present the translator with further challenges. In

---

11   Landers (2001: 151) stresses the importance of preserving all impolite uses of the SL in the TT and Wright (1960) adopts this approach throughout her translation of Raymond Queneau's (1938) *Zazie dans le métro*.

Je pince les fesses des messieurs dans le métro, the word *messieurs* is misplaced, inappropriate, and therefore comical. Use of the noun *mecs* or *hommes* would have been much less entertaining. In my attempt to preserve this amusing clash of registers I produced the following: 'I pinch gentlemen's bums in the *métro*'. Had I used one register only – 'I pinch guy's bums' or 'I pinch men's bottoms' – some of the humour of the original would have been lost. In the same vein, the correct and standard language used in the first sentence of the second paragraph is countered by the later use of sexual argot: *D'un oeil furtif, il passe en revue les mains inertes et innocentes de ses voisins, persuadé [...] qu'il a été peloté par un homo*. Once again, it was appropriate to remain close to the tone and language of the ST when rerendering this entire sentence. Hence: 'Furtively, he then inspects the perfectly still and innocent hands of the people next to him, convinced that he's been touched up by some gay'.

Thus, Sarraute's voice, which dominates '*Pince-fesses*', contains many contradictions both between sentences and within individual utterances, and this results in a sense of instability throughout the article. In order to recapture this disharmony in the TT it was necessary, at all times, to rerender closely the multi-tonality of Sarraute's voice, but to employ a balance of close and freer translation strategies in order to preserve its heteroglossic nature.

Those instances in '*Pince-fesses*' where Sarraute addresses her narratees directly are similarly multidimensional and disharmonious. They too are multi-tonal and heteroglossic and therefore give rise to a similar range of translation difficulties. When Sarraute adopts a reassuring but ironic tone towards her narratees, her language assumes an elevated register: *Pour peu que vous vous fendiez alors d'un petit sourire égrillard et narquois*. Nevertheless, when she provides her audience with some explanation, her tone becomes informal: *Si je vous parle de ça aujourd'hui c'est parce que*. I was particularly close in my translation of both of these. However, when she seemingly confides in her narratees she uses a standard register of language – *Je vais vous faire un aveu* – and I translated this with the equivalent TL expression, 'I've got a confession to make', as discussed above.

Sarraute uses a different tone of voice, but an equally standard register of French, when inciting her narratees to action: *Essayez, vous verrez, c'est à mourir de rire.* I rerendered this by applying the principle of modulation and produced: 'Try it. You'll see, you'll kill yourself laughing'. I was most free, however, in my handling of the sentence, *Vous vous rappelez cette fille dans le Doubs, Maryse.* In this instance, Sarraute appeals to her SL audience's knowledge of a past event in France, with which the TL audience would undoubtedly not be familiar. While remaining close to the content, tone, and relatively standard register of the SL in my TT, I translated this comment obliquely, rephrasing the original in the form of an explanation, rather than a question: 'This girl lived in eastern France and was called Maryse'. Therefore, when recapturing dialogic narrator-narratee addresses throughout *'Pince-fesses'*, it was once again necessary to remain constantly close to the multiple tones of these utterances, but to adopt a range of approaches to the translation of the distinct registers in which they are written.

Multidimensionality and disharmony manifest themselves in other ways throughout *'Pince-fesses'*. Sarraute's intertextual reference and her uses of French cultural terms also contribute towards the complex nature of this ST and require attention on the part of the translator. Where *L'Huma* is cited, I preserved the name of this magazine in my TT, further clarifying it by providing the name in full – *L'Humanité* – and by supplementing the reference with an explanatory footnote. This particular translation strategy serves to make the translator visible and to foreignize the TT. I considered this strategy appropriate for a number of reasons. First, there is no TL equivalent of this publication. Second, as it was an article in *L'Humanité* which inspired Sarraute to write *'Pince-fesses'*, this instance of intertextuality is particularly significant. And third, an understanding of the militant nature of this magazine is important if the action taken by the Communist Youth Movement is to be properly contextualized. Therefore, the TL audience would, I felt, benefit from a description of this. Similarly, at times I directly transferred cultural terms (*le métro*), italicizing these in order to reinforce the original French setting in which *'Pince-fesses'* was written. However, I replaced other terms with functional TL equivalent, for instance, 'Women's Lib'. for *M.L.F.*, where this involved no semantic loss in the TT. My approach, like that of Stroumza (1998), therefore incorporates both foreignizing and domesticating translation strategies, despite

Schleiermacher's (1813, in Lefevere 1992a) belief that both these approaches are fundamentally incompatible. My overall approach to the translation of such references and terms was, then, an entirely heterogeneous one.

As Sarraute refers to both present and past time in this article (present and past attitudes, immediate action which can avenge past generations, a current magazine article which recounts past events), each mention of time is relational. Each one is connected to other time frames and is a further cause of instability in the ST. For the most part, it was possible to translate these closely in the TT. However, one such sentence contained a duality of meaning and was thus slightly ambiguous. In the following, it is unclear whether the pronoun *on* refers to people in general, or whether it is used by the author as a means of referring impersonally to her own former attitudes: *Au début – les miens remontent à l'époque héroïque du M.L.F. – on n'ose pas, on hésite, on a peur de prendre une gifle.* I interpreted the sentence in the former sense and used the simple past tense, so as to better convey the notion of past time in the TL. Thus: 'In the beginning – I'm going back to the pioneering days of Women's Lib. – you didn't dare, you hesitated, you were afraid to get a slap in the face'.

Last, mentions of other places in the ST are both spatially relational, as they exist in relation to other places, and entirely chronotopic, as they are used in close connection with references to certain time frames. At times, a close translation of these was possible (*Suède, États-Unis*). At other times, however, alternative translation strategies were needed. I directly transferred 'Besançon' to the TT as, even if members of the TL audience are not familiar with this town, they will infer from the previous sentence that it is situated in eastern France. Again, this approach foreignizes my TT by retaining the French quality of the original text. TI rewrote Sarraute's *Ici, ça fait rigoler* as 'In France, it makes people laugh' and I translated *dans le Doubs* obliquely and discreetly as 'in eastern France', domesticating my translation in this instance, as discussed previously. Thus, rerendering of temporal and spatial connection and disruption in *'Pince-fesses'* required that I draw on a considerable range of translation strategies.

Extract 4: *Allô Lolotte, c'est Coco* (1987: 93–6)

Situated midway through Sarraute's first novel, this extract is preceded by a conversation between Lolotte's son, Patrice, and her father, regarding their imminent summer holidays. Patrice has informed his grandfather that he is to be sent alone to a house in Brittany and minded by a young au pair. Annoyed and unhappy, the old man has ordered his grandson to leave. In the present extract, Sarraute discusses and disagrees on the content and quality of her novel with her characters, one of whom is also her editor. The passage opens with a clear narrative voice, but Sarraute switches abruptly to the use of reported indirect speech to describe Patrice's anger at her treatment of her characters, and her subsequent argument with Patrice during which he criticizes her work. She then addresses her audience directly, voicing her upset at this attack, and explains her decision to call her editor, Françoise Verny, for advice. In the ensuing dialogue between Sarraute and Verny, which appears in direct speech, Sarraute suspects that Verny has not read her manuscripts properly, and so accuses her of not taking her work seriously. When Verny does insinuate that the scripts are of a poor standard, Sarraute is further vexed. She again addresses her audience and, in a fit of rage, resolves to have Patrice killed in a motorbike accident. The passage is followed by Sarraute's broader discussion of road deaths in France.

This extract, which contains a constant interplay of voices and is acutely self-reflexive, gives rise to a number of translation challenges. In his 1929 *Problems of Dostoevsky's Poetics*, Bakhtin (1929/1984: 6–7) defined the polyphonic novel as one in which 'equal consciousnesses [and] independent [and] fully valid voices' coexist. Judged according to this criterion, the present text constitutes a prime example of polyphony. These consciousnesses and voices in the extract, which are individually self-aware and interrelated, are now considered, as are the most appropriate means of recapturing these in the TT. Moreover, the present commentary demonstrates that, in this text, dialogue and interrelationships occur at many other levels of the SL and the ST, thus also contributing to its interactive nature. The translation issues and challenges which each of these poses are now discussed, and potential solutions proposed.

In this ST, Sarraute's own consciousness and voice are noteworthy. This author is highly self-aware and thoroughly interactive; her behaviour is always conditioned by her relationships with her characters, editor, friends, and readers. In the present extract, Sarraute's function is complex. She acknowledges authorship of her novel; she is its 'real author' (Baldick 1990: 146). However, she frequently assumes the role of narrator, speaks to her readers argues with her characters, and relinquishes her narratorial authority. Therefore, in this extract, Sarraute could be classed as a linguistic site in which contending voices clash, rather than a true authorial presence. Sarraute's complexity is reinforced by her multivoicedness. At times, she uses a clear narrative voice in order to set the scene (*Il est colère, là, Patrice, vraiment furax* [Now Patrice is angry, really livid]), and to describe her own actions (*Je l'ai envoyé promener* [I told him where to go]). At other times, however, she uses reported speech to rehearse her characters' words (*Non, mais qu'est-ce qu'elle se croit, cette nana – la nana, c'est moi* [Just who does that bird think she is – the bird's me]). She also enters into explicit dialogue with her editor and addresses her audience directly, which is discussed later. Indeed, due to this multivocality in the ST, it is often unclear who is speaking. For instance, the sentence *Voilà un type, oui, qui a des choses à dire et qui les dit merveilleusement* may express either Sarraute or Patrice's opinion of Woody Allen. Similarly, when Sarraute anticipates the question, *Un peu moins quoi?*, she may be assuming that either Patrice or her audience requires explanation of the neologism in her text. Despite her unstable position, at the end of this particular extract Sarraute appears to emerge as independent and fully in control; she decides autonomously on the fate of her character: *Je vais réagir vite fait. Tant pis pour lui. Je le supprime* [I'm going to react sharpish, and it's his bad luck. I'm going to do away with him].

On an initial reading, this text appears to pose particular difficulties for the translator; as Sarraute is a chameleonic figure – her voice and position are in a permanent state of flux –, the translator has no stable model to emulate. Nevertheless, it was largely possible to remain close to the language of the ST in order to preserve Sarraute's self-consciousness, to recapture the medley of voices which she uses, and to retain any instances of ambiguous language, such as those detailed above. In *Allô Lolotte*, the characters share a number of similarities with Sarraute herself. Patrice is self-conscious – he is aware that he is a character in Sarraute's work, and Verny participates fully and consciously in her role as editor of the novel. These individuals interact both with Sarraute and with one another. If this suggests a degree of interdependence amongst characters, Sarraute nonetheless senses Patrice and Verny as 'independent consciousnesses' who are also 'valid' (Bakhtin 1929/1984). She describes Patrice's anger and his criticism of her work: *Ils sont nuls, vos dialogues, ma pauvre dame, plats comme un trottoir, écrits avec un fer à repasser. Ils vont quand même pas publier ça! C'est complètement débile.* In this instance, it was possible to remain close to the meaning and tone of Patrice's comments, but necessary to translate some of the idiomatic SL expressions with appropriate TL equivalents. Hence: 'The conversations you write are useless, you stupid old woman. Flat as a pancake, dull as dishwater. They'll never publish that! It's totally pathetic'. Furthermore, Sarraute recognizes the need for Patrice to simmer down after his outburst, implying that his behaviour is beyond her control: *Patrice, il n'y a plus rien à en tirer. Faut lui laisser le temps de se calmer.* Again, I rerendered this language with colloquial TL equivalents: 'You can't do any more with Patrice. You've gotta give him time to calm down'. Sarraute suggests that Verny is equally valid and independent. She seeks her opinion on her manuscripts, and so values her advice. However, she realizes that her editor / character has not bothered to read her work properly. *Tu l'as pas lue, la scène des godasses, alors? Non, mais c'est pas vrai!* [So you didn't read the scene with the shoes, then? I don't believe it!]. Moreover, she allows Verny to use her own voice to insult her work. Once again, it was appropriate to remain close to the idiom and tone of the SL when rerendering these comments in my TT.

The remaining participants in Sarraute's text are those who exist on an extra-textual level, that is, her readers. This extract contains a clear narrative voice and addresses its readers (or narratees) explicitly, thus heightening their self-awareness. In her interaction with these individuals, Sarraute assumes solidarity between herself and her audience. She writes: *Vous me connaissez, je m'angoisse pour un rien*, suggesting that a bond already exists between them. In addition, at the end of this extract, Sarraute presumes that readers of *Allô Lolotte, c'est Coco* are already familiar with her articles in *Le Monde*. She also anticipates their responses to her work, and their need for explanation. Thus, she treats the members of her audience as independent and valid people. When rerendering these addresses it was possible to remain close to the meaning and tone of the ST, making only minor modifications to the SL, as demonstrated in the following: *La faute à qui? A moi, figurez-vous, oui, moi, l'auteur* which becomes 'And who's to blame? Me, would you believe it, yes, me, the author'.

The interactive nature of this extract is reinforced by many of its other features. These pose a number of translation challenges which require a range of solutions. As Sarraute is aware not only of her own self and role but also of her writing process, her text is self-conscious: *Comment je vais le sortir de là, maintenant, hein?* [How am I going to get him out of there now, eh?]; *Je l'ai déjà récrite vingt-cinq fois [cette scène]* [I've already rewritten [this scene] twenty-five times]; *J'ai jeté je ne sais pas combien de brouillons* [I've thrown out I don't know how many rough drafts]. On the whole, such instances of self-consciousness can be closely transferred to the TT. Nevertheless, when the ST becomes intertextual, or indeed intergeneric and intercultural, the task of the translator becomes more complex. As the film, *La Rose pourpre du Caire*, was originally made in the TL, I literally translated the title back into English: *The Purple Rose of Cairo* I also supplemented this with the oblique explanation, 'that Woody Allen film', as the film was produced in the 1980s and would therefore probably be unknown to some contemporary readers. Although Woody Allen is a familiar name in the TL culture, those of the Italian playwright, Pirandello and the French actor, Coluche, are not. As these figures provide the ST with an intercultural dimension, and are directly relevant to Patrice's nature and to the fate of this character, I considered it important to further explain them in the form of footnotes. As I employed a combination of strategies when transferring this intertextuality, my approach is closely in line with that of Stroumza (1998).

Sarraute's novel, a written text, is largely composed of spoken language which is itself multidimensional and dialogic. When this language is so colloquial, heteroglossic, and indeed playful, translation of the ST proves a particularly challenging task. In my attempt to recapture the colloquialisms and idioms of the SL in my TT, I sought equivalent uses in the TL such as:

Je l'ai engueulé	I had a real go at him
Il me débine	He slags me off
Pourquoi il ramène sa fraise, celui-là?	Why's he shoving his oar in?

At times, however, I was slightly more adaptive in my rerenderings: *Enfin, Françoise, ça va pas la tête?* [Françoise, are you daft or what?] and *Mais ça, c'est mon côté maso* [But hey, that's my masochistic side for you]. On occasion, pronunciation is lax, and it appears that words have been phonetically transcribed. In such instances, a degree of adaptation was also necessary in order to fully recapture this in the TL.[12] For example, *T'as qu'à rectifier le tir. Cette scène, y a qu'à la reprendre* became 'You've just gotta change your approach. Just go back over that scene'.

Much of the language used in this extract is mildly impolite and I sought to preserve all SL expletives in the TT:[13]

Je ne leur fais faire que des conneries à mes personnages.	I always make my characters do bloody stupid things.
Et s'il avait raison, ce petit con!	What if *the little bugger* was right!

Further, certain synonyms, of different degrees of vulgarity, are used in the text and it was necessary to maintain this heteroglossia in the TL. Thus: *Il n'en a rien à cirer* was rerendered as 'He doesn't give a monkey's', whereas *Tu t'en fous de ce que j'écris* became 'You don't give a shit about what I write'. Similarly, I wanted to distinguish between *[Patrice] trouve que c'est de la crotte* and *Il achète souvent de la merde, le public*, so used the terms 'cack' for *crotte* and 'crap' for *merde*. While this text is largely heteroglossic, it also contains one instance of polyglossia. Sarraute's use of 'bye-bye' feels slightly exotic in the ST. As the expression belongs to the TL and direct

---

12   This technique was identified in Wright's 1960 translation of phonetically transcribed conversations which feature in Queneau's *Zazie* (1938).

13   Bakhtin (1929/1984: 5) believed such vulgar language to belong to a particular branch of folk humour named 'Billingsgate'.

transferral of this to the TT would have lost its original foreign resonance, I rerendered it with the Italian *ciao*.[14]

Sarraute's playful use of language adds a further dimension to the present extract and I allowed myself to be equally creative in my rerendering of this. Her neologism *diplopotame* (*diplomate* + *hippopotame*) became 'diplopotamus' (diplomat + hippopotamus) and I translated her *papy-sitter* as 'grampy-sitter'. This text also contains two puns. Despite wide acknowledgement that these are often impossible to translate (Girard 2001; Landers 2001), I attempted to rewrite them. Thus:

Il m'a fait tout *un cinéma* [...]. Je lui ai même conseillé d'y retourner *au cinéma* et de revoir *La Rose pourpre du Caire*.	He made *a real scene*. I even advised him to go and watch a few *scenes* from that Woody Allen film, *The Purple Rose of Cairo*, again.
Tu vas aller *t'éclater* [...] contre le premier camion venu.	You'll have a *smashing* time [...]. You're going to *smash* [...] into the next lorry which comes along.

Notions of time and space in this extract are also multidimensional and interrelated. Within the narrative, time is progressive and logical. However, on a heterodiegetic level, references are made both to past events and conversations and to future plans, and there is thus some sense of temporal disruption in the ST. It was necessary to pay attention to Sarraute's switching of tenses and use of time phrases, but close linguistic transferral of these was possible (Crowther 1976; Wynne 2002). For the most part, space is comparably stable and progressive in the text. This said, references to other places are made and cause some disruption in the extract. When rerendering these places in the TL, I felt it appropriate to use a combination of translation strategies. I was most close in my handling of *Sciences-Po*. As it is a particularly important cultural reference in the ST, I transferred

14   Where Queneau (1938) uses TL words in *Zazie*, Wright (1960) also re-renders these in a third language (German) in her TT, thereby preserving the exoticism of the original words.

the name directly to my TT, italicized it in order to reinforce its foreign quality, and provided explanation of this in a footer. I also rerendered *le Midi* closely in the TL with 'the south of France'. I did, however, feel some rewriting to be necessary in the translation of *boulevard Malesherbes*. Rather than explaining the precise location of this Parisian boulevard in a footnote, a strategy which I thought would overburden my TT, I reworded this in order to convey the way in which the name was originally used. Hence: *L'effet catastrophique que [...] aura boulevard Malesherbes* became 'The disastrous effect that [...] will have in their household'.

Extract 5: *Maman coq* (1989: 7–11)

This text, the second novelistic extract of my collection, is composed of the opening pages of Sarraute's second novel, *Maman coq*, and falls into two parts. The first takes the form of a dialogue between two characters; one who is irritated at having spent an entire day doing chores and looking after an unwell baby, and the other who has just returned home late that evening. As the couple bicker, the reader is led to believe that the former character is a woman, and the latter a man. However, at the end of the conversation it emerges that the reverse is the case. The characters speaking were in fact the male and female protagonists of Sarraute's first novel, *Allô Lolotte, c'est Coco* (1987) – JJ, a househusband, and Lolotte, a career woman. The second part of the extract opens with Sarraute's voice. Sarraute addresses her readers directly, rebuking them for not having read *Allô Lolotte*, and discusses the difficulties encountered by new writers. In this narrative passage, she draws parallels between authors, who attempt to sell their works, and prostitutes, who sell themselves. She then recounts two personal anecdotes from the early days of her writing career, describing her feelings of self-doubt and failure.

This extract shares certain similarities with the previous one. First, although there is a greater distinction in this text between the consciousnesses and voices of the characters (part one) and those of Sarraute (part two), all participants in this extract are nevertheless 'independent' and 'equal' (Bakhtin 1929/1984: 6–7), and are both individually self-conscious and socially constructed (Voloshinov 1927). Second, this extract contains many other interactive qualities at a number of levels. Parts one and two of the extract are now examined in turn in order to demonstrate how the participants in the text are both self-aware and interactive in character, and to highlight other important manifestations of self-consciousness, dialogue, interactivity, and interrelationships in this passage.

In part one, the characters are entirely independent of Sarraute – there is no interaction with, or apparent intervention from, their creator. Despite Sarraute's 'covertness' (Baldick 1990: 146; Rimmon-Kenan 1983/1997: 96), she is the 'real author' of this text. An 'implied author' presence can also be felt throughout this part of the present extract. The characters are also independent of one another – man and woman argue as equals, with 'fully valid voices' (Bakhtin 1929).[15] These characters are highly self-conscious (*dans un livre on y est* [we are in a book]). As was the case in the previous extract, instances of character self-awareness in this text lend themselves to close linguistic transferral. The characters are also always inherently dialogic, as they constantly interact with, and exist in relation to, one another. The linguistic challenges to which their conversation gives rise are later discussed.

This part of the extract is self-conscious, dialogic, and interactive in numerous other ways, that is, on textual, linguistic, cultural, spatial, and temporal levels. First, JJ draws attention to the genre, style, and publisher of the work:

> D'abord, dans *un livre* on y est. Deuxièmement, tu vas pas commencer à me prendre la tête à cause *du style de ce bouquin*. Pour les réclamations, le guichet Sarraute est ouvert vingt-quatre heures sur vingt-quatre *aux Éditions Flammarion*.

15   Not only do these comical male and female characters argue as equals, but the stereotypical, gendered roles which they appear to perform are also reversed at the end of their conversation and the reader's expectations are consequently flouted. Thus, Sarraute destroys the traditional gender divide, as was the case in Extract 3.

Firstly, we are in *a book*. Secondly, you're not going to start doing my head in over *its style*. If you've got any complaints, the Sarraute desk is open twenty-four hours a day *at Flammarion*.

Once again, it was mostly possible to closely preserve the text's sense of self-reflexivity in the TT. As I transferred the publisher's name, Flammarion, to my TT, I did consider clarifying this in a footnote. However, given that this reference occurs in the first page of the novel, I felt that it would be more subtle, and therefore more appropriate, to first translate the title of the work and then follow this with an oblique explanation: 'Published by Flammarion'. This text is not only self-conscious, but is also aware of what is other; it contains an instance of intergenericity. When listing his activities of the day, including his care of the baby, JJ mentions *le rot de vingt heures*, which is reminiscent of the daily French news programme, *Le Journal de 20 heures*, on TF1. I closely recaptured this displaced and amusing allusion with 'the 8 o'clock burp', which has similar connotations in the TL culture.

Second, as this part of the extract is made up entirely of a spoken dialogue, oral language dominates this written text. Sarraute erodes the divide between spoken and written discourses in this text (see also Extracts 1 and 4). In the opening lines, language is acutely self-aware:

> – *C'est à cette heure-ci que tu rentres?*
> – *Qu'est-ce que ça veut dire, ça? C'est à cette heure-ci que tu rentres? Où tu crois que t'es? Dans une pièce de théâtre? Dans un film? Dans un livre? Tu peux pas dire: T'as vu l'heure qu'il est*, comme tout le monde?

I attempted to rerender this self-consciousness quite closely in my TT, recapturing both JJ's bizarre turn of phrase, and the contrasting way in which his question would usually be worded. Hence:

> – *You come home at this hour?*
> What's that supposed to mean? *You come home at this hour?* Where d'you think you are?
> In a play? A film? A book? Can't you say, '*Have you seen what time it is?*', like everyone else?

The spoken language which this extract contains is highly dialogic. It is multi-tonal (Bakhtin 1970–1) and conveys sarcasm (*Alors, on peut savoir d'où tu viens, là?* [So, may one ask where you've been?]), panic (*Alors, si c'est ça que tu veux, retrouver le bébé mort demain matin dans son berceau...!* [So, if that's what you want, to find the baby dead in his cot tomorrow morning!]), and calm reassurance (*Mais non, voyons, tout ira bien. Faut pas te mettre dans des états pareils* [Of course I don't. Come on, now. It'll all be fine. You shouldn't get yourself in such a state]). In these instances, it was again necessary to translate the SL relatively closely in order to fully recapture its multi-tonality in the TT.

Where the characters' language is of a particularly colloquial register, I often translated this closely: *T'écoutes même pas quand je te parle* [You don't even listen when I'm speaking to you]. At times, I sought equivalent words (*le toubib* [the quack]) and expressions (*Tu vas pas commencer à me prendre la tête* [You're not going to start doing my head in]). However, where vocabulary used in the ST is inventive (*pauvre petit choupinet*), I was similarly creative in my translation [poor little sweetie-weetie].

Thus far, the instances of dialogue and interactivity discussed have been firmly rooted in the SL culture; two self-conscious, socially constructed French characters communicate using self-conscious, (dialogic) French language.

The French context of this ST is reinforced by the presence of certain cultural references, *métro* and *minitel*, both of which I directly transposed to the TT and italicized in order to preserve their Frenchness in my foreignizing translation. I supplemented the latter noun with an explanatory footnote (Home terminal of the French telecommunications system which links telephone users to a database), as I considered it to be an important cultural term with no TL equivalent.

This first part of the extract is, however, by no means entirely mono-cultural. Indeed, the third area of the text in which dialogue and interactivity occur is that of culture, and this is communicated powerfully in the SL. Towards the end of their conversation, Lolotte and JJ imitate the German accent, create a humorous German name, and refer to a woman who was a known figure in Nazi Germany:

– Nous afons les moyens de le faire roter!
– A fos ordres, Frau Strumpfhelfeldkommandant Lolotte! Quand t'auras fini de jouer à la chienne de Buchenwald!

Recapturing these lines in the TT required implementing a number of translation techniques. I directly transferred *Frau Strumpfhelfeldkommandant* in order to maintain the humour of this German name.[16] I then attempted to transpose the exaggerated German accent onto my English translation. This is the approach which I adopted to transposing the Guadeloupian accent imitated in Extract 1. Here, I relied on my own ('A' level) knowledge of the language: 'Vee 'av veys off mekking him burp!'. Last, I considered a variety of approaches to the rerendering of *la chienne de Buchenwald*.[17] I contemplated translating this name literally as 'the Buchenwald bitch' and providing an explanatory footer, but thought that this would appear stilted and would interrupt the reader of the TT unnecessarily. Rather, I decided to rewrite this reference obliquely with the following. *Quand t'auras fini de jouer à la chienne de Buchenwald* [When you've stopped playing at some Nazi in a concentration camp!]. Clearly, unlike the original term, this rerendering does not contain the concept of the prison guard as a vamp-like female. However, as I felt that an attempt to preserve this would appear un-natural in the TT (When you've stopped playing at some vamp-like guard in a concentration camp), I favoured my first rerendering.

Fourth and finally, the notions of time and space in this part of the extract are also relational. The conversation takes place in the present time and in the couple's home, but JJ and Lolotte discuss what they have done during the day and where they have been. The text is therefore not only chronotopic but, as there is a dialogue between its chronotopes; it is definable as 'polychronotopic' (Pearce 1994: 71–2). All instances of spatial and

---

16 Such lengthy names and compound nouns which are usual in German are also parodied in Voltaire's (1759) *Candide* and are directly transferred to the TT by his English translators (Butt 1947; Cameron 1997).

17 'La chienne de Buchenwald' was the nickname which prisoners of Buchenwald gave to Lise Koch, prison guard and wife of Lagerkommandant S.S. <http://permanent. nouvelobs.com/cgi/debats/aff_mess?id=200102220039&offs=239>.

temporal connectedness and consequent disruption, which are important features of postmodernism (Harvey 1989), could be closely transferred to the TT. Thus, rerendering of self-consciousness, dialogue, interactivity, and interrelationships in this part of the TT required application of a number of translation strategies. This apparent sense of disruption is heightened in the transition between parts one and two of the extract. As the second part opens, abrupt changes in voice, style, and subject matter occur, together with marked shifts in time and space.

Part two again raises many translation issues. Sarraute becomes a highly 'overt' narrator (Baldick 1990: 146; Rimmon-Kenan 1983/1997: 96). She writes in the first person and uses her voice, which dominates this part of the extract, to demonstrate her independence as an individual, and to suggest a certain equality between her own voice and those of her characters Sarraute is entirely self-aware. She fully acknowledges her role as an author, refers explicitly to her characters, describes the difficulties experienced by new authors, and recounts two personal anecdotes. Thus, she provides her novel with an autobiographical dimension and is an 'intrusive author' (Baldick 1990: 112). As was the case in the previous extract, all instances of self-consciousness in this text could be transferred closely to the TT.

Moreover, Sarraute is evidently a socially constructed being; her own self has been formed through past experiences and involvement with other people, and during interaction with her readers (Bakhtin 1979). She anticipates her readers' reaction to her characters' dialogue and their poor knowledge of her first novel, chides them, provides them with explanations and, at times, befriends them. When transferring such addresses, I paid particular attention to the tone and register of the original utterances, remaining close to their tone and seeking equivalent registers in the TL to those used in the SL. Thus, *Ça vous en bouche un coin, hein! Vous ne vous attendiez pas à les voir dans ces rôles-là* becomes 'You're gobsmacked, aren't you? You weren't expecting to see them in those roles'. Similarly, *Ah! Ne me dites pas que vous faites partie de ces chiens qui l'ont snobée, [...], ma Lolotte* is translated as 'Oh don't tell me you're one of *those swines* who snubbed my Lolotte'.

As in the first half of this extract, instances of self-consciousness, dialogue, interactivity, and interrelatedness in this part of the text also occur on textual, linguistic, spatial, and temporal levels, and each of these raises specific issues and challenges for the translator. First, Sarraute makes self-conscious, intertextual references to her column in *Le Monde* and to her first novel, *Allô Lolotte*. I transferred these directly to my TT as my audience will already be familiar with these texts, having read extracts one to four of my collection. However, I did clarify one reference to the front cover of *Allô Lolotte*, as I believed this to reinforce the intertextual nature of the original reference, of which members of the TL culture could not be expected to be aware.

This intertextuality is extended as Sarraute looks beyond her own work and mentions other writers such as Plantu, Sulitzer, and d'Ormesson. I directly transferred the name *Plantu* to my TT, as this is explained in the text itself, but I investigated the precise nature of this man's work, and subsequently translated his profession, *caricaturiste*, as 'political cartoonist', rather than simply as 'cartoonist'. By contrast, I rewrote the reference to *Sulitzer et d'Ormesson* as 'successful authors – academics and financial experts', as I did not feel that more detailed explanations of these individual writers would necessarily enhance my readers' appreciation of this text. Second, the language which Sarraute uses is heteroglossic and thus comparably multidimensional. Individual words belong to both standard and slang registers (*le canard* [the rag]), and at other times their meaning is context-dependent (*un confrère* [another newspaper], not 'a colleague'). Certain vulgar words (*ma petite crotte* [my crappy little article];[18] *le salopard* [the bastard]) are also juxtaposed with otherwise polite uses of language, and I attempted to preserve these closely in the TL. Moreover, the text contains multiple smutty puns. Inspired by translations of sexual argot in Pilard's *Rude French* (2002), I attempted to recapture these double entendres in the TL, creating equivalent plays on the roles of writers, prostitutes, and their respective customers:

---

18   I considered rerendering this as 'cacky', as I had already translated *crotte* as 'cack' in Extract 4, but decided that this would sound rather unusual. I also debated using the TL term 'shitty', but decided against this word as it is more offensive in the TL than is *crotte* in the SL. Furthermore, as I had translated *tous les emmerdes* in part one of this extract as 'all the shit', I wanted to preserve the contrast between these SL words in my TT.

Elle faisait le tapin, ma Lolotte.	My Lolotte was touting for customers.
Dur, dur [...] de se vendre.	It's really tough to sell yourself.
C'est comme tout, ça s'apprend. Faut que ça rentre!	It's like everything else, it's something you learn. You've gotta let it sink right in!
Appâter le client.	To lure the clients.
Soixante-neuf balles.	Sixty-nine francs.

At times, the double entendres are particularly concentrated in the ST: *[Les chalands] Vous passez, vous regardez, vous palpez, vous jetez un coup d'oeil distrait sur la réclame qu'ils nous ont collée au derrière, vous reniflez, vous reposez d'un air dégoûté et... vous levez la voisine!* I rerendered such a dynamic use of language with the following: 'You customers walk past, look, have a feel, glance absent-mindedly at what's on its rear, sniff, put it back with a look of disgust and then... you pick up the next one!'.

Sarraute also uses repetition as a playful device in her text. At times, such wordplays could be transferred to the TT relatively closely. *Je lèche la devanture, mine de rien, ou plutôt, mine d'une nana qui se regarde dans la vitrine* became 'I gaze at the window, looking all casual, or rather, looking like a bird who's looking at herself in the window'. However, at other times, a freer approach was necessary in order to rerender these. *C'est pas parce que les affaires sont pas bonnes que j'en suis une mauvaise, d'affaire* [If business is bad, that doesn't mean I'm no good]. I also rewrote certain language in the TL to imitate both the idiomatic quality of the SL (*Moi, rien* [Me? Zilch]) and Sarraute's adaptation of SL terms (*papa poule et maman coq* [doting dad and modern-day mum]). I bore in mind the content of the entire novel, *Maman coq* (1989), when rewriting the latter term.

Third, time and space are also interconnected in the second part of this extract; each time frame exists in relation to others. As an 'intrusive narrator' (Baldick 1990), Sarraute describes her characters in the present, refers to the past to explain the early stages of her career, discusses current activity in Amsterdam in the present, and concludes with a second anecdote relating to her past, which she tells in the present historic. This temporal connection could be closely transferred to the TT. Space, as a concept, is similarly relational and equally unstable. Mentions are made of various bookshops in France and a book fair in Brussels, a street in Paris and the streets of Amsterdam. As time and space are intrinsically connected, the text is distinctly chronotopic. While many such references to places could be closely translated, I paid particular attention to two of these. I directly transferred *La Foire du Livre* to my TT and italicized this; I felt that the reference exoticized my TT, and that members of the TL audience who were not familiar with the term could nevertheless infer its meaning from the context in which it appears. I also left the street name *rue St Denis* in my translation to preserve its ST context, but supplemented this with a footnote to fully explain to my audience the connotations of the original reference. Thus, similarly to the first part of the extract, this second part poses a wide range of translation issues and challenges which have called for a comparable range of solutions.

Extract 6: *Mademoiselle, s'il vous plaît!* (1991: 137–40)

My sixth extract is situated approximately three quarters of the way through Sarraute's third novel, *Mademoiselle, s'il vous plaît!*, and is preceded by a scene in which Tatoune and Poupette, the novel's two middle-aged female protagonists, discuss both their work in the French department store, *Les Galeries Lafayette*, and Poupette's infatuation with their boss, Mr Maximilien. The present extract is divisible into three sections. In the first, Sarraute describes Poupette's son Jean-Marc who, like many busy adults, has little time for his mother. Instead, he showers Poupette with presents, the latest of which is a holiday to Venice, courtesy of the travel company which he owns. The second section is composed of a conversation between mother and son. Jean-Marc has telephoned Poupette from his office and they talk about her holiday to Italy. Throughout the call he patronizes his mother, speaking to her as if she were a child. In the third and final section, Tatoune and Poupette are on holiday in Venice and are sitting in a restaurant where they are about to eat. Tatoune tries to talk to her friend, but in vain; Poupette is daydreaming about her ideal man, with whom she would rather be spending her holiday. Tatoune, who then tries to decipher the Italian menu alone, has difficulty communicating with the native waiter; she becomes irritated and resorts to using pidginized French and a hotchpotch of other European languages in an attempt to make herself understood. As the extract ends, Poupette, who is no longer daydreaming, protests at the calorific dishes which her friend is ordering. In the following scene, Poupette expresses concerns about her weight and the two friends set about their sightseeing in Venice.

This extract shares a number of similarities with the previous two novelistic texts discussed. It qualifies as polyphonic as it contains a plurality of consciousnesses and voices, i.e. it is multivoiced, and it also displays many other instances of dialogue, interactivity, and interrelatedness (Extracts 4 and 5). Furthermore, it falls into distinct, yet interrelated, parts (Extract 5). The present commentary considers the three sections of this ST individually in order to establish how each one is multivoiced and otherwise interactive and multidimensional, and to determine both the translation challenges which these features of the text pose, and the solutions which they require. However, unlike the previous two commentaries, examination of this extract focuses on the distinction between, and coexistence of, intra- and interculturalism. It seeks to demonstrate that, as the latter becomes more prominent in the ST, translation challenges are multiplied and a wider range of solutions is called for.

In section one, dialogue and interactivity occur on a predominantly intracultural level. In this paragraph, multivoicedness is, for instance, rooted in the SL culture. There is a constant oscillation in the ST between the voice of Sarraute, the French narrator, and other French voices, including those of characters, which appear in reported speech. These could be preserved by remaining close to the lexis and syntax of the SL in the TT. Moreover, these voices express themselves in intraculturally multidimensional language. Use of French is heteroglossic. Sarraute's opening sentence, which is written in a standard and correct register and which I translated closely, contrasts starkly with her later use of colloquialisms, which I sought to rerender with equivalent TL expressions, for example, *Christelle avait mis le holà* became 'Christelle put a stop to that' and *ça lui coûte pas un rond* was recaptured as 'It doesn't cost him a penny'. In this paragraph, use of the SL is also multi-tonal and dialogic. The tone is at first factual, but as the voice changes, it l becomes condescending, as can be witnessed in the following: *A quoi tu veux jouer ma petite maman?* [What do you want to play, mummy?]; *Tu vas en faire un parent gâté* [You'll turn her into a spoilt parent] and *Elle leur a fait une grosse bêtise* [She was a very silly girl]. At the close of the paragraph, the tone again becomes neutral and factual. I sought to recapture this multi-tonality in my TT by remaining close to the tone of the SL at all times.

Despite this emphasis on the SL culture, instances of interculturalism do begin to emerge in this section of the extract. Sarraute uses the TL noun *package tours*, which she italicizes in order to highlight its 'polyglossic' (Bakhtin 1934–5/1981: 364) quality in her ST. I retained this term in my translation, but removed the original italics in order to naturalize and domesticate its use and to avoid its looking obscure in the TT. However, where Sarraute refers to the American soap, *Santa Barbara*, I not only preserved this name in my TT, but also clarified it in a footnote. I considered this appropriate for two reasons. First, American series frequently feature on French television and I wanted to draw attention to this. And second, I believed that mention of the time at which the programme was produced and popular would help to situate this extract within the original time frame in which *Mademoiselle, s'il vous plaît* was written. In this first section, interculturalism is also evident at the level of the chronotope. Although the text is written principally in the present tense and is set in France, references are made to the characters' past holiday in Marrakech and to Poupette's forthcoming trip to Venice. It was possible to preserve these switches of tense in the TL, and to translate closely the names of those foreign places mentioned.

An abrupt cut to the second section of the extract follows.[19] Once again, much of the dialogue and interactivity apparent in this section

---

19 Temporal and spatial disconnection are particularly apparent in the transitions between the three sections of the extract and create a powerful sense of fragmentation in the ST; this novel is polychronotopic (Pearce 1994: 71–2).

occurs on the level of the SL culture; it is largely intracultural. The two
stylized characters, mother and son, who speak on the telephone, are both
French and communicate through use of dialogic French language.[20] It was
possible to preserve the voices of these stereotypical characters in the TT
by paying particular attention to their multidimensional use of French,
and by implementing a number of translation strategies. Their dialogue is
multi-tonal. Poupette's sensible, adult tone contrasts with the exaggerated,
patronizing attitude of her son. Their conversation also contains a more
creative use of language; *fifils*, as opposed to the standard *fils*:

> – Et toi, tu [...] es libre [...] de venir avec moi?
> – Moi? Enfin, voyons, ma petite chérie, quelle idée! Il travaille ton fifils, il doit
> aller à son bureau, tu le sais bien.

While I preserved these tones closely in the TL, I rewrote *fifils* as 'sonny-
wonny'. Given that *fifils* is used three times in this part of the extract, I felt
that any longer translation of it, such as 'mummy's (little) darling boy',
would appear awkward in the TL and would lose the punch and humour
of the original term.

In addition to this, the characters' use of language is also heteroglossic, as it contains use of colloquial, sub-standard registers. It was equally
possible to preserve this closely in the TL:

T'es absolument libre de...	You're absolutely free to...
Et toi, tu l'es, libre?	And what about you? Are you free?
Libre de quoi?	Free for what?
Ben de venir avec moi?	Er, to come with me?

However, when language in this section is playful, I attempted to be
similarly adaptive in my rerendering of the SL. Hence:

20   As was the case in the two previous novelistic extracts, in Extract 6 much speech (a
      primary genre) is incorporated into this written text (a secondary genre) (Bakhtin
      1970–1/1986: 62).

Rapport à Lucien, *rapport au* magasin, *rapport à...*	Lucien *relies on* her and there's the shop and...
*Rapporte-t'*en à moi.	You can *rely on* me.

Such instances of intraculturalism notwithstanding, in this section of the extract, interculturalism is clearly beginning to assume greater importance. Here, time and space are again intrinsically linked. The characters' conversation, which takes place in the present, refers to Poupette's future holiday, including the sights which she will visit, the person who will accompany her, and the means of transport by which they will travel. Jean-Marc compares this trip with Poupette's past holidays in France and suggests that his mother try to dream about Venice that night, painting an idyllic picture which she will be able to visualize. It was largely possible to preserve in my TT these varied references to times and places. For instance, I used a literal approach to translating the names of famous Venetian sights. Nevertheless, when rerendering *dans ce trou perdu en Auvergne*, I adopted an oblique strategy in order to preserve the Frenchness of this place in my TT while also explaining it discreetly: 'in that god forsaken hole in the Auvergne region', thereby both foreignizing and domesticating my TT.

The references to foreign places which are made in the first and second sections of the extract do indeed anticipate the whole tenor of section three, to which there is another abrupt cut. If elements of intraculturalism are still present here, due to the powerful sense of foreignness and exoticism in this section, there is a marked shift in emphasis from intra- to interculturalism.

In section three Sarraute, the narrator, intervenes only once. However, as in the previous section, this part of the extract contains a strong implied author presence. Essentially, the voices in this section belong to members of the SL culture – Tatoune and Poupette. Nevertheless, an important element of this passage is Tatoune's attempt to communicate with an Italian waiter. If the waiter's voice is not actually heard, his presence does provide the ST with a distinctly intercultural dimension. As this part of the text is composed almost entirely of oral language,[21] intra- and interculturalism are

---

21   As Bakhtin (1941/1981: 5) explained, the novel 'squeezes out some genres and incorporates others into its peculiar structure'. This passage incorporates not only the

particularly apparent on a linguistic level. First, Tatoune and Poupette's use
of French is heteroglossic, and I sought to recapture this with similar TL
uses. Their pronunciation is lax (*T'as tes lunettes?* [You got your glasses?])
and their language also contains the following colloquialisms:

le [...] Machin	the [...] Whatsit
Qu'est-ce que c'est que ce charabia?	What's all this gobbledygook?
Tu comprends ce qu'il dit, toi? Moi, pas un mot.	D'you understand what he's saying? I don't get a word of it, me.

However, when Tatoune strives to talk to the Italian waiter, translation of her unidirectional speech gives rise to a greater range of challenges.
Tatoune pidginizes her mother tongue when she asks *Vous pas avoir carte
français?* I rerendered this by creating a comparable pidginization of the
TL: 'You no have French menu?'. Irritated, she then uses a hybrid of words
belonging to four European languages. This is indeed the most extensive
and highly concentrated example of polyglossia in all of Sarraute's writings.
I approached these lines by translating closely Tatoune's uses of French
words into English, and vice versa, but directly transposed all Italian and
German words to my TT, as these would have the same exotic effect on
my TL audience as they would on the original readership. I also retained
in my translation both Sarraute's use of italics, in order to maintain the
visual texture of the language, and her erroneous uses of Italian, as these
would also be amusing to TL readers with knowledge of this language.
Errors include *francesca* (rather than the correct *francese*), *englese* (instead
of *inglese*), and the addition of the letter 's' to plural nouns which should
end in 'i' in Italian: *spaghetti, gnocchi, ravioli*. Last, Sarraute's play on the
expression, *c'est du chinois*, provides an apt and entertaining conclusion to
this extract and it was necessary to recreate this in the TL. Thus, *Sorti de là,
le reste, c'est du chinois. Et moi, manger avec des baguettes, merci bien, mais*

---

speech genre, but also imitations of other written genres which are intracultural (a
birth certificate) and which I translated closely, and intercultural (items from an
Italian menu), which I directly transposed to my TT.

non merci!, which translates literally as 'Apart from that, the rest is Chinese. And me, eating with chopsticks, thanks very much, but no thanks!', became 'Apart from that, the rest's all Greek to me. And I don't fancy eating Greek right now, thanks very much!'.

I adopted a similar range of translation strategies in order to rerender in my TT both French and foreign cultural terms which occur in this section. Again, these are both intra- and intercultural. I attached a footnote to explain the significance of the French film star, Alain Delon, with whom contemporary TL readers would probably not be familiar. Where Tatoune and Poupette's boss, the Frenchman Maximilien, is mentioned, I also explained this in a footnote. As my audience will not be reading this extract within the context of the novel of which it is part, I thought it appropriate to provide such contextual information. By contrast, I rewrote the names of other people belonging to the SL culture. In the TL there are no exact equivalents of the organizations for which these people work, but I wanted to avoid overburdening my translation with further explanatory footers. I therefore rerendered *P.-DG du Crédit Lyonnais* ou *de la Lyonnaise des Eaux* ou *des Eaux et Forêts* as 'CEO of a large bank or environmental agency'.

Where references are intercultural, I at times transposed these directly. The actor, de Niro, is widely known in the TL culture, as are traditional Italian dishes (*spaghetti, gnocchi, ravioli*). At other times, however, I translated these relatively closely. For instance, I preserved the original description of stereotypical Italian behaviour and provided a TL equivalent of the offensive racial term which is used in the original: *Oui, bon, ça va, vous fatiguez pas à gesticuler comme ça... On a toujours l'impression qu'ils s'adressent à des sourds-muets, les Ritals* therefore became 'Yes, all right, that's enough! There's no need to wave your arms round like that... You always get the impression that the Eyeties are talking to the deaf-and-dumb'.

Finally, in this, the third principal chronotope of the extract, time occurs mainly in the present tense and the scene is set in one location: the Italian restaurant. This time and space could be closely recaptured in translation. Nevertheless, this section of the text contains a further subdivision, or chronotope. Poupette dreams of another imaginary time, which is conveyed in reported speech and through use of the conditional tense, and of other places. I modified Sarraute's original use of tense in my TT in order to recapture this other time frame: *Il serait assis là [...] Il l'aurait invitée à dîner* thus became 'She's imagining him sat there [...] She's imagining that he's asked her to dinner'. When translating the names of other places, I sometimes remained close to these, as in *le Grand Canal* [the Grand Canal], and at other times was oblique in my approach i.e *Ugo [...] de la Tour du Pin* [Ugo [...] from la Tour du Pin region].

Extract 7: *C'est pas bientôt fini!* (1998: 50–2)

The fourth and final novelistic extract in my collection is situated one quarter of the way through Sarraute's sixth novel, *C'est pas bientôt fini!* Prior to this passage, Didier and Vincent, two teachers at the *Collège Raymond-Fourneron*, a multi-ethnic school in a deprived suburb of Paris, talk in the staffroom. Didier attempts to discuss their pupils' grades, but his colleague, who is not interested, begins to daydream.

In the present extract, Vincent recalls accompanying the school's social worker, Ségolène, to a dilapidated tower block on a local housing estate, where she was to visit a Malian family. In the stairwell, Ségolène was almost knocked over by two boisterous teenagers, one of whom was truanting from the *collège*. Impressed by Ségolène's handling of the situation, Vincent was suddenly smitten with her. At her request he then left, allowing her to carry out her visit alone. An abrupt cut back to the staffroom follows, as Didier speaks to Vincent and interrupts his thoughts. Remembering his visit, Vincent mentions the numerous satellite dishes in the estate. He believes that the foreign channels which non-native pupils watch are detrimental to their learning French, and that these children should watch more French television if they are to better master the language. In response, Didier reminds him that the French used on television is not always of a correct register; it contains *franglais, franjeune*, and *verlan* (Pilard 2002: 89–90). This extract, and the chapter from which it emanates, conclude as Vincent agrees that, if pupils are to understand such slang, they must first have a reasonable command of standard French.

Certain parallels may be drawn between this extract and the previous one. Extract 7 is composed of separate, yet interrelated, sections. These contain a number of voices, and multiple manifestations of multidimensionality which occur both within and beyond the French language and culture. This commentary discusses the two principal sections of the extract in turn, focusing on particular issues within these. First, highlighting the intra- and intercultural nature of both sections, it explores how, in each of these, multidimensionality and interactivity are communicated through various voices, that is, how they are reflected not solely in the language which these voices use, but also in the issues which they discuss. Second, it presents the ways in which intra- and interculturalism are also apparent in the space, or location, of both sections. In each instance, this commentary outlines significant translation issues which arise, and proposes strategies which enable the above to be fully recaptured in the TT. Thus, it demonstrates that, despite the many points of comparison which exist between Extracts 6 and 7, the translation issues and challenges to which Extract 7 gives rise, especially those which occur in its latter section, are quite distinct from those which emerged in the previous extract. Rerendering of this extract therefore requires an equally distinct blend of translation strategies.

Section one of the extract centres on a scene in which two French professionals visit an underprivileged and multicultural area of Paris. Different strata of French society come into contact with one another in a carnivalesque fashion, and indigenous French people interact with foreign others. This is reflected in the voices of the text, namely in the language and the content of the participants' utterances. This section of this text is multivoiced; the voice of the narrator alternates with those of the characters, which feature in reported speech.

Sarraute's narrative voice is intraculturally multidimensional. Her use of language is multi-tonal; the factual tone in which she sets the scene differs from the chattiness of her later lines. It is also heteroglossic, as more standard uses of French are juxtaposed with less formal idioms: *Si elles s'entendent? Comme chien et chat* [And do these two women get on? No – they fight like cat and dog].

Furthermore, at times, this voice anticipates its French audience's reactions and need for clarification: *Où ça?; Si elles s'entendent?; Signe d'amitié ou de dépit?* All instances of intracultural multidimensionality in Sarraute's voice could be recaptured relatively closely in the TT, and where the SL contains such idiomatic uses, I sought equivalents in the TL. This strong sense of intraculturalism notwithstanding, the narrator's voice does have an important intercultural dimension. Sarraute uses her voice to describe Koebé and her Malian family, and Karim, a lively young African boy. I translated these descriptions closely and transposed the names of these people in order to fully preserve the exoticism of the ST in my translation. On one occasion, I supplemented my TT with a footnote. As the term *femme-relais* is an African one, with no equivalent in the Western world, I rerendered *Koebé, une femme-relais, une Malienne* as 'Koebé, *a duty-wife*, a Malian woman' and provided my reader with an explanation of this translation. By attaching this footnote and writing it in the first person, I make myself highly visible as translator.

In section one, Sarraute also presents the voices of her characters through use of reported speech. Sarraute's decision not to use inverted commas when reporting her characters' words creates an impression of indistinct and merging voices in the ST, which I replicated in the TT. Once again, these voices have both intra- and intercultural qualities. Ségolène uses the SL to communicate with her French colleague and with the African boy, and adopts very different tones of voice when addressing these two people. I attempted to recapture closely both Sarraute's description of this phenomenon, and the way in which it manifests itself in Ségolène's speech. Hence:

> [Elle] leur lance sur le ton familier, rude, et vaguement enjoué d'une Mamma habituée à rabrouer sa nichée: Pouvez pas faire attention, non? En voilà des manières! Tiens, Karim! Je croyais que tu étais malade. Ça n'a pas l'air d'être bien méchant, cette otite, dis donc! [...] Allez, file... Dou-ce-ment!

> [She] calls out to them in the familiar, harsh and vaguely cheerful tone of a Mama who's used to ticking off her brood: Can't you watch where you're going? What manners! Oi, Karim! I thought you were ill. Hey, that ear infection of yours doesn't look too bad! [...] Go on, clear off... Care-ful-ly!

Last, in this section of the extract, intra- and interculturalism are reflected in the sense of space, or the location, of the ST. As the extract begins, there is a cut from the professional environment of the French staffroom, to a poor estate which houses immigrant families. This section of the extract is chronotopic as notions of time and space within it are intrinsically linked; Vincent's daydreaming focuses entirely on his past visit to the housing estate. Sarraute's description of this visit does, however, take place in the present tense, thus giving a sense of immediacy to the dream. It was possible to closely preserve in the TT both these shifts in time and space and Sarraute's vivid description of locations.

The second section of the extract opens with a cut back to a scene which is set in the present time and in the staff room. Similarly to the first half, this portion of the text contains elements of intra- and intercultural multidimensionality which are conveyed through the voices in the text; they are reflected in their language and in the subject of their conversation. The French which Sarraute's two characters speakis intraculturally multidimensional and could often be recaptured closely in the TT and through use of TL equivalents. Their French is heteroglossic, incorporating as it does non-standard uses and colloquialisms: *Hé! Ho!* [Hey there]; *Elle est d'un nul!* [It's useless]; *C'était n'importe quoi* [It was a load of rubbish]. Didier also uses the meaningless SL filler *machin* on four occasions during their conversation, which I replaced consistently with the comparable TL use of 'like'. For instance: *On peut savoir où tu étais machin?* [Can I ask where you were, *like?*] and *T'as vu [...] sur la violence à l'école machin?* [Did you see [...] on violence in schools, *like?*]. I also sought equivalent TL uses to rerender vulgar language (*On se fout de ce que disent les présentateurs* [It doesn't bloody matter what the presenters say]), and to recapture playful uses of SL idioms in my TT (*Ils sont tous logés à la même enseigne. Une enseigne toute déglinguée mais raccordée à un satellite* [They're all in the same boat – a boat which is falling to pieces but connected to a satellite]). However, where pronunciation of the SL is lax, I was, at times, slightly freer in my rerendering and substituted this pronunciation with grammatical inaccuracies in the TL: *T'as remarqué, il y a au moins dix enceintes paraboliques sur chaque barre dans la cité* therefore became 'Have you noticed, *there's* at least ten dishes on each tower block on the estate'.

The subject of Didier and Vincent's conversation does, nevertheless, render this portion of the text interculturally multidimensional. The characters' discussion of their foreign pupils' poor command of French includes mentions of foreign television channels, which I translated closely, and of a specifically French programme. In the latter case, Didier refers to, and insults an episode of *La Marche du Siècle*, a serious, analytical programme which debates current social and political issues in France. I decided not to overburden my TT by explaining the precise nature of this programme in a footer. I also felt that it would be unreasonable to replace this reference with an approximate TL equivalent, such as *Panorama*, as Didier's comments regarding the original programme are highly critical. Instead, I adopted a neutral and oblique strategy: *T'as vu 'La Marche du Siècle' sur la violence à l'école machin l'autre soir? C'était n'importe quoi* [Did you see *that discussion programme* the other night on violence in schools, like? It was a load of rubbish].

Moreover, when Vincent suggests that exposure to French television may improve non-native pupils' language skills, this intercultural awareness prompts Didier's acutely self-conscious, intracultural consideration of the complex, heteroglossic nature of their own mother tongue. The following lines present a wealth of translation issues and challenges (see also Ellender 2006b: 158–60):

> – La question n'est pas là, voyons, Didier! On se fout de ce que disent les présentateurs, les invités, tout ça. L'important c'est qu'ils le disent en français.
> – C'est pas du français, c'est du franglais ou du franjeune. On dit d'une situation qu'elle est sérieuse au lieu de grave. On dit habiter sur Marseille au lieu de à machin. On dit appart, com, perso, kit, cata et pack machin... Tout juste si on ne parle pas le verlan.
> – Ça ne serait déjà pas si mal. A Fourneron, sorti de deux trois mots, keuf, meuf, laisse béton, le verlan, personne ne le comprend. Normal. Pour parler le français à l'envers, faut commencer par savoir le parler à l'endroit.

The principal translation difficulty of this passage resides in the fact that the sub-languages, or varieties, of the SL which are discussed self-consciously and used in the ST either do not have exact equivalents or do not exist at all in the TL. As close translations of these would therefore have been artificial and inaccurate, I rewrote / adapted them entirely,[22]

---

22   In this respect, my approach is closely in line with that of the poststructuralist, Philip E. Lewis. Of Lewis's work Venuti (2000: 341) writes: 'It goes beyond literalism to

thereby domesticating my TT. The three varieties of the SL which feature are *franglais*, *franjeune*, and *verlan*. First, although *franglais* is a concept which exists in the TL, English speakers do not view this with the same hostility as do francophones, who often fear invasion of their language by Anglicizms. Thus, I sought 'emprunts' (Vinay & Darbelnet 1958) whose presence is equally powerful in the TL, and opted for Americanizms. This required that I replace instances of *franglais* which occur in the ST with commonly used Americanizms in the TL.

Second, I adopted a similar approach to my rerendering of *franjeune*, as these modern uses of the SL are equally untranslatable. I rewrote this term as 'yoof speak', and replaced examples of *franjeune* with comparable, trendy uses of the TL. In this context, literal translations of *L'important c'est qu'ils le disent en français* and *C'est pas du français* would also have been inappropriate; in the TT, it is no longer the French language which is being discussed. Consequently, I rewrote these mentions of, and one later reference to *le français*, with a neutral, decontextualized, alternative: 'our language'.[23]

Third, it was particularly awkward to rerender *verlan* in the TL, as there is no equivalent form of English slang which functions in this way, that is, by inverting the syllables of words. Given this, I thought it appropriate to use English 'back slang' in my TT, a type of slang which literally spells words backwards. In order to do this, I took each example of *verlan* (for instance *keuf*), reversed the syllables to form the usual slang word (*flic*), translated this into English ('cop' – abbreviation of 'copper', or 'policeman'), and spelled this backwards ('poc'). Furthermore, as *verlan* is such an important branch of French slang, I provided a short explanation of this in a footnote to my TT, using the instances of *verlan* which feature in the ST as examples. Again, by attaching this footnote, I make myself visible as translator.

---

advocate an experimentalism: innovative translating that samples the dialects, registers and style already available in the translating language to create a discursive heterogeneity which is defamiliarizing but intelligible to different constituencies in the translating culture'.

23　This is a striking example of the ultimate paradox of translation, as identified by Derrida. As Derrida (in Collins & Mayblin 1996: 106–7) pointed out, the simple but self-conscious French sentence, *Oui, oui, ce sont des mots français* [Yes, yes, these are French words] can never be fully translated; it is a sentence which derails translation.

Due to this rewriting of the SL, all context-dependent and culture-bound words which occur in the ST also needed to be removed. In the same way that I rewrote references to *le français* in my TT, I replaced the name of the school, *Fourneron*, with the word 'here'. Implementing all of the above, I produced the following rerendering of the previously quoted passage:

> – Come on, Didier, that's not the point! It doesn't bloody matter what the presenters and guests and that lot say. What's important is that they say it in our language.
> – It's not our language. It's full of Americanizms and yoof speak. They say chill out instead of relax. They say wicked instead of great, like. They say pad, gen., guys, nightmare, gear and caboodle, like… And that's when they're not using back slang.
> – That wouldn't be so bad. Apart from two or three words – poc, namow, ti tegrof – nobody here understands back slang. And that's natural. If you're going to speak our language back to front, you've got to start by speaking it the right way round.

As was the case in the first section of the extract, in this latter half, intra- and intercultural multidimensionality are also apparent in the location of the ST. Although references are made to the housing estate in Vincent's daydream, this passage is situated in the staffroom of the *Collège Raymond-Fourneron*; the passage is polychronotopic. Explicit mentions of these two places gave rise to certain translation issues. I rerendered *Dans une barre aux Œillets* obliquely as 'In a tower block on the Les Œillets estate'. Moreover, as was previously discussed, I replaced the reference to the school, *Fourneron*, with the word 'here'; I was obliged to rewrite the self-conscious discussion of the SL in the TL and, as a consequence, to remove any context- or culture-bound terms in my TT.

Extract 8: *Des Hommes en général et des Femmes en particulier* (1996: 111–15)

My eighth extract is taken from *Des Hommes en général et des Femmes en particulier*, the only one of Sarraute's works of its kind. In this social critique, Sarraute treats all aspects of the sexes and of the complex relationship between them. This particular passage is composed of the latter part of the eleventh of twenty-four chapters which constitute the work. Chapter eleven, entitled *Parlez-moi d'amour* [Talk to me about love], begins with a discussion of the idiosyncratic nature of sexual partnerships and the compatibility of individuals, before swiftly moving on to cover a range of loosely related topics. The rapid succession of subjects and the humour which characterize the first part of this chapter, and indeed the entire work, also feature prominently in the present extract. Here, Sarraute first discusses teenage girls' interest in sex, and the way in which young girls read teen magazines in order to learn about, and master, sexual behaviour. She recounts an incident in Great Britain, and parodies a magazine quiz which tests adolescent males' understanding of their girlfriends' sexual pleasure. Sarraute then compares the attitudes of young people towards relationships in different milieux of French society, and the sexual appetites of males and females. She adds a socio-historical dimension to her text, discussing the traditions of mixed-generation relationships and arranged marriages. Moving forward in time, Sarraute suggests that, despite the sexual revolution of the 1970s, women remain disadvantaged in relationships and, for certain reasons, she concludes, will always end their days alone in the bedroom.

This extract, and the work of which it is part, provide a comparative, relational treatment of the genders, focusing on the fundamental biological and social differences which exist between males and females. Exploration of this extract reveals that dialogue, interrelationships, and multidimensionality are not apparent solely in the subject matter of the text, but also at many other levels of the ST. In view of this, the present study details instances of intertextuality and intergenericity in the extract, the dialogic language which is used by the text's participants as different genders, societies, and cultures are discussed, and the presence of temporal and spatial relativity in the ST.

Extract 8 contains a rich medley of intertextual, and indeed intergeneric, references. In the opening lines, Sarraute names four girls' magazines in the SL culture and follows these closely with those of four comparable TL publications. I transferred all eight of these references directly to the TT, thus preserving the sense of intertextual and intercultural comparison contained in the original. Similarly, I transferred directly to my TT references to literary figures (Molière) and to established works of literature (Colette's *Chéri*). In the first instance, I considered no further explanation necessary, as Molière is an internationally known writer. By contrast, I supplemented the reference to Colette's novel with a footnote, as it is an important work in the SL culture, whose plot is of direct relevance to the present ST. By adopting this approach, I increased my visibility as a translator.

When rerendering Sarraute's reference to an article which had appeared in the magazine, *Paris-Match*, the previous summer, I was, however, considerably freer in my approach. As I had decided to replace the names of SL personalities mentioned in the ST (to be discussed later), I also considered replacing that of the SL magazine and using an approximate TL equivalent, such as *Hello*. Nevertheless, as a particular article is referred to in the original, and as the subject which it discusses may not have been covered in an edition of *Hello* the previous summer, it may have been inaccurate to use this name as a substitute for *Paris-Match*. Instead, I rewrote this reference neutrally. Hence, *Phénomène longuement analysé à partir de quelques exemples genre [...], dans Match, l'été dernier* became 'This phenomenon was analysed at length *in a magazine* last summer, using a few examples like [...]'.[24]

Instances of intertextuality and intergenericity in the extract are not restricted to isolated references to SL texts. Where Sarraute describes in general terms other genres of text or other media, her words could be translated literally: *Contrairement à ce qu'on voit à la télé et au cinéma* [Unlike what we see on TV and at the cinema].

More significantly, in this extract Sarraute parodies[25] titles of magazine articles. Drawing inspiration from editions of the magazine, *Cosmopolitan*,

24   I confronted similar issues when rerendering the name of the French television pro-
      gramme, *La Marche du Siècle*, in Extract 7.

25   Bakhtin (1941/1981: 5) stated that: 'The novel parodies other genres (precisely in their
      role as genres); it exposes the conventionality of their forms and their language, it
      squeezes out some genres and incorporates others into its own peculiar structure,
      reformulating and re-accentuating them'. This is a clear illustration of Bakhtin's
      (1929, in Lodge 1990: 59–60) 'varidirectional double-voiced discourse'. However, as
      this is precisely what Sarraute does in *Des Hommes*, a non-novelistic text, this text is
      evidence that important features which Bakhtin identified in the novel are far from
      genre-specific.

I translated some of these titles closely: *Mon petit ami a couché avec mon frère* [My boyfriend slept with my brother]; *Je me suis tapé cent mecs* [I've had a hundred blokes]. However, I rerendered one of these more playfully, in order to preserve the raunchy and amusing nature of the original title in my TT: *Les hommes se débraguettent* [Men get unzipped].

This extract also contains an extended parody. Sarraute burlesques a quiz in a teenage magazine, and does so in a carnavalesque sense. In my attempt to fully recapture the ribaldry and the humorous effect of the ST and make the TT immediately accessible to my audience without over-burdening the text with footnotes, I adapted and rewrote some of the SL terms. At times, I also exaggerated the innuendos contained in the original:

> Vous voulez savoir si la libido de votre petite amie s'accorde à la vôtre? Faites le test ci-dessous. [...] la question 13: Son orgasme à elle, pour vous, c'est, A: un coucher de soleil. B: un boeuf bourguignon. C: le 14 Juillet. D: l'Arlésienne. E: la grosse Bertha.

> To find out if your girlfriend's libido matches yours, try the test below. [...] question 13: In your opinion, what's her idea of an orgasm? Is it A) a sunset. B) a slap-up meal. C) a summer bank holiday. D) a rousing piece of classical music. E) a huge missile-firing weapon?

Interrelationships and multidimensionality are equally apparent in the voices of the text's participants. If the extract is dominated by the clear, discursive voice of the narrator, Sarraute does, at times, disrupt her own narrative flow by inserting her own comments and personal opinions randomly into the text. At times, Sarraute is therefore an 'intrusive narrator' (Baldick 1990: 112). Instances of this occur in the first sentence of the second paragraph and in the last sentence of the penultimate paragraph, and could both be rerendered closely in the TT. Multivoicedness also occurs in the text as Sarraute reports the words of others through use of indirect speech. It was possible to translate this closely, as is illustrated in the last sentence of the second paragraph. Moreover, Sarraute anticipates the responses of her readers (or narratees), thus adding a further dimension to this multivocality. I also translated these closely: *On? Qui ça on?* [We? Who's we?].

The voices in this extract are particularly significant. They are the media through which all language in the text is articulated, much of which is also

multidimensional. The language which the text's participants use is explicitly heteroglossic. Sarraute's informal, idiomatic and, at times, vulgar words
could be translated closely, using a combination of literal methods and
transposition: *Entre deux débutants, ça relève davantage de la maladroite et
tâtonnante boucherie que de la fusion magique et savante* [When both parties
are novices, it's more about shoving it in awkwardly and by trial and error
than about fusing together magically and skilfully]. Such language contrasts
starkly with the exaggeratedly affected speech of imaginary members of
the upper classes, represented by Sarraute in reported direct speech. It was
possible to preserve the register of this speech very closely in the TL. *Dis,
chérie, sois mignonne* therefore became 'I say, darling, be a dear'.

Furthermore, language in the ST is, on occasion, distinctly self-conscious. Where Sarraute displays awareness of the SL in her *ce qui est très
tendance, comme on dit*, I translated the first part of her comment as 'a
very fashionable thing to do', but omitted the latter part in my text. As
the English expression which I use is not particularly noteworthy in the
TL, it would not have been appropriate to draw attention to it in the TT.
Rendering her work polyglossic, Sarraute also demonstrates her knowledge
of the heteroglossic nature of the TL: *'Have sex' comme disent les Anglo-
Saxons par opposition à 'make love'*. I transferred these expressions directly to
the TT, leaving them in inverted commas to emphasize the fact that English
was not the principal language of the ST and thereby foreignizing the TT.

Interrelationships and multidimensionality are not only apparent in
the texts, genres, voices, and language which feature in this extract. These
voices, and the language which they use, discuss the opposition of the genders and, in doing so, draw on a range of French and British social and cultural terms, many of which also raise certain issues and challenges for the
translator. For the most part, Sarraute's comparing and contrasting of the
sexes could be transferred closely to the TT. However, in the concluding
paragraph of the extract, when men and women are presented in blatant
opposition to one another, I added the TL nouns, 'men' and 'women', in
order to reinforce both this distinction between, and solidarity within, the
genders (my emphases):

N'empêche, la différence d'âge jouera forcément dans les deux sens à l'avenir puisque, aussi bien, on est libre d'en changer à sa guise. On? Qui ça on? Ben... *Eux*, à vrai dire. *Nous*, [...] on n'a plus tellement le choix.

Be that as it may, in the future, age difference between partners is bound to work both ways, seeing that we are, just as well, free to chop and change as we please. We? Who's we? Er... in actual fact, they are – *the men*. *We women* [...] don't really have a choice anymore.

Sarraute's juxtapositions of the genders are also multi-tonal; at times accurate and considered, but largely light-hearted and comical. It was possible to closely preserve entertaining descriptions of male and female adolescents' behaviour (paragraphs one and three).[26] By contrast, where Sarraute uses names of fruits symbolically in her text to describe relationships between older women and younger men, I adopted a more creative and imaginative approach in order to rerender these images in the TT: *mais qu'une poire blette séduise un fruit vert* therefore became 'but if a shrivelled prune seduces an unripe banana'.

Given that Sarraute discusses and juxtaposes attitudes towards sexual relationships and behaviour within different sectors of French society, her text also assumes a socially relational dimension. I translated descriptions of the classes closely, and sought TL equivalents to the narrator's uses of socially-bound terms:[27]

Les fils de bourgeois songent d'abord à décrocher [...] des diplômes [...] tout en affichant parfois, pas souvent, une 'fiancée' de leur âge. Et les gosses des banlieues accordent plus d'importance à leur bande et à leur territoire qu'à la chasse aux minettes.

The sons of the middle classes think first and foremost about getting qualifications [...] while sometimes, but not often, also parading a 'fiancée' of their own age. And the young lads of the suburbs attach more importance to their gang and territory than to chasing trendy young chicks.

26 The only word which I replaced in this passage was *Jules*. In the SL this noun is both a male Christian name and a synonym of 'boyfriend'. I considered the TL 'Guy' to be an appropriate equivalent of the SL word.

27 I also adopted this approach when rerendering *promis* [betrotheds] in the TT.

Moreover, on several occasions throughout the ST, Sarraute adopts a satirical and deliberately affected tone in her portrayal of the upper classes. In order to fully recapture this in the TT, I remained particularly close to the phrase structure of the French in my rerendering. Such calques make the foreign identity of the ST visible in the TT:

> Depuis Abraham, les vieux mâles s'adjugeaient à plaisir des jeunes femelles qui leur étaient souvent livrées par leurs pères. Solide et confortable tradition que Molière, déjà, tournait en dérision. Celle de mariages arrangés en fonction de la dot ou au contraire de la fortune qu'un barbon laisserait en héritage à sa veuve. Joyeuse.

> Ever since the time of Abraham, old men where taking young women at their whim, women who were often handed to them by their fathers. A strong, comfortable tradition which was ridiculed as far back as Molière; the tradition of arranging marriages according to the dowry or, conversely, the fortune, which some greybeard was to leave to his widow. What a joy.[28]

This said, a number of references to aspects of the SL culture did not, I felt, lend themselves to such a close approach. I therefore rewrote these in my TT. For instance, neither the most basic, nor one of the most prestigious, French university qualifications which Sarraute mentions has an exact equivalent in the TL culture. Thus, *Les fils de bourgeois songent d'abord à décrocher, de Deug en agrég, des diplômes* became 'Throughout their time at university, the sons of the middle classes think first and foremost about getting qualifications.'[29]

I was yet freer when rerendering the names of French personalities which Sarraute uses as examples of couples in which the woman is older than her male partner. As a decision to transfer these names directly to the TT would have required that I supplement this sentence with four footnotes, I substituted these French couples with equivalent partnerships in the TL culture, as in the following example: *Phénomène longuement analysé à partir de quelques exemples genre Édith Piaf et Théo Sarapo ou Alain-Fournier et*

---

28   Sarraute's use of *joyeuse* is ambiguous; it may refer to the tradition described, or to the happy widow who is left a generous amount of money by her husband. I re-rendered this as 'What a joy', which I felt best conveys the tone of the SL.

29   I also expanded and rephrased cultural terms in this manner when rewriting Sarraute's burlesque magazine quiz, as discussed above.

Mme Simone, dans Match, l'été dernier [This phenomenon was analysed at length in a magazine last summer, using a few examples like *Joan Collins and Percy Gibson*, or *Barbara Windsor and Scott Harvey*].

As aspects of British culture are referred to in the ST, this extract also contains a degree of interculturalism. In such instances, the translation issue was one of transferring names and terms which belong to the TL culture but appear in the ST, back into their original TL context. At times, it was possible to transfer these directly (Jack Nicholson). However, where Sarraute uses French terms to describe concepts which also exist in the TL culture, I used TL equivalents: *un élu conservateur* [a conservative Member of Parliament]; *ce brave député* [this nice M.P.]. I also reworded certain French terms used: *Il réclame le carré blanc, ce brave depute: cette publication est déconseillée aux enfants de moins de seize ans*[30] therefore became 'This nice M.P. is calling for this publication to be classed as unsuitable for children under sixteen'. Given the range of strategies which I implement when rerendering both SL and TL cultural terms in the TT, my approach resembles closely that of Stroumza (1998).

Extract 8 is also underpinned by temporal and spatial interrelationships. The narrator alternates descriptions of attitudes and behaviour in the present tense, with explanations of events which have taken place in the recent past. She then makes a chronological leap back to Biblical times, before moving forward again to describe trends in behaviour through the seventeenth, eighteenth, and nineteenth centuries. When this extract, and the chapter of which it is part, conclude by referring to the future, Sarraute also likens life to a journey. With the exception of one mention of time which I rewrote in my TT, in order to make it more immediately accessible to a wider audience: *Après l'hécatombe de 14–15* [After the massacres *of the First World War*]. I remained close to all uses of tense and all time phrases employed in the SL. Such flux is also apparent on a spatial level in the ST. From British toilets to French bedrooms, and from the territories of suburban gangs to the homes of the middle classes, these references, which also serve to frame the extract, could all be transferred closely to the TT.

---

30 *Le carré blanc*: A sign on French television which indicates that a programme is suitable for adults only.

Extract 9: *'P(o)ur homme'* – Article for *Psychologies*,
September 2000

'P(o)ur homme' is the first of two articles in my collection which were
published in the magazine, *Psychologies*. This text centres on a dialogue
between Alain and Mouna, a man and woman who live together and have
recently returned from holiday. The precise nature of the pair's relationship
is, however, unclear. Alain initiates the present conversation by questioning
Mouna about her irritability, which has lately become worse. Her anger is
fuelled by Alain's mispronunciation of the French sound 'ou'; this speech
impediment, and subsequent confusion of the sounds 'ou' and 'u', recur
throughout *'P(o)ur homme'*. Alain and Mouna then speak about their holiday and about a man, Fabien, whom they met whilst away. When Alain
insults the homosexual Fabien, Mouna is defensive and dismisses Alain's
comments. Nevertheless, her attitude soon changes. Annoyed that Fabien,
whom she found very attractive, has not bothered to stay in touch with her,
she herself begins to insult him. Alain finally convinces Mouna that Fabien
is indeed gay, and the pair make their peace. As harmony is restored, Alain
loses his speech impediment and Mouna pretends to acquire it, imitating
it affectionately.

This article is inherently unstable; the characters' relationship is
ambiguous and their conversation acrimonious. The text is also humorous throughout since the speech and attitudes of these individuals are, at
all times, exaggerated. In turn, instability and humour are reflected powerfully in the dialogue and interrelationships which are present at numerous levels of the ST; those of genre, voice, character, language, culture,
time and space. The present pages seek to demonstrate that, owing to the
multidimensional nature of *'P(o)ur homme'*, this relatively short text gives
rise to some complex translation issues and requires that an exclusive set
of strategies be implemented.

Like so many of Sarraute's writings, this text is significant for its intergenericity and generic instability. Although it is a written article, *'P(o)ur
homme'* is composed entirely of a spoken dialogue between its two characters. This generic indistinctiveness could be closely preserved by retaining

the original format of the ST in the TT. The characters' speech is dialogic, and the true identity of their voices, uncertain. Sarraute, the 'real author' (Baldick 1990), uses these puppet-like individuals to communicate her own exaggerated vision of certain types of personality.[31] In Bakhtinian terminology, the present scene would class as a 'Ritual Spectacle'; a comic show of the market place (1938). It was possible to recapture the fluctuating and carnivalesque (Bakhtin 1929) nature of these characters by paying close attention to their use of language.

Alain and Mouna's dialogic language is thoroughly multidimensional, which renders it unstable and entertaining. First, it is heteroglossic. Individually, these characters use contrasting registers which could be closely preserved with TL equivalents: *J'en ai rien à cirer* [I don't give a monkey's] is, for instance, juxtaposed with the more impolite *Je m'en fous* [I don't give a shit]. I also translated closely the vulgar insult, *con*, which appears four times in the ST, with the corresponding TL term, 'bastard'.[32] If some less vulgar, but equally amusing, colloquialisms could also be rerendered closely with TL equivalents – *Moi, tu sais, les pédés...* [Personally, you know, *poofs*...] –, others required a more adaptive approach. Thus, I expanded in my TT those SL uses with no equivalent in the TL: *Tu deviens d'un beauf, mon pauvre Alain!* [You're becoming a really small-minded little petty bourgeois, my dear Alain!]. I was also more creative when recapturing slovenly uses of the SL, writing TL words as if to phonetically transcribe laxly pronounced English. Hence *Je sais pas* became 'I dunno', and *Comment tu le sais?* was rerendered as 'How d'you know?'.

31 Thus, Sarraute's work again shares clear similarities with that of Dostoevsky. As Bakhtin (1929/1984: 93). wrote of Dostoevsky's articles: 'This striving of Dostoevsky to perceive each thought as an integrated personal position, to think in voices, is clearly evidenced even in the compositional structure of his journalistic articles. His manner of developing a thought is everywhere the same: he develops it dialogically, not in a dry, lyrical dialogue, but by juxtaposing whole, profoundly individualized voices. Even in his polemical articles he does not really persuade but rather organizes voices, yokes together semantic orientations, most often in the form of some imagined dialogue'.

32 In the context of the carnival, Bakhtin (1929/1984: 5) believed such amusing uses of vulgar words to belong to a particular branch of folk humour; that of 'Billingsgate'.

Second, the characters' conversation contains multiple opposed tones, which are often confrontational, exaggerated, and therefore comical. In my attempt to fully preserve these tones in the TT, I also adopted a range of close and freer translation methods. In the SL, tone is used to convey reproach (*Tu aurais pu me le dire*, which I translated literally as 'You could have told me!') and a desire for reconciliation (*Allez, viens faire la paix*, which I rerendered with the TL equivalent, 'Come on, come and make up!'). Where tone communicates victimization: *Lâche-moi avec ça, tu veux?*, this could also be translated with a TL equivalent, 'Will you stop going on at me about that?'. However, when tone is defensive in nature, I employed a combination of literal translation and equivalent uses to preserve this. *Où est le problème? Nulle part. Pourquoi j'aurais un problème?* [What's the problem? There isn't one. Why should I have a problem?]. By contrast, where the impression is one of attack, I used the process of modulation to recapture this in the TL: *C'est d'un grotesque cette attitude de mari jaloux, c'est d'un plouc!* [You've got the attitude of a jealous husband – it's so ridiculous and so uncouth!].

The third and most significant linguistic feature of the ST is, without doubt, Alain's mispronunciation of the SL sound 'ou'. Plays on the sounds 'ou' and 'u' oppose correct and incorrect pronunciation and are humorous both for the irritation and disharmony which they cause, and for the frequency with which they occur. Given the non-equivalence of SL and TL sounds, close translation of this linguistic playfulness was clearly impossible. Rather, it was necessary to totally rewrite this in the TT, if the ST was to 'survive' in the TL (Benjamin 1923) and if 'dynamic equivalence' was to be achieved (Nida 1964). My immediate feeling was to replace mispronunciation of the SL with poorly enunciated English, omitting the final sounds of SL words, for instance: *'P(o)ur homme'* [F' real men]. However, when Alain protests at Mouna's criticism of his speech and claims that he is not to blame for this defect – *Lâche-moi avec ça, tu veux? C'est pas de ma faute si je...* –, it becomes apparent that this is not due to laziness, but to a speech impediment. I thus recaptured this in the TT by allowing the English sound 'r' to be mispronounced as 'w'. I felt that this was particularly appropriate when rerendering the title of the article, *'P(o)ur homme'* [For (weal) men], and other uses of *p(o)ur* in the text: *Il n'est pas pur toi* [He's not a weal man, he's not wight for you]; *Pur de bon? Oui, là, pur be bon?* [Weally? Yes, weally!]. Use of this TL impediment also enabled me to preserve mispronunciation of the female protagonist's name (Mouna / Muna, Maria / Mawia) and indeed to compensate for Alain's speech defect throughout my TT, as is illustrated in the following:

Je vudrais bien savoir ce qui peut te mettre dans un état pareil. C'est vrai, je ne peux plus uvrir ma gueule sans que tu me sautes dessus tutes griffes dehors...	I'd weally like to know what's getting you into such a state. Honestly, I can't open my twap now without you pouncing on me with your claws out...

At times, Mouna draws attention to this impediment, rendering it self-conscious. I attempted to recapture this device, and the confusion and laughter to which it gives rise, by making the TL equally self-aware:

– *Alors u est le problème?* – *Où? Où est le problème? Nulle part. Pourquoi j'aurais un problème?*	– So what's the pwoblem? – Problem! What's the problem? There isn't one. Why should I have a problem?
– *Ça devient infernal la vie avec toi, Mouna.* – *Mouna, c'est ça! Tu vois quand tu veux...*	– Living with you is getting unbearable, Maria. – Maria, that's right! You see, when you want to...

Nonetheless, due to the non-equivalence between the source and target languages, on one occasion I was required to completely rewrite a portion of the original dialogue in order to fully recapture this self-reflexivity in the TL:

> – Qu'est-ce que tu as en ce moment, Muna? Tu es d'un irritable, tu te fâches pur un rien... Il y a quelque chose qui ne va pas?
> – Mouna, pas Muna!
> – Ben oui, Muna, c'est bien ce que j'ai dit. Tu me cherches des pux ou quoi?
> – Pas pux, poux! Choux! Roux! C'est agaçant, à la fin, cette façon que tu as de prononcer les 'ou'...

> – What's the matter with you at the moment, Mawia? You're so iwitable, you get angwy over nothing... Is there something wrong?
> – Maria, not Mawia!
> – Well yes, Mawia, that's what I said. Are you cwiticizing me, or what?
> – Not cwiticize, criticize! Cry! Crack! It's really annoying, the way you pronounce 'r's...

A further point of interest in the ST is the characters' tendency to refer, self-consciously and amusingly, to aspects of their own culture. In order to rerender such instances of intra-culturalism and related humour, I implemented a range of translation strategies. I remained particularly close to the French concept of the *PaCS* in my TT. Through application of the principle of modulation *Ils sont pacsés depuis Noël* became 'They signed a *PaCS* at Christmas time'. I also supplemented this translation with a footnote, as the *PaCS* is an important SL concept with no exact equivalent in the TL culture. However, when Mouna mentions the French Rock singer, Johnny Hallyday, who has a similar speech defect to that of Alain, in connection with the satirical French puppet show, *Les Guignols*, I adopted an alternative strategy. I substituted these references with appropriate names in the TL culture (adaptation); Jonathan Ross, who mispronounces the TL sound 'r', and the English television programme, *Spitting Image*, which is in the mould of *Les Guignols*:

C'est agaçant, à la fin, cette façon que tu as de prononcer les 'ou'... Tu essayes d'imiter la marionnette de Johnny Hallyday *aux Guignols* ou quoi?	It's really annoying, the way you pronounce 'r's... Are you trying to imitate Jonathan Ross's puppet on *Spitting Image*, or what?

I adopted exactly this approach when dealing with the name of the French boy-band, *2B3*. Rather than adding a further footnote to my text, I replaced this name with that of an equivalent band which would be likely to be immediately comprehensible to the TL audience. For instance, *Tu te languis après Mister 2B3, c'est ça?* became 'Are you pining for Mr Boyzone, is that it?'. This said, I was most free when recapturing Mouna's reference to the French politician of the U.M.P., La Mère Boutin Mention of this woman would not have the same resonance for the TL reader as it would for the SL audience, and I thought explanation in the form of a footnote would lose the humour of the original reference. I therefore rewrote this, alluding to the outbreak of homophobia which occurred in 1999 at the time of Boutin's campaign against the *PaCS*. *On croirait entendre la Mère Boutin!* was therefore rerendered as 'You sound like *a right homophobe!*'.

Last, notions of time and space within this article are thoroughly relational and therefore contribute, in part, to the text's inherent sense of instability. While the characters' dialogue is set within the present time, the subject of their past holiday occupies the majority of their conversation. All such references to time, and time phrases, could be closely preserved in the TT. Similarly, if this dialogue is set in one space (the characters' home), allusions are constantly made to the place where they spent their holiday, and I again preserved all such allusions closely in the TT. However, where Alain refers to one particular holiday venue, *[le] bar de la paillotte*, I rerendered this more freely in the TL as '[the] beach bar'.

Extract 10: *'Et toi, pour qui tu votes?'* – Article for *Psychologies*, June 2002

The second of my chosen articles from *Psychologies*, and final extract of this collection, is set immediately after the 2002 presidential elections in France. *'Et toi, pour qui tu votes?'* is based on a dialogue between Lili and Roger, a couple with fundamentally left-wing beliefs, who are discussing political parties and individual politicians in their country. Lili leads their conversation, asking Roger a series of questions about his personal views. In his responses, he displays sound political knowledge and expresses some strong opinions. Roger, who has voted for the Left for most of his life, has become disillusioned with all politicians in recent years. He expresses his dislike of Chirac, the Right, and the present government. He is, moreover, similarly critical of the Left, insulting individual members of the *Parti socialiste* and explaining to Lili how these individuals should otherwise have acted. He concludes that, whatever their particular allegiances, all politicians have one of two intentions: to remain in power or to return to it. In the light of Roger's comments, Lili likens his attitude to that of Le Pen.

'Et toi, pour qui tu votes?' illustrates once more the dialogue-inspired, multidimensional nature of Sarraute's writings. This text displays a certain iconoclasm by appearing to react against established political institutions. Furthermore, by seemingly encouraging a 'suspension of [...] hierarchical precedence' in France (Bakhtin 1965/1984: 10), it also promotes a sense of

social disorder. The tenor of this article is, then, one of instability, much like that of Extract 2. As the present commentary seeks to demonstrate, multidimensionality and instability also manifest themselves variously at a number of levels of 'Et toi', that is, in relation to its genre, characters, language, culture-specific subject matter, and the time and space in which it is located. Grounding itself in Bakhtinian thought, this commentary pinpoints significant instances of multidimensionality and instability which occur at these levels. It identifies the translation issues and challenges to which each of these gives rise, and proposes appropriate strategies which enable the peculiar qualities of Sarraute's text to be fully rerendered in the TT. In this connection, it posits that, due to the particular nature of 'Et toi', the overall approach to this ST should differ quite considerably from that which was adopted when rerendering the previous nine extracts.

First, this article is generically unstable; it reacts against conventional written norms as it incorporates language of an oral nature. Consequently, it blurs the boundary which commonly exists between spoken and written discourses and the resulting effect is one of instability in the text, a tendency which is apparent in all genres of Sarraute's writings, especially Extracts 1 and 9. This could be fully recaptured in translation by preserving the original format of the ST in the TT. Second, the conversation on which this ST centres takes place between two individuals whose speech is both dialogic and unstable. As Lili and Roger are Sarraute's own constructs, they function as her own mouthpieces. Again, Sarraute is the 'real author' of this article. In addition, there is a clear 'implied author' presence (Rimmon-Kenan 1983/1997: 87) throughout 'Et toi?'. The true identity of these voices is thus ambiguous and contributes further to the sense of disruption which prevails in 'Et toi'. The slippery nature of these characters could be maintained in the TT by paying close attention to their various, sometimes dissonant, uses of language.

Language constitutes the third source of multidimensionality and instability in this article, and raises diverse issues for the translator. Lili and Roger discuss serious, political subject matter in an informed manner, yet the informal, colloquial language which they use throughout their conversation is opposed to, and therefore contrasts starkly with, such seriousness. In my attempt to preserve this informal register closely in the TT, I used a combination of literal translation and some TL equivalents. Hence,

Et toi, pour qui tu votes? [What about you? Who're you voting for?] and *Pour la gauche, j'ai l'impression que c'est mal barré* [I get the impression the Left's up the creek!]. On occasion, I was, however, more adaptive in my rerenderings of the characters' informal, idiomatic language: *Ouais, ben, la cure d'opposition, très peu pour moi* [Yeah, well, I don't really want the Left to take time out]. And when preserving imagery contained in the ST: *Il a beau avoir été blanchi, il fait encore tache, là* [He may well have had his name cleared, but he's really blotted his copybook].

Roger's informal language frequently becomes vulgar. In order to fully preserve this in the TT, I often remained close to the SL and used TL equivalents: *Avec son putain de bilan et sa campagne à la con* [What with his sodding report and his bloody stupid campaign]. At times, I adopted a slightly freer approach. *Je vous ai mis dans la merde, alors démerdez-vous sans moi* therefore became 'I got you into the shit, so you can get out of it by yourselves'. At other times, however, it was necessary to entirely replace certain vulgar uses in the TL. I considered rerendering Roger's *Chirac avec sa batterie de casseroles au cul* as 'Chirac and hise team of useless arse-licking idiots'. Nevertheless, I felt that, by attempting to preserve the coarseness of the SL in the TT, I would, in this instance, distort the original meaning of Roger's words. I thus referred to an alternative part of the anatomy in the TL: 'Chirac and his team of useless idiots at his elbow'.

In '*Et toi*' it is not only subject matter and language use which clash; contrasting registers of language are themselves juxtaposed. Indeed, the explicitly heteroglossic quality of the characters' language reinforces the instability of this text. Within individual sentences, Lili and Roger employ vocabulary and expressions of very distinct and discordant registers, which I again recaptured through use of TL equivalents, as in the following:

La faute à qui, ça? A tous les inconscients comme toi qui *ont éliminé* Jospin.	Who's to blame for that? All those fools like you who eliminated Jospin.
Fallait les entendre *vitupérer* contre la cohabitation, *les socialos*.	You should've heard the Lefties railing against cohabitation.

In one instance, I also preserved such registers by applying the principle of modulation:

– Il méritait une leçon, Jospin, avec son putain de bilan et sa campagne à la con. – *Une leçon, peut-être, pas un renvoi.*	– Jospin deserved a lesson, what with his sodding report and his bloody stupid campaign. – *Maybe he did, but he didn't deserve to be dismissed.*

The culture-specific subject which the characters discuss is the fourth area of the ST in which instability occurs and which gives rise to particular translation issues. As this article is firmly rooted in a French political context, and marked differences exist between the political systems of the SL and TL cultures, I transposed certain references directly to my TT (*Matignon*), italicizing some to exoticize them in my TT, and provided an explanation of each term in a footer. I also explained a reference to Strauss-Kahn in a footnote. By employing this strategy, I make myself visible as translator.

Sarraute's use of proper names throughout the ST creates further translation issues. These many names belong to a number of opposed political parties and convey a certain sense of instability and confusion in the text. This confusion will be especially apparent amongst TL readers. Given that these names are, once again, deeply embedded in the SL culture, I felt that it would not be feasible to substitute these with TL names and thereby recontextualize the TT. Rather, I transferred all proper names directly to my text. In the interests of concision and clarity, I attached a foreword to my TT, grouping all names cited in the ST according to the political parties to which they belong and detailing the precise nature of these elections and the time at which they took place. Such information is vital if the TL reader is to fully understand the content of the original text. I decided that, by providing this in a foreword, I would avoid both overburdening my TT with numerous footnotes, and confusing my reader by leaving explanation until the end of the text in an attached endnote.

Moreover, the characters' discussion of these politicians appears iconoclastic and therefore extremely unstable. Roger not only condemns politicians collectively (*Et ce gouvernement! Rien que des minables!* [And this government! What a pathetic lot they are!]), but names and insults many individuals. However, it should again be stressed that Sarraute's irreverence is always playful, and encourages social transition and change rather than destruction (Chapters 1 and 2). Drawing inspiration from other satirical publications in the SL and TL cultures (*Le Canard Enchaîné*; *Private Eye*), I translated all such abuse closely, using equivalent TL terms:

Entre ce *ramollo* de Hollande et cet *arriviste* de Fabius.	What with that spineless creature, Hollande, and that ruthless go-getter, Fabius.
Encore un coup de cette *vacharde* et *ramenarde* de Martine Aubry, je te parie.	I bet you that's another of that nasty, boastful Martine Aubry's tricks.
Cet *escroc* de Chirac.	That con-man, Chirac.
Que Chirac et *ses tocards* prennent leurs responsabilités.	Let Chirac and his losers face up to their responsibilities.

Finally, temporal disruption and instability are apparent throughout this article. Lili and Roger's conversation is set in the present and discusses the political situation at that time, but also contains frequent references to past and future events. I preserved all uses of tense and related time phrases closely in the TT. Unlike the majority of Sarraute's writings, '*Et toi*' is not, however, spatially relative nor unstable. As this text is set exclusively in France, the translation issue was one of preserving the original location of the ST in the TT. This arose naturally as I adhered closely to the above-discussed cultural references. Where one particular place in the SL country is mentioned (*Matignon*), I provided additional explanation of this in a footnote, as also discussed previously.

Table 6 The Text

Features of the ST	Range of translation solutions employed	Explanation and justification of approaches adopted	Translation theorists who have influenced my approaches	Practising translators who have influenced my approaches
A) Literary / Generic Issues				
Self-conscious genre	Close. Characters are aware of the genre of the text in which they appear (5)	Could be translated closely in the TL	Vinay & Darbelnet (1958) ('Literal')	Grossman (2004)
Explicit intra- and intergeneric references	Direct transfer. Names of four teen magazines (8)	Will be easily understood by TL audience as these are contrasted with names of TL publications in the text		Crowther (1976)
	Direct transfer + footnote. *L'Huma* (3); *Chéri* (8)	Important SL texts whose nature and content are relevant to the content of STs 3 and 8	Venuti (1995)	Grossman (2004); Radice (1982)
	Close + footnote. *La Rose pourpre du Caire: The Purple Rose of Cairo* (4)	Film was originally a TL text. Footnote provides clarification for contemporary TL audience	Venuti (1995)	
	TL equivalent. Les Guignols: *Spitting Image* (9)	Reference to SL television programme is related to ST character's speech impediment. TL speech impediment must refer to TL show. (See also Table 6 B)	Vinay & Darbelnet (1958) ('Equivalents')	Stroumza (1998)

	Rewrite. 'La Marche du Siècle': 'that discussion programme' (7)	SL programme is criticized in the ST. Would be unreasonable to replace with a TL programme and criticize this in the TT	Lefevere (1992b)	Stroumza (1998)
	Rewrite. 'Phénomène longuement analysé [...], dans *Match*, l'été dernier': 'This phenomenon was analysed at length in a magazine last summer' (8)	Cannot use name of TL publication as this may not have covered the subject matter in question last summer	Lefevere (1992b)	Stroumza (1998)
Generic playfulness	Close. ST does not conform to usual generic norms (1) (9) (10)	Can be preserved by retaining the original format of the ST in the TT	Nida (1964)	
Generic imitation / parody	Close. Titles of articles in teen magazines (8)	Humour transferred in close translation		
	Adapt. One title 'Les hommes se débraguettent': 'Men get unzipped' (8)	Makes TL more idiomatic and reinforces parody in the TT		Bell (1973); Stroumza (1998)
	Adapt / expand. Four multiple-choice answers in magazine quiz (8)	Humour reinforced and made immediately accessible to TL audience. (See also Table 8 A)		Bell (1971); Wright (1958)
	Rewrite. Poetry / rhyme (2)	Literal translation impossible. Rhyme rewritten and reintegrated into TT to reinforce impression of generic cacophony	Lefevere (1992b)	Stroumza (1998); Wright (1958)

Features of the ST	Range of translation solutions employed	Explanation and justification of approaches adopted	Translation theorists who have influenced my approaches	Practising translators who have influenced my approaches
B) Linguistic Issues				
Self-conscious language	Close. 'C'est à cette-heure-ci que tu rentres? [...]' (5)	Possible to closely preserve bizarre nature of expression and subsequent self-consciousness of this in the TL	Nida (1964)	Bell (1973)
Hetero-glossia in the SL (+ self-conscious language)	Close. Current / dated (2); bourgeois / banlieues (8); politics / colloquialisms (10)	Possible to closely preserve distinct and contrasting registers in the TL	Berman (1985)	
	Adapt. Lax pronunciation. 'T'as tes lunettes?': 'You got your glasses?' (6); 'Je sais pas': 'I dunno' (9)	Some adaptation required in the TL	Vinay & Darbelnet (1958) (combination of techniques)	Wright (1960)
	Adapt. Use of idioms (4) (5) (6) (7) (9)	Adaptation required	Vinay & Darbelnet (1958)	Bell (1973)
	Rewrite (+ footnote). Certain varieties of the SL: 'franglais', 'franjeune', 'verlan' (+ self-consciousness) (7)	SL / TL non-equivalence. Language varieties must be rewritten in English	Lefevere (1992b); Lewis (1985)	Emerson (1984); Nétillard (1973)

Use of vulgar language	Close. 'J'en ai rien à cirer' vs. 'Je m'en fous': 'I don't give a monkey's' vs. 'I don't give a shit' (4) (9)	Contrasting registers have functional equivalents in TL	Vinay & Darbelnet (1958) ('Equivalents')	Landers (2001); Pilard (2002); Wright (1960)
	Adapt. 'vieux con': 'silly bugger' (2); 'ce petit con': 'the little bugger' (4). BUT 'sale con': 'bastard' (9); 'salaud': 'bastard' (5)	Non-equivalence of SL and TL expletives. Rerendering depends on context and precise nature of individual utterances	Tabakowska (1990)	
	'crotte'; 'cack'; 'merde': 'crap' (4) 'tous les emmerdes'; 'all the shit'; 'ma petite crotte': 'my crappy little article' (5) 'Ce sont des mal baisées': 'They're in need of a good shag' (3)			
Linguistic playfulness	Equivalent + compensation. 'On peut aussi donner dans la chinoiserie: veuve Mao pour Yvette Roudy': 'You could also get unnecessarily complicated and use foreign references: "widow Mao" for Yvette Roudy' (2)	As TL equivalent results in loss of SL pun, this must be compensated for in the TT	Lefevere (1992b)	Bell (1973)
	Adapt. Pidginization of the SL. 'Vous pas avoir carte français?': 'You no have French menu?' (6)	Grammatical inaccuracies can be recreated in the TL		

Features of the ST	Range of translation solutions employed	Explanation and justification of approaches adopted	Translation theorists who have influenced my approaches	Practising translators who have influenced my approaches
	Rewrite. Neologisms. 'diplopotame': 'diplopotamus' (4); 'papy-sitter': 'grampy-sitter' (4); 'choupinet': 'sweetie-weetie' (5); 'papa poule et maman coq': 'doting dad and modern-day mum' (5); 'fifils': 'sonny-wonny' (6)	Playful use of SL can be mirrored in the TL	Lefevere (1992b)	
	Rewrite. Puns. 'cinéma' (4); 's'éclater' (4); multiple double-entendres (5); 'chinois' (6)	Impossible to translate closely such uses of the SL. Rewriting is dictated by semantic and lexical non-equivalence between the SL and TL	Landers (2001); Lefevere (1992b)	Bell (1999); Girard (2001); Stroumza (1998)
	Rewrite. Titles of articles, including playful uses of the SL (1) (2) (3) (9)	These can be recreated in the TL	Nida (1964); Lefevere (1992b)	
	Rewrite. Plays with SL sounds 'u' and 'ou' (+ self-consciousness) (9)	SL sounds and speech impediment do not exist in the TL. Decision to rewrite also has impact on rerendering of certain SL cultural references (Table 8)	Benjamin (1923); Lefevere (1992b); Venuti (1995)	Wright (1958)

Category	Examples / technique	Description	Vinay & Darbelnet (1958) (combination of techniques)	Landers (2001)
Multitonality	Close. Variety of dissonant tones juxtaposed in the ST (1–10) (especially 3 and 10)	These can be closely preserved in the TT	Vinay & Darbelnet (1958) (combination of techniques)	Landers (2001)
Hetero-glossia (other)	Adapt. SL spoken with foreign accent. Guadeloupian (1); German (5)	Must transpose foreign accents from SL to TL words	Berman (1985)	
Polyglossia	Direct transfer. Words from Italian menu, including erroneous uses (6)	Preserve linguistic hybrid, exoticism and humour of the ST	Berman (1985); Venuti (1995)	
	Direct transfer. TL expressions 'Have sex' / 'make love' (8)	Retain inverted commas to preserve in the TT Sarraute's awareness of the TL		
	Transfer and naturalize. *Package tours*: package tours (6)	ST italics removed in the TT. No need to draw attention to this term in the TL		Hammond (1994)
	Equivalent use. 'bye-bye': 'ciao' (4)	'bye-bye' has foreign resonance in ST but not in the TT. Use of 'ciao' is current in the TL yet also exotic		Wright (1960)

Table 7 The Participants

Features of the ST	Range of translation solutions employed	Explanation and justification of approaches adopted	Translation theorists who have influenced my approaches	Practising translators who have influenced my approaches
A) Author (or narrator)				
Portrayal / position	Close. Sarraute is self-conscious, her self-view sometimes unclear, her opinions conflicting, and her position unstable (4) (5)	All of these qualities can be preserved by remaining close to the language and content of the ST in the TL	Vinay & Darbelnet (1958) (combination of techniques)	Crowther (1976); Grossman (2004)
	Close + footnote. Sarraute's cultural origin (1)	Footnote provided to explain autobiographical dimension of the ST	Venuti (1995)	Grossman (2004)
B) Characters				
In relation to the author (or narrator)	Close. Sarraute attempts to control her characters but they sometimes remain fiercely independent (4)	Such tendencies can be closely translated in the TL	Vinay & Darbelnet (1958) (combination of techniques)	Landers (2001)
Proper names	Direct transferral. French names (2–10) French / foreign names (7)	Preserve Frenchness of ST in the TT Preserve multiculturalism of ST in the TT		Stroumza (1998) Wright (1960)

	Example	Explanation	Theorist	References
C) Readers (or narratees)	TL equivalent. 'Jules': 'Guy' (8)	Dual meaning of SL 'Jules' (male Christian name / term for 'boyfriend') needs to be preserved in the TL		Belmont & Chabrier (1972); Cohen (1955); Landers (2001)
Addresses and responses	Close. Sarraute addresses her audience and anticipates reactions to herself / her work (2) (3) (4) (5) (7) (8)	Can be maintained by adhering to the language and tones used in the ST. There is no need to modify or adapt these	Vinay & Darbelnet (1958)	
D) Gender				Crowther (1976); Stroumza (1998)
Portrayal	Close. Sarraute addresses males and females, alternately takes the side of each sex and presents her characters, who are often gendered stereotypes, in relation to one another (3) (8)	These tendencies are communicated semantically, in the behaviour and actions of the characters, and linguistically, through their speech. It was possible to preserve these in the TT by remaining in close proximity to the content and language of the ST		
	Adapt. 'Eux [...]. Nous [...]': 'The men [...]. We women [...]' (8)	Addition of TL nouns to clarify male and female pronouns used in the SL		
	Rewrite. 'qu'une poire blette séduise un fruit vert': 'if a shrivelled prune seduces an unripe banana' (8)	Symbolic uses of fruits replaced with alternatives in the TL to recapture the concept of mixed-generation relationships and the sexual connotations contained in the ST	Nida (1964)	

Table 8 Social, Cultural, and Political Issues

Features of the ST	Range of translation solutions employed	Explanation and justification of approaches adopted	Translation theorists who have influenced my approaches	Practising translators who have influenced my approaches
A) The SL Culture			Bassnett & Lefevere (eds. 1990; 1998). (Relationship between culture and translation)	
Proper names	Direct transfer + footnote. 'Coluche' (4); 'Alain Delon' (6)	Important cultural references which are relevant to content of ST but probably unknown to TL audience	Venuti (1995)	Stroumza (1998)
	Direct transfer + foreword. Multiple names of politicians quoted randomly (10)	Names are rooted in French political context and so cannot be substituted with names of politicians in the TL culture. Foreword used to provide TL readership with clarification before embarking upon the TT	Berman (1985); Venuti (1995)	Ledoux (1958); Nabokov (1964)
	Close. Insulting of politicians (2) (10)	Important to preserve iconoclasm of the ST in the TT		Landers (2001)

Example	Comment	Reference(s)
		Cohen (1955)
Close + footnote. 'Veuve Mao': 'Widow Mao' (2)	Footnote makes reference immediately accessible to contemporary TL audience	Venuti (1995)
TL equivalents. 'Séguéla': 'Max Clifford' (2) 'Edith Piaf et Théo Sarapo ou Alain-Fournier et Madame Simone': 'Joan Collins and Percy Gibson or Barbara Windsor and Scott Harvey' (8)	Use of approximately equivalent individuals in the TL culture entails no loss in the TT and avoids overuse of footnotes	Venuti (1995); Vinay & Darbelnet (1958) ('Equivalents')
'Johnny Hallyday': 'Jonathan Ross' (9)	TL personality with TL speech impediment is required in the TT	
Rewrite. 'Des expressions telles que sagouin, ça prouve qu'on a lu Mauriac, ça fait cultivé': 'Expressions which prove that you're well-read and which look cultured' (2)	Mauriac is mentioned in relation to use of the SL word 'sagouin'. Translation of this term would not be noteworthy in the TL and, when translated, the word would no longer be associated with this writer. Rewriting of this sentence avoids complicated and unnecessary footnotes	Lefevere (1992b); Venuti (1995)
Rewrite. 'I.V.G. pour V.G.E.': 'V.E.D. (Vehicle Excise Duty) for V.G.E. (Valéry Giscard d'Estaing)	Use of TL acronym which contains similar letters to the original. Explanation of the two acronyms used in the TT is also provided as these will be less familiar to the TL readership than are the SL acronyms to the SL audience	Lefevere (1992b)

Features of the ST	Range of translation solutions employed	Explanation and justification of approaches adopted	Translation theorists who have influenced my approaches	Practising translators who have influenced my approaches
	Rewrite. 'Sulitzer et d'Ormesson': 'academics and financial experts' (5) 'On croirait entendre la mère Boutin': 'You sound like a right homophobe' (9)	Oblique explanation avoids any loss in the TT and removes need for footnotes		Stroumza (1998)
Cultural terms and references	Direct transfer. 'Le Métro' (3) (5)	Term is likely to be familiar to TL audience. Italics exoticize the TT / Possibly not familiar to TL audience, but meaning can be inferred from context. Term exoticizes TT without alienating its readership	Venuti (1995) / Berman (1985)	Hammond (1994)
	'La Foire du Livre' (5)	Important cultural information which may not be understood by TL audience. (Exoticism)	Venuti (1995)	Grossman (2004); Manheim (1983)
	Direct transfer + footnote. 'Sciences-Po' (4); 'minitel' (5); 'PaCS' (9); 'Matignon' (10); 'cohabitation' (10)	These involve no loss in the TT	Venuti (1995)	Stroumza (1998)

TL equivalents. 'MLF': 'Women's Lib' (3); 'un élu conservateur': 'a conservative Member of Parliament' (8); 'un député': 'an M.P' (8); '2B3': 'Boyzone' (9)	TL functional equivalent (droit de seigneur) sounds unnatural in the TL and may not be familiar to younger readers of the TT	Lefevere (1992b)	Stroumza (1998)
Rewrite. 'droit de cuissage': 'the sexual harassment of employees by their employers (3)	Neither of the French university qualifications named has an exact equivalent in the TL culture. Additional explanation of these French terms would not enhance the TL audience's appreciation of the text	Lefevere (1992b)	Stroumza (1998)
Rewrite. 'De Deug en agrég': 'Throughout their time at university' (8)	Cultural terms dealt with obliquely to reinforce humour contained in the ST and to make all references immediately accessible to a contemporary TT readership	Lefevere (1992b) Nida (1964)	
Rewrite. Cultural terms used in quiz: 'un boeuf bourguignon, le 14 Juillet, l'Arlésienne, la Grosse Bertha': a slap-up meal, a summer bank holiday, a rousing piece of classical music, a huge missile-firing weapon' (8)			

Features of the ST	Range of translation solutions employed	Explanation and justification of approaches adopted	Translation theorists who have influenced my approaches	Practising translators who have influenced my approaches
B) Other cultures				
Language	Various approaches (1) (5) (6) (8)	See Heteroglossia (other) and Polyglossia (Table 6)		
Proper names	Direct transfer. 'Frauhelfeldkommandant Lolotte' (5)	Retains foreign and humorous effect of original	Nida (1964)	Butt (1947); Cameron (1997); Wright (1960)
	Direct transfer. African Christian names. 'Koebé'; 'Karim' (7)	Preserves impression of multicultural community in the TT	Nida (1964)	
	Direct transfer. 'Woody Allen' (4); 'de Niro' (6); 'Jack Nicholson' (8)	TL audience will be familiar with famous English and American personalities		
	Direct transfer + footnote. 'Pirandello' (4)	Italian playwright may be unknown to anglophone readers	Venuti (1995)	Stroumza (1998)
Cultural terms and references	Direct transfer. Italian food / dishes (6)	Preservation of these creates the same foreignizing effect on the TT audience as that which is experienced by French readers	Nida (1964); Venuti (1995)	

Close. Italian stereotypes (6)	These exist throughout the Western world		Stroumza (1998)
TL equivalent. 'Les Ritals': 'Eyeties' (6)	Equivalent term of racial abuse is used in the TL	Vinay & Darbelnet (1958) ('Equivalents'); Lefevere (1992b); Venuti (1995)	Landers (2001); Pons (1965); Wright (1960)
Approximate translation (+ footnote). 'une femme-relais': 'a duty-wife' (7)	This concept does not exist in the West. It is appropriate to preserve the 'foreignness' of this term and to explain it in a footnote		
Rewrite. 'La chienne de Buchenwald': 'some Nazi in a concentration camp' (5)	Captures most of the connotations of the original and avoids both an unnatural translation and the need for a footnote	Venuti (1995)	
Rewrite. 'Il réclame le carré blanc': '[He] is calling for this publication to be classed as unsuitable for children under sixteen' (8)	SL term is used in the ST to describe an event in the TL culture. This needs to be transferred back to its original context in the TT	Venuti (1995)	

Table 9 Time and Space

Features of the ST	Range of translation solutions employed	Explanation and justification of approaches adopted	Translation theorists who have influenced my approaches	Practising translators who have influenced my approaches
A) Time	Close. Tenses and time-related phrases, where time is either stable or disrupted in the ST (1–10)	Close translation is appropriate on most occasions		Crowther (1976); Hammond (1994)
	Equivalents. '[...] on n'ose pas, on hésite, on a peur de prendre une gifle': [...] you didn't dare, you hesitated, you were afraid to get a slap in the face' (3)	Uses of SL and TL tenses do not correspond exactly. Simple past tense better conveys notion of past time in TL		
	Adaptation. Certain uses of tense in the SL. 'Il serait assis là... Il l'aurait invitée à dîner...': 'She's imagining him sat there... She's imagining that he's asked her to dinner' (6)	Adaptation / expansion is required in order to fully convey in the TL the uses of tense in the SL		
B) Space References to places	Direct transfer. 'Besançon' (3)	Preserves text's original French setting. Even if SL audience does not know Besançon, they can infer that it is a French town from the context in which it appears	Venuti (1995)	Wright (1960)
	Direct transfer + footnote. 'Rue St Denis' (5); 'Matignon' (10)	Maintains Frenchness of original texts in the TTs. Provides important cultural information, enhancing TL audience's appreciation of the text	Venuti (1995)	Manheim (1983)

	Direct transfer + oblique. '[...] en Auvergne': '[...] in the Auvergne region' (6); '[...] de la Tour du Pin': '[...] from the Tour du Pin region' (6); '[...] aux Œillets': '[...] in the Les Œillets estate' (7)	Retains original French references. Provides subtle explanation of places which do not require detailed explanation in footers	Vinay & Darbelnet (1958) ('Adaptation')	Hammond (1994)
	Close. 'En Suède et aux États-Unis': 'In Sweden and the United States' (3); 'Le Midi': 'the South of France' (4); 'Marrakech' / 'Venise' / Venetian sights (6)	Standard TL translations can be used	Vinay & Darbelnet (1958) ('Literal')	Cohen (1955); Crowther (1976); Hammond (1994):
	Rewrite. 'Ici': 'In France' (3)	Sarraute's use of 'ici' refers to France and so cannot be translated as 'here' for TL readers who live elsewhere	Lefevere (1992b)	Wynne (2002)
	Rewrite. 'Le Doubs': 'Eastern France' (3); 'boulevard Malesherbes': 'their home' (4); 'le bar de la paillotte': 'the beach bar' (9)	Rewriting provides explanation of places cited in the ST and avoids overburdening the TT with footnotes	Lefevere (1992b)	Stroumza (1998)
Setting of the ST	Close. Political context (2) (10)	Setting must be preserved when ST is deeply embedded in French political context	Venuti (1995)	
	Rewrite. Self-conscious uses of SL (including references to places). 'A Fourneron [...] le verlan, personne ne le comprend': '[...], nobody here understands back slang' (7)	The TL must become equally self-conscious and related references to places must also be adapted to the TL culture	Lefevere (1992b)	Grossman (2004); Manheim (1983)

Explanation of Tables

Table 6, 'The Text', is sub-divided into two sections: 'Literary and Generic Issues' and 'Linguistic Issues'. The first of these illustrates that certain textual features of Sarraute's writings can always be rendered closely in the TL (self-conscious genre, generic playfulness) and that this approach has been inspired by a number of theoretical methodologies (Vinay and Darbelnet) and by the approaches of certain practising translators (Grossman). This section of the table does, however, suggest that there are many more literary and generic features (intra- and intergeneric references, generic imitation and parody) which lend themselves to a broader range of translation approaches. My use of these was influenced by the work of some very diverse theorists (from Nida and Vinay and Darbelnet, to Lefevere and Venuti) and practitioners (from Crowther, Grossman, and Radice, to Bell, Stroumza, and Wright).

Similarly, as emerges in the second section of Table 6, some of the linguistic features of Sarraute's texts could always be rerendered closely in the TL (self-conscious language, multi-tonality). This approach, which was determined with reference to the above-mentioned theorists, was also adopted by such practitioners as Bell and Landers. Nevertheless, other (dialogic) uses of language in Sarraute required that I adopt very different strategies. Where Sarraute pidginizes the French language, uses neologisms and puns, plays with sounds in the SL, and imitates foreign accents, I was similarly playful with the TL. When formulating my approach, I drew on the theoretical works of Berman, Benjamin, Lefevere, and Venuti, and on the TTs of Bell, Stroumza, and Wright. Moreover, other dialogic language in Sarraute, that is, various instances of heteroglossia and polyglossia, could, I felt, be best rerendered through use of a variety of translation strategies. In such cases, I referred specifically to the work of Berman, Lefevere, Lewis, Tabakowska, and Venuti, and to translations by Bell, Emerson, Nétillard, Pilard, and Wright.

My seventh table demonstrates that, when rerendering issues pertaining to the text's participants (author (or narrator), characters, readers), similar trends emerge. For instance, it was, at all times, possible to recapture closely in the TT the portrayal and position of the socially constructed author (or narrator), her relationship with her interactive characters, and the ways in which she both addresses her readers (or narratees) and anticipates their responses to herself and to her work. Once again, the practicable methodologies of Vinay and Darbelnet, and certain concepts discussed by Venuti, guided me in this process, as did the translations of a number of practitioners, including those of Belmont and Chabrier, Cohen, Crowther, and Grossman. This said, when rerendering in my TTs the names of the text's participants and the portrayal of their genders, I implemented a greater range of translation strategies and, in doing so, consulted the work of a variety of academics and practising translators.

Recapturing those features of Sarraute's writings which relate to social, cultural, and political issues required use of a slightly different balance of translation approaches. As is demonstrated in Table 8, no features of Sarraute's texts which occurred in this category, be these within French or other societies and cultures, lent themselves to exclusively close or free translation. Rather, it seemed appropriate to rerender each of these, including proper names and cultural terms and references, by applying a considerably broader selection of techniques. These ranged from direct transferrals of SL items and provision of explanatory footnotes or a foreword, through use of close translation methods and TL equivalents, to complete rewritings of the original. As was the case in the two above categories, when recapturing social, cultural, and political issues in this collection of TTs, I took inspiration from an amalgam of theorists and practitioners, amongst whom: Butt, Cameron, Ledoux, Manheim, Nabokov, and Pons.

The findings recorded in my eighth and final table, 'Time and Space', are more in line with those in Tables 6 and 7. Certain temporal features (use of contrasting tenses and time-related phrases) could mostly, but not exclusively, be recaptured closely in my ten TTs. By contrast, transferral of references to space, or places, which are made in the collection of STs required that I employ a wider spectrum of techniques, and these were influenced by a number of the above-mentioned theorists and practitioners.

Thus, the ten preceding commentaries and my four sets of tabulated empirical findings (Tables 6 to 9) indicate three important conclusions. First, although certain significant features of Sarraute's writings can be rerendered by employing either entirely close, or solely free, translation strategies, in the majority of cases, the translation issues and challenges to which individual features of these STs give rise cannot always be dealt with in one uniform manner. The way in which each and every peculiar quality of these STs can be best rendered in the TL must, therefore, be judged separately, according to its particular nature and context. Second, by extension, as each polyphonic ST is such a *sui generis* dialogic medley, the rerendering of such texts requires application of an equally unique and eclectic blend of translation solutions. When I spoke to Sarraute, she stressed that, if rerendered in the TL, her writings must be entirely rewritten. However, this second conclusion reinforces the suggestion made in Chapter 3 that this is not necessarily the most appropriate approach to adopt towards rerendering her work. Finally, when recapturing in the TL individual (dialogic) features of Sarraute and, indeed, extended and entirely polyphonic extracts from Sarraute's writings, the translator can be greatly assisted by reference to elements of both translation theory and practice. The present findings therefore fully support the theses of Chapters 3 and 4.

Conclusion

As written works are always deeply imbued with the ideologies and values of the society in which they are produced (Medvedev 1928), the 'archetypal' postmodern text is a thoroughly fragmented and unstable entity (Eagleton 1987; Hassan 1985) which crosses generic boundaries and flouts discursive norms, calling into question the roles of the text's participants, hybridizing and satirizing societies and cultures, and playing with notions of time and space. Similarly, the transfer of any text from one national language to another reflects the ethos of a given period (Gentzler 2001) and approaches to this have consequently multiplied over time. Thus, if translation has always been a challenging process, it appeared to become particularly so in the late twentieth century. Not only are translators now frequently confronted with fragmented, decentred STs, so too are they operating in a climate in which a plethora of conflicting approaches to translation coexist (Gentzler 2001; Munday 2001; Venuti 2000).

Against this background, *Preserving Polyphonies* contended that, to date, translation theory currently offers no satisfactory response to the multidimensional challenge of rerendering postmodern texts. If many theorists now recognize the impossibility of achieving complete equivalence in translation and, when rerendering the fragmented, decentred postmodern text, a process of 'rewriting' is instead deemed more appropriate (Lefevere 1992a; 1992b), examination of a number of key concepts from some of the major phases of translation theory nevertheless suggests that such an approach may not always be the most suitable. Through both detailed investigation and practical application, this work therefore set out to determine effective means by which the translator may read and analyse the postmodern ST and subsequently preserve its many intricacies in the TL.

The writings of the contemporary French journalist and novelist, Claude Sarraute, which epitomize fragmented, unstable and dynamic postmodern texts and which had, hitherto, been neither studied in depth nor translated into English, were taken as the medium through which to explore this issue. With reference to those insights gained through personal contact with Sarraute (Landers 2001: 86–8), this writer's background was first outlined and a potted history of her career provided in order to trace the evolution of her work from the journalistic to literary, or novelistic, genre. It was suggested that, over the years, Sarraute has striven to forge her own identity as a columnist and novelist, producing her own distinctive, idiosyncratic, reactive and subversive texts. Four key areas of Sarraute's writings were then considered – 'The Text', 'The Participants', 'Social, Cultural, and Political Issues', and 'Time and Space' –, so as to demonstrate both the close relationship which exists between her journalistic articles and her later literary texts, and the development of her work. Throughout her career, Sarraute has produced open, fluctuating and humorous texts which transcend a number of established norms and boundaries and are, at times, distinctly iconoclastic.

It was established that certain of the key tenets of the work of the Bakhtin Circle, namely those of dialogism and the polyphonic text (Bakhtin 1929), constitute a suitable paradigm which can assist in theorizing post-modern writings as involved as those of Sarraute. The concept of dialogism, which unifies the Circle's work (Pearce 1994; Todorov 1939/1995) and which draws on the notions of dialogue, interactivity, interrelatedness and power-inscribed relationships, can help to account for a wide range of the unstable and dynamic qualities apparent in the four above-mentioned areas of Sarraute's work. The present study was thus essentially Bakhtin-driven. The quadripartite approach to the classification of Sarraute's writings, which became a leitmotif throughout *Preserving Polyphonies*, was a product of the Bakhtin Circle's work and later served as a benchmark against which to assess the success of my translations of Sarraute. In contrast to a number of other studies which tend to employ only one or two aspects of Bakhtinian philosophy when analysing a given ST (Berman 1985; Kumar & Malshe n.d.; Muhawi n.d.; Tabakowska 1990), this work applied the Circle's thought in a variety of ways (Pearce 1994; Todorov 1981/1984) in order to theorize the postmodern text before proposing solutions to the exclusive translation issues to which each of its particular features gives rise. Thus, it intended to provide a wide-ranging response to this multidimensional challenge.

Given the dynamic character and multiple complexities of Sarraute's work, it was deemed necessary to determine how one can effectively read, and subsequently translate, these writings. A rapid review of an eclectic range of theories of textual and stylistic analysis and reader-response criticism suggested that few established approaches in these fields can satisfactorily account for the reading of texts as intensely dispersed and variegated in character as those of Sarraute. For instance, while the hermeneuticians acknowledge the interactive role of the reader, they tend to presume that written texts have a definite 'core' and an authorial figure whose intention is clearly defined (Spitzer 1962), neither of which is the case in Sarraute. Similarly, if thinkers belonging to the formalist and structuralist movements adopt a rigorous approach to textual analysis, they generally attach little importance to the reader's role in this process; their approach is essentially static rather than dynamic. A more appropriate strategy for reading Sarraute should, it appears, both acknowledge the context-bound nature of these texts (Foucault 1969, 1971; Van Dijk 1995), and combine a subjective and open approach to their reading with systematic and close methods of analysis (Fish 1970; Riffaterre 1966).[1]

In this connection, it was suggested that, despite some fundamental differences between Bakhtin and Derrida, when considered collectively, aspects of their work can offer a more fruitful framework in which to examine texts such as Sarraute's. Bakhtin (1970–1/1986: 75) acknowledged the interactive role of the reader and advocated not solely a dynamic approach to literary analysis (1941/1981: 8) but also 'a *sociological* stylistics' (1934–5/1981: 300).[2] Moreover, Derridean thought can both account for individuality in the reading of such writings, and assist identification of the peculiar qualities of polyphonic texts themselves. In his coining of the neologism *différance*, Derrida posits that the very nature of words renders

[1]   As each *act of reading* is a unique dialogue between the reader and the text, it would, nevertheless, be impossible to recommend an exact boundary, or desirable balance, between systematization and subjectivity of approach.

[2]   Despite his advocation of dynamic and sociological approaches, Bakhtin, unlike theorists such as Fish (1970), Riffaterre (1966), and Spitzer (1962), did not propose precise methodologies of textual and stylistic analysis.

impossible any complete representation of meaning in language; consequently, all written texts lend themselves to infinite possible interpretations.
It is on this term that his deconstructionist method is also founded. Derrida
(1967a) argues that, as all concepts in society are grounded in language, and
as language is inescapably unstable, all conceptual hierarchies in society can
be destroyed, or deconstructed. When applied to this study, the concept
of *différance* encourages the reader to form a thoroughly communicative,
interactive relationship with Sarraute's writings, reading her texts subjectively, or *openly*, and supplementing them with new meaning. Moreover,
adoption of Derrida's approach enables *close* stylistic analysis of Sarraute's
texts. By breaking down the text into its smallest components, deconstructing and interrogating it, the analyst can, it was argued, maximize their own
understanding of Sarraute and thus become a well-informed interlocutor
of her polyphonies.

The notions of dialogue and interlocution are equally fundamental to
the process of translation (Kelly 1979; Mounin 1963; Robinson 1991; Youzi
2006); as interlocutor, the translator enters into a dynamic, communicative relationship with the ST. At this juncture it was posited that, if the
translator is to preserve in the TL the peculiar qualities of the polyphonic
ST, they are required to employ particular instruments, and to possess
certain insights, which can be supplied by translation theory.[3] Due to the
multivoiced, heterogeneous, satirical and ludic character of postmodern,
polyphonic texts, it may seem appropriate to adopt a free, adaptive and
comparably playful approach to their rerendering. Interestingly, when asked
about the most suitable method of translating her work, Sarraute herself
was emphatic that: *Il faut pas le traduire, il faut le récrire.* [...]. *Il faut trans-
poser complètement* [You shouldn't translate it, you should rewrite it [...].
It should be completely transposed]. These firm beliefs notwithstanding,
detailed examination of a number of key concepts from some of the major
phases of translation theory (from the Bible-centred approaches of Cicero

---

3   Owing to the unique and dynamic nature of the *act of translation*, it would also be
     impossible to establish where the translator's subjective involvement in this process
     should end, and where his debt to theory should begin.

and St Jerome, to the dynamic and deconstructionist work of Bakhtin and Derrida respectively) sought to establish that, while the translator of Sarraute's work can, at times, rewrite elements of her STs (Lefevere 1992b), at other times they are actually required to implement a very close translation approach and to demonstrate a high degree of linguistic precision. As each of Sarraute's polyphonic text is such a *sui generis* amalgam of distinct features, no single translation theory or unified translation approach can fully assist their rerendering. Rather, the translator would be better advised to interact with, and apply, an eclectic blend of translation approaches (Ellender 2006b: 160–1).[4] These range from elements of Nida's (1964) formal and dynamic equivalence and Vinay and Darbelnet's (1958) seven-part translation methodology to Lefevere's (1992a; 1992b) concept of rewriting, Lewis's (1985) Derrida-influenced abusive fidelity and Venuti's (1995) domesticating and foreignizing strategies. For these reasons it would, moreover, be impracticable to predetermine the precise combination of theoretical translation insights and practical translation instruments which any one translator of a given (polyphonic) text could reasonably draw on and implement. This recommendation sits closely in line with recent thinking on translation. In the concluding chapter of his *Contemporary Translation Theories*, Gentzler (2001: 203) recalls past and present 'dialogues' between translation scholars of different persuasions before pronouncing himself 'in favour of the implementation of multiple theories of translation from a variety of disciplines and discourses'. He states that: 'We are at the verge of an exciting new phase of research for the field, one that is forcing scholars to combine theories and resources from a variety of disciplines and which is leading to new insights' (ibid.: 203). Venuti (2000: 333–4) arrives at similar conclusions when summarizing the contents of his anthology.[5]

---

4   In Chapters 3 and 5 it was argued that, if the translator is to be eclectic, he can avoid contradictions in his approach by clearly establishing at the outset the *skopos* of his TTs (Vermeer 1989), the nature of his TL audience, and his resulting translation strategy.

5   Although, in his discussion of Translation Studies as an interdiscipline, Munday (2001: 190) expresses some reservations (individual translators do not, in his opinion,

In Translation Studies, the mutually complementary nature of theory and practice is also being increasingly acknowledged (Chesterman & Wagner 2002; Gentzler 2001; Hartley 2004; Robinson 2012). In order to complement the preceding theoretical investigation, the question of rerendering polyphonic texts was examined from a practical perspective. An eclectic body of some thirty STs which are definable as polyphonic and their corresponding TTs were referred to. Using the four recurring categories it was illustrated how the particular qualities of these works, which are also features of Sarraute's writings and can be theorized by referring to the work of the Bakhtin Circle, had been rerendered variously in the TL. When rerendering Sarraute's writings, it was demonstrated that the translator can learn important lessons and make informed pragmatic choices by drawing on the TTs of other practising translators of polyphonies. These include Crowther's 1976 translation of Lainé's *La Dentellière*, Nabokov's 1964 translation of Pushkin's *Eugene Onegin* and Radice's 1982 translation of Erasmus's *Praise of Folly*, all of which are based on a predominantly close approach. Of equal interest and assistance are Bell's 1973 translation of Goscinny's *Astérix chez les Bretons*, Grossman's 2004 translation of Cervantes's *Don Quixote*, Stroumza's 1998 translation of Fielding's *Bridget Jones's Diary* and Wright's 1958 translation of Queneau's *Exercices de Style*, which combine some close rerenderings with much more radical, inventive and playful rewrites. Again, no uniform approach, or exact combination of practical translation strategies, can therefore be prescribed to any one translator of any one (polyphonic) ST. Building on this argument,[6] and on the useful instruments and relevant insights which the translator can acquire by referring to the work of diverse theorists, a balanced framework was proposed in order to guide the rerendering of Sarraute.

---

have the necessary expertise in a sufficiently wide range of areas to render their work truly interdisciplinary), like his contemporaries, he recognizes the advantages of adopting such an integrated approach which can 'bridge the gap between linguistic and cultural studies'.

6   Chapter 4 sought to explain these findings. In doing so, it argued that choice of translation strategy is always determined by multiple factors which are at play at each level of the dialogic process of translation.

Unlike previous translation theory which, to date, offers no satisfactory nor sufficiently wide-ranging response to the multidimensional challenge of rerendering postmodern texts, *Preserving Polyphonies* sought to establish that, by adopting an approach to the reading and analysis of the ST which is dynamic, subjective and systematic, and by implementing a heterogeneous blend of theoretical and practical translation strategies, the translator, as interlocutor of the postmodern, polyphonic text, can ensure that their methodology is sufficiently thorough and balanced. Accordingly, when rerendering in English my collection of ten extracts from Sarraute's writings, I first read each of these dynamically and interactively, supplementing them with my subjective interpretations. I then engaged in close stylistic analyses of these writings, so as to gain an appreciation of their various qualities. When subsequently embarking upon their translation, I made a number of decisions based on my existing knowledge, was inspired by other sources of information,[7] and drew on those insights which I had gained during my study of translation theory and practice. Individually and collectively, my resulting TTs were produced, and Sarraute's original polyphonies preserved, by employing a unique combination of translation strategies, from close rerenderings (heteroglossia in Extracts 1 and 2 and political figures in Extracts 2 and 10), to much freer and adaptive rewritings of poetry (Extract 2), symbolic use of language (Extract 8), and a speech impediment (Extract 9). My translations were, then, not only entirely personal, which was reflected in my deliberate use of the first person throughout my commentaries, but also carefully considered responses to Sarraute's writings.

Thus, in order to respond effectively to any one postmodern, polyphonic ST, the translator/interlocutor, a dynamic, interactive being, can situate themselves, and is at liberty to negotiate their exact position, within a Bakhtinian-cum-Derridean framework and a contemporary Translation

---

7   As a socially constructed being, I was influenced by many other factors and sources when rerendering Sarraute. These ranged from my existing knowledge of German (Extract 5), through the poetry of Benjamin Zephaniah (Extract 1) and an edition of Berlitz's travel guides (Extract 7), to recent copies of magazines such as *Cosmopolitan* (Extract 8) and *Private Eye* (Extract 10).

Studies paradigm. As Robinson (1991: 100) advocates when devising his Bakhtin-inspired, dialogic method of translation: 'What we need is a conception of relation and dialogue that commingles not only sound and sense, and not only self and other, but also theory and practice'. The dialogue is, as it were, never-ending.

Bibliography

Álvarez, Roman, & M. Carmen África Vidal (eds). 1996. *Translation, Power, Subversion* (Clevedon: Multilingual Matters).

Auerbach, Erich. 1946. *Mimesis: The Representation of Reality in Western Literature*, trans. by Willard R. Trask, 1968 (Princeton, NJ: Princeton University Press).

Baker, Mona (ed.). 1998. *The Routledge Encyclopedia of Translation Studies* (London: Routledge).

Bakhtin, Mikhail. 1929. *Problems of Dostoevsky's Poetics* / 1961. *Toward a Reworking of the Dostoevsky Book*, ed. and trans. by Caryl Emerson (Minneapolis: University of Minnesota Press).

———. 1934–41. *The Dialogic Imagination: Four Essays by M.M. Bakhtin*, ed. by Michael Holquist, trans. by Caryl Emerson, 1981 (Austin: University of Texas Press) ('Epic and Novel', 1941; 'From the Prehistory of Novelistic Discourse' 1940; 'Forms of Time and of the Chronotope in the Novel' 1937–8; 'Discourse in the Novel' 1934–5).

———. 1965. *Rabelais and His World*, trans. by Hélène Iswolsky, 1968/1984 (Bloomington, IN: Indiana University Press).

———. 1979. *Speech Genres and Other Late Essays*, ed. by Caryl Emerson and Michael Holquist, trans. by Vern W. McGee, 1986 (Austin: University of Texas Press).

Baldick, Chris (ed.). 1990. *The Concise Oxford Dictionary of Literary Terms* (Oxford: Oxford University Press).

Barthes, Roland. 1968. 'The death of the author' in *Image, Music, Text*, 1979, trans. by Stephen Heath (London: Fontana) pp. 142–8.

———. 1970. *S/Z* trans. by Richard Miller, preface by Richard Howard (London: Cape).

———. 1981. *The Pursuit of Signs: Semiotics, Literature, Deconstruction* (London: Routledge).

Bassnett, Susan. 1980/1991 rev edn. *Translation Studies* (London: Routledge).

———. 1997. *Translating Literature* (Cambridge: D.S. Brewer).

———. 2003. 'Theory and practice: the old dilemma', *ITI Bulletin*, November-December, pp. 18–19.

Bassnett, Susan, & André Lefevere (eds). 1990. *Translation, History and Culture* (London: Pinter).

———. 1998. *Constructing Cultures: Essays on Literary Translation* (Clevedon: Multilingual Matters).

Bell, Anthea. 25 February 1999. 'Astérix, my love'. Electronic Telegraph, issue 1371. <http://www.asterix-international.de/asterix/mirror/asterix_my_love.htm> (accessed 18.05.04).

Benjamin, Walter. 1923. 'The task of the translator', in *Illuminations* 1968/1973, ed. and intro. by Hannah Arendt, trans. by Harry Zohn (London: Fontana) pp. 69–82.

Berman, Antoine. 1985. 'Translation and the trials of the foreign', trans. by L. Venuti, in L. Venuti (ed.), 2000, pp. 284–97.

Breakwell, Glynis. M. 1990. *Interviewing and Problems in Practice*, BPS Books (London: Routledge).

Burgess, Anthony. 1962/2000. 2nd edn. *A Clockwork Orange* (London: Penguin).

——. 1972/1993. *L'Orange Mécanique*, trans. by Georges Belmont and Hortense Chabrier (Paris: Robert Laffont).

Céline, Louis-Ferdinand. 1934/1952. *Voyage au bout de la nuit* (Paris: Gallimard).

——. 1983. *Journey To the End of the Night*, trans. by Ralph Manheim (New York: New Directions).

Cervantes, Miguel de. 1906/1975. *Don Quixote*, trans. by Peter Motteux, intro. by L.B. Walton (London: Everyman's Library).

——. 2004. *Don Quixote* trans. by Edith Grossman, intro. by Harold Bloom (USA: HarperCollins; London: Secker & Warburg).

Chesterman, Andrew, & Emma Wagner. 2002. *Can Theory Help Translation? A Dialogue Between the Ivory Tower and the Wordface* (Manchester: St Jerome).

Chouliaraki, Lilie, & Norman Fairclough. 1999. *Discourse in Late Modernity: Rethinking Critical Discourse Analysis* (Edinburgh: Edinburgh University Press).

Collins, Jeff, & Bill Mayblin. 1996/2000. *Introducing Derrida* (Cambridge: Icon Books).

Cronin, Michael. 1996. *Translating Ireland: Translation, Languages, Cultures* (Cork: Cork University Press).

——. 2006. *Translation and Identity* (London: Routledge).

Culler, Jonathan. 1975/1989. *Structuralist Poetics: Structuralism Linguistics and the Study of Literature* (London: Routledge).

Cupitt, Cathy. [n.d.]. 'Throne of Blood: Is it Shakespeare?' pp. 1–6. <http://www.geocities.com/Area51/Hollow/2405/tob.html?20065> (accessed 05.02.06).

Derrida, Jacques. 1967a. *De la Grammatologie*, Collection Critique (Paris: Minuit).

——. 1967b. *L'Écriture et la Différence* (Paris: Seuil).

——. 1968. 'La Différance' in *Les Marges de la Philosophie*, 1972 (Paris: Minuit) pp. 1–31.

——. 1974. *Glas* (Paris: Galilée).

——. 1985a. 'Des tours de Babel', in J.F. Graham (ed.). 1985. *Difference in Translation* (Ithaca, NY: Cornell University Press).

——. 1985b. *The Ear of the Other: Otobiography, Transference, Translation: Texts and Discussions with Jacques Derrida*, ed. by Christine V. McDonald, trans. by Peggy Kramuf, 1988 (Lincoln: University of Nebraska Press).

Dickens, Charles. 1837–8/2003. *Oliver Twist* (or *The Parish Boy's Progress*), ed., intro., and notes by Philip Horne, Penguin Classics (London: Penguin).

——. 1973/2003. *Les Aventures d'Olivier Twist*, trans. by Francis Ledoux 1958 (Paris: Gallimard).

Dostoevsky, Fyodor. 1868. *The Idiot*, trans. 1913/1964 (Surrey: Bookprint).

Eichenbaum, Boris. 1926. 'The theory of the "Formal Method"' in *Russian Formalist Criticism: Four Essays* 1965, trans. by Lee T. Lemon (Lincoln: University of Nebraska Press), pp. 99–140.

Ellender, Claire. 2006a. *Preserving Polyphonies: Responding to the Writings of Claude Sarraute*. PhD thesis. Lancaster University.

——. 2006b. 'Rerendering the dialogic writings of Claude Sarraute: translate or re-create?', in *Translation and Creativity: How Creative is the Translator?* Proceedings of the Fifth Annual Translation Conference, University of Portsmouth 2005, ed. by Ian Kemble and Carol O'Sullivan (Portsmouth: University of Portsmouth), pp. 154–62.

Erasmus, Desiderius. 1509. *Praise of Folly and letter to Martin Dorp*, trans. by Betty Radice, intro. and notes by A.H.T. Levi, 1971/1982 (Harmondsworth: Penguin).

Even-Zohar, Itamar. 1978. 'The position of translated literature within the literary polysystem', in L. Venuti (ed.) 2000, pp. 192–7.

Fairclough, Norman. 1995. *Critical Discourse Analysis: The Critical Study of Language*, Language in Social Life Series (London: Longman).

Fielding, Helen. 1996. 2nd edn. *Bridget Jones's Diary* (London: Picador).

——. 1998. *Le Journal de Bridget Jones*, trans. by Arlette Stroumza, Éditions J'ai Lu (Paris: Flammarion).

Fish, Stanley. 1970. 'Literature in the reader: Affective stylistics', in J. Tompkins (ed.). 1980, pp. 70–100.

——. 1976. 'Interpreting the *Variorum*', in J. Tompkins (ed.) 1980, pp. 164–84.

Foucault, Michel. 1969. *L'Archéologie du savoir* (Paris: Gallimard).

——. 1970. 'What is an author?' in *Language, Counter-Memory, Practice* ed. Donald F. Bouchard, trans. by Donald F. Bouchard and Sherry Simon, 1977 (Ithaca, N: Cornell University Press), pp. 124–7.

——. 1971. *L'Ordre du discours: leçon inaugurale au collège de France, prononcée le 2. décembre 1970* (Paris: Gallimard).

Freund, Elizabeth. 1987. *The Return of the Reader. Reader Response Criticism* (London: Methuen).

Genette, Gérard. 1972/1988. *Narrative Discourse Revisited*, trans. by Jane E. Lewin, 1988 (Ithaca, NY: Cornell University Press).

Gentzler, Edwin. 2001. rev 2nd edn. *Contemporary Translation Theories* (Clevedon: Multilingual Matters).

Gide, André. 1914/1922. *Les Caves du Vatican*, Collection Folio (Paris: Gallimard).

———. 1927/1969. *The Vatican Cellars*, trans. by Dorothy Bussy (London, New York: Penguin).

Girard, Alexandra. 2001. 'On the relative (un)translatability of puns'. ForeignExchange Translations <http://www.multilingualwebmaster.com/library/puns_translation.html> (accessed 10.07.02).

Goscinny, René, & Albert Uderzo. 1961/1995. *Astérix le Gaulois* (Paris: Dargaud).

———. 1966/1995. *Astérix chez les Bretons* (Paris: Dargaud).

———. 1968/1992. *Astérix aux Jeux Olympiques* (Paris: Dargaud).

———. 1969. *Asterix the Gaul*, trans. by Anthea Bell and Derek Hockridge (London: Hodder Dargaud).

———. 1969/1995. *Astérix en Hispanie* (Paris: Dargaud).

———. 1971. *Asterix in Spain*, trans. by Anthea Bell and Derek Hockridge (London: Hodder Dargaud).

———. 1976. *Asterix at the Olympic Games*, trans. by Anthea Bell and Derek Hockridge (London: Hodder Dargaud).

———. 1973. *Asterix in Britain*, trans. by Anthea Bell and Derek Hockridge (London: Hodder Dargaud).

Gray, John. 1992. *Men Are from Mars, Women Are from Venus: A Practical Guide for Improving Communication and Getting What You Want in Your Relationships* (London: HarperCollins).

Halliday, Michael A.K. 1964. 'Descriptive linguistics in literary studies', in Donald C. Freeman (ed.) 1970 (New York: Holt, Rinehart & Winston) pp. 57–72.

Harvey, David. 1989. *The Condition of Postmodernity: An Enquiry into the Origins of Cultural Change* (Oxford: Blackwell).

Hatim, Basil, & Ian Mason. 1990. *Discourse and the Translator* (London: Routledge).

———. 1997. *The Translator as Communicator* (London: Routledge).

Hawkes, Terence. 1977/1978. *Structuralism and Semiotics* (London: Methuen).

Hermans, Theo. 1999. *Translation in Systems* (Manchester: St Jerome).

Holquist, Michael. 1990. *Dialogism: Bakhtin and His World* (London: Routledge).

Houellebecq, Michel. 1994. *Extension du domaine de la lutte*, Éditions J'ai Lu (Paris: Flammarion).

———. 1998. *Whatever*, trans. by Paul Hammond (London: Serpent's Tail).

———. 2001. *Platforme*, Éditions J'ai Lu (Paris: Flammarion).

———. 2002. *Platform*, trans. by Frank Wynne (London: Vintage).

Iser, Wolfgang. 1974. 'The reading process: a phenomenological approach', in J. Tompkins (ed.) 1980, pp. 50–69.

Jakobson, Roman. 1959. 'Closing statement: Linguistics and poetics', in T. Sebeok (ed.) 1960. *Style in Language* (Cambridge, MA: MIT Press), pp. 350–77.

——. 1959. 'On linguistic aspects of translation', in L. Venuti (ed.) 2000, pp. 113–18.

Jerome (St Jerome). 395 CE / 1997. 'De optime genere interpretandi' (Letter 101, to Pammachius), in *Epistolae D. Hieronymi Stridoniensis* (Rome: Aldi F.) (1565), pp. 285–91, trans. P. Carroll as 'On the best kind of translator', in D. Robinson (ed.) (1997) *Western Translation Theory from Herodotus to Nietzsche* (Manchester: St Jerome), pp. 22–30.

Kelly, Louis. 1979. *The True Interpreter* (Oxford: Basil Blackwell).

Kramsch, Claire. 1998/2000. *Language and Culture* (Oxford: Oxford University Press).

Kumar, Amith, & Milind Malshe. [n.d.]. 'Lyric polyphonies and multiple translations: a Bakhtinian perspective' <http://www.hss.iitb.ac.in/TCITI/Amith.doc> (accessed 08.04.06).

Lainé, Pascal. 1974. *La Dentellière*, Collection Folio (Paris: Gallimard).

——. 1976. *A Web of Lace*, trans. by George Crowther (London: Abelard).

Landers, Clifford E. 2001. *Literary Translation. A Practical Guide* (Clevedon: Multilingual Matters).

Lefevere, André (ed.). 1992a. *Translation/History/Culture: A Sourcebook* (London: Routledge).

——. 1992b. *Translation, Rewriting and the Manipulation of Literary Fame.* (London: Routledge).

Lewis, Philip E. 1985. 'The measure of translation effects', in L. Venuti (ed.) 2000, pp. 264–83.

Lodge, David. 1990. *After Bakhtin: Essays on Fiction and Criticism* (London: Routledge).

——. 1992. *The Art of Fiction* (London: Penguin).

Medvedev, Pavel Nikolnevich. 1928. *The Formal Method in Literary Scholarship: A Critical Introduction to Sociological Poetics*, trans. by Albert J. Wehrle, 1978 (Baltimore: Johns Hopkins University Press).

Mounin, Georges. 1963. *Les Problèmes théoriques de la traduction* (Paris: Gallimard).

Muhawi, Ibrahim. [n.d]. 'Towards a folkloristic theory of translation' <http://www.soas.ac.uk/Literatures/satranslations/Muhawi.pdf> (accessed 08.04.06).

Munday, Jeremy. 2001. *Introducing Translation Studies. Theories and Applications* (London: Routledge).

Newmark, Peter. 1981. *Approaches to Translation* (Oxford: Pergamon Press).

——. 1988/1998. *A Textbook of Translation* (Hemel Hempstead: Prentice Hall Europe).

Nida, Eugène. A. 1964. *Towards a Science of Translating* (Leiden: E.J. Brill).

Niranjana, Tejaswini. 1992. *Siting Translation. History, Post-Structuralism and the Colonial Context* (Berkeley: University of California Press).

Papargyriou, Eleni. 'Translating intertextuality or cultural reference: Yoryis Yatromanolakis' Greek novel *Eroticon*' <http://people.brunel.ac.uk/~acsrrrm/entertext/4_3?ET43Spapargyriou.doc> (accessed 08.04.06).

Pearce, L. 1994. *Reading Dialogics* (London, New York: Arnold).

Pilard, Georges. (ed.) 2002. *Rude French. An Alernative French Phrasebook* (Edinburgh: Chambers Harrap).

Pushkin, Alexander. 1964/1990 2nd paperback edn. *Eugene Onegin*, trans. and intro. by Vladimir Nabokov, Bollingen Series LXXII, 2 vols (Princeton, NJ: Princeton University Press).

——. 1977/2003 rev edn. *Eugene Onegin*, trans. by Charles Johnston (London Penguin).

Queneau, Raymond. 1938/1996. *Zazie dans le métro*, Collection Folio (Paris: Gallimard).

——. 1947/2000. *Exercices de Style*, Collection Folio (Paris: Gallimard).——. 1958/1979. *Exercises in Style*, trans. and preface by Barbara Wright (London: John Calder).

——. 1983. *Zazie in the metro. A novel by Raymond Queneau*, trans. by Barbara Wright (London: John Calder).

Rabelais, François. 1534–8/1972. *Gargantua (Extraits)*, Classiques Larousse (Paris: Larousse).

——. 1955. *Gargantua and Pantagruel*, trans. and intro. by J.M.Cohen (London: Penguin).

Reiss, Katharina. 1981. 'Type, kind and individuality of text: decision-making in translation', trans. by S. Kitron, in L. Venuti (ed.) 2000, pp. 160–71.

Reynolds, Jack, & Jonathan Roffe (eds). 2004. *Understanding Derrida* (London: Continuum).

Riffaterre, Michael. 1959. 'Criteria for style analysis', *Word XV*, pp. 154–74.

——. 1966. 'Describing poetic structures: two approaches to Baudelaire's "Les Chats"', in J. Tompkins (ed.) 1980, pp. 26–40.

Rimmon-Kenan, Shlomith. 1983/1997. *Narrative Fiction: Contemporary Poetics* (London: Routledge).

Robinson, Douglas. 1991. *The Translator's Turn* (Baltimore: Johns Hopkins University Press).

——. 2012. *Becoming a Translator: An Introduction to the Theory and Practice of Translation*. 3rd edn (London: Routledge).

Ruquier, Laurent. [n.d]. Site Officiel. Liste des Chroniqueurs: Claude Sarraute <http://www.ruquier.com/bande/chroniqueurs_detail.html?Cle=5&mnu=menu6&smnu+M6_1&sltaction+LIST_ACTIF> (accessed 17.07.05).

Sarraute, Claude. 1960, June. Interview with *Le Monde* in *Céline et son art*. 1957–61 <http://www.louisferdinandceline.free.fr/art/art2.htm> (accessed 15.08.02).

——. 1985. *Dites Donc!* (Paris: Lattès).

——. 1987. *Allô Lolotte, c'est Coco*, Éditions J'ai lu (Paris: Flammarion).

——. 1989. *Maman Coq* (Paris: Flammarion).

——. 1991. *Mademoiselle, s'il vous plaît!*, Éditions Livres de Poche (Paris: Flammarion).

——. 1993. *Ah! L'amour, toujours l'amour!*, Éditions Livres de Poche (Paris: Flammarion).

——. 1995. *Papa qui?*, Éditions Livres de Poche (Paris: Flammarion).

——. 1996. *Des Hommes en général et des Femmes en particulier* (Paris: Plon).

——. 1998. *C'est pas bientôt fini!*, Éditions Pocket (Paris: Plon).

——. March 1998 – December 2004. *Psychologies* (73 articles) <http://www.psychologies.com/cfml/chroniqueur/1_chroniqueur.cfm?ide=4> (accessed 05.01.03).

——. 2000. *Dis, est-ce que tu m'aimes?* (Paris: Plon).

——. 2003. *Dis-voir, Maminette* (Paris: Plon).

——. 2005. *Belle Belle Belle* (Paris: Plon).

Saussure, Ferdinand de. 1916/1964. *Cours de linguistique générale* (Paris: Payot).

Simon, Sherry. 1996. *Gender in Translation. Cultural Identity and the Politics of Transmission* (London: Routledge).

Snell-Hornby, Mary. 1988. *Translation Studies. An Integrated Approach* (Amsterdam: John Benjamins).

Spitzer, Leo. 1948/1962. *Linguistics and Literary History. Essays in Stylistics* (New York: Russell & Russell).

Spivak, Gayatri. 2000. 'The politics of translation', in L. Venuti (ed.) 2000, pp. 397–416.

Steiner, George. 1975/1998 3rd edn. *After Babel: Aspects of Language and Translation* (London: Oxford University Press).

Sterne, Laurence. 1912/1991. *Tristram Shandy* (London: Everyman's Library).

——. 1946/1982. *Vie et opinions de Tristram Shandy*, trans. by Charles Mauron, preface, bibliography and notes by Serge Soupel (Paris: Flammarion).

Swift, Jonathan. 1940/1991. *Gulliver's Travels* (London: Everyman's Library).

——. 1965/1976 rev edn. *Les Voyages de Gulliver*, trans. by Jacques Pons (Paris: Gallimard).

Tabakowska, Elzbieta. 1990. 'Linguistic polyphony as a problem in translation' in Susan Bassnett & Andre Lefevere (eds), pp. 71–6.

Todorov, Tzevetan. 1939. *Mikhail Bakhtin: The Dialogical Principle*, trans. by Wlad Godzich 1995, Theory & History of Literature (Minneapolis: University of Minnesota Press).

Tompkins, Jane. (ed.). 1980/1992. *Reader-Response Criticism: From Formalism to Post-Structuralism* (Baltimore: Johns Hopkins University Press).

Twain, Mark. 1885/1994. *The Adventures of Huckleberry Finn*, Penguin Popular Classics (London: Penguin).

——. 1973/1999 rev edn. *Les aventures de Huckleberry Finn*, trans. by Suzanne Nétillard 1973, illustrations by Nathäele Vogel 1982, Folio Junior (Paris: Gallimard).

Van Dijk, Teun. A. 1995. *From Text Grammar to Critical Discourse Analysis*, Unpublished paper (University of Amsterdam).

Venuti, Laurence. 1995. *The Translator's Invisibility. A History of Translation* (London: Routledge).

——. 1998. 'Strategies of translation' in M. Baker (ed.), pp. 240–3.

——. (ed.). 2000. *The Translation Studies Reader* (London: Routledge).

Vermeer, Hans. 1989. 'Skopos and commission in transational action', in L. Venuti (ed.) 2000, pp. 221–32.

Vice, Sue. 1997. *Introducing Bakhtin*. (Manchester: Manchester University Press).

Vinay, Jean-Paul & Jean Darbelnet. 1958. *Comparative Stylistics of French and English: A Methodology for Translation*, ed. and trans. by Juan C. Sager & M-J Hamel, 1995 (Amsterdam: John Benjamin).

Voloshinov, Valentin. 1927. *Freudianism: A Critical Sketch*, ed. in collaboration with N.H. Brunst, trans. by I.R. Titunik, 1976 (Bloomington, IN: Indiana University Press).

——. 1929. *Marxism and the Philosophy of Language*, trans. by Ladislav Matejka and I.R. Titunik, 1973 (New York: Seminar Press).

Voltaire. 1759/1990. *Candide*, annotations and notes by Jean Goldzink, Classiques Larousse, Texte Intégral (Paris: Larousse).

——. 1947. *Candide* (or *Optimism*), trans. by John Butt, Penguin Classics (London: Penguin).

——. 1997/2001. *Candide*, trans. by Norman Cameron, Penguin Popular Classics (London: Penguin).

Weber, Jean (ed.) 1996. *The Stylistics Reader. From Roman Jakobson to the present* (London: Arnold).

Wright, Barbara. [n.d]. 'Reading Raymond Queneau'. On-line edition. No. 9. <http://www.centerforbookculture.org/context/no9/wright.html> (accessed 10.07.02).

Youzi, Li. 2004. 'On the subjectivity of the translator' (Unpublished thesis, Nanjing University, China) <http://www.towerofbabel.com/features/subjectivity/> (accessed 08.04.06).

Zephaniah, Benjamin. 1992/1995. *City Psalms* (Newcastle-upon-Tyne: Bloodaxe).

Zlateva, Palma. 1990. 'Translation: text and pre-text "adequacy" and "acceptability" in crosscultural communication' in Susan Bassnett & Andre Lefevere (eds) pp. 29–37.

Index

NEW TRENDS IN TRANSLATION STUDIES

In today's globalised society, translation and interpreting are gaining visibility and relevance as a means to foster communication and dialogue in increasingly multicultural and multilingual environments. Practised since time immemorial, both activities have become more complex and multifaceted in recent decades, intersecting with many other disciplines. *New Trends in Translation Studies* is an international series with the main objectives of promoting the scholarly study of translation and interpreting and of functioning as a forum for the translation and interpreting research community.

This series publishes research on subjects related to multimedia translation and interpreting, in their various social roles. It is primarily intended to engage with contemporary issues surrounding the new multidimensional environments in which translation is flourishing, such as audiovisual media, the internet and emerging new media and technologies. It sets out to reflect new trends in research and in the profession, to encourage flexible methodologies and to promote interdisciplinary research ranging from the theoretical to the practical and from the applied to the pedagogical.

New Trends in Translation Studies publishes translation- and interpreting-oriented books that present high-quality scholarship in an accessible, reader-friendly manner. The series embraces a wide range of publications – monographs, edited volumes, conference proceedings and translations of works in translation studies which do not exist in English. The editor, Dr Jorge Díaz Cintas, welcomes proposals from all those interested in being involved with the series. The working language of the series is English, although in exceptional circumstances works in other languages can be considered for publication. Proposals dealing with specialised translation, translation tools and technology, audiovisual translation and the field of accessibility to the media are particularly welcomed.